# Radical Schooling for Democracy

'Neil Hooley's new book offers a philosophical vision of radical schooling for democracy in terms of criticizing neoliberal and dehumanizing reform of education. It is an outstanding contribution to reconstruct the idea of public education through a comprehensive and fascinating approach to pragmatism and the public good.'
— *Masamichi Ueno, Professor of Education, Daito Bunka University, Japan*

*Radical Schooling for Democracy* proposes that formal education around the world has a serious philosophical weakness: as the ideology of neoliberalism increasingly dominates economic and, as a consequence, educational and social life, formal education has adopted a narrow, rational and economic purpose for all students. Hooley argues that, under these circumstances, schooling is inherently frustrating and alienating for vast numbers of children as they are systematically removed from the big ideas and practices of history and knowledge of which they and their communities are a part and are instead inducted into a technical and superficial rationality of human existence.

*Radical Schooling for Democracy* begins with a progressive and contemporary overview of philosophical and sociological thought during the European Enlightenment and identifies a framework of understanding that is extremely weak in education. This action framework of integrated philosophy, sociology and epistemology generates an 'action theory' that not only accounts for human progress but also has the potential to radically change the nature of schooling. A number of theorists who generally support a 'theory of action' are considered, ranging from Aristotle, Marx, Dewey and Freire to Habermas. From this analysis, the curriculum, pedagogical, assessment and research constructs of schooling are detailed such that a coherent and integrated model of education as an attribute of being human can be articulated rather than being seen as a disparate derivative from other disciplines.

With its coverage of internationally relevant issues, this book will be essential reading for academics, graduate students, policymakers and researchers in education, philosophy, sociology and epistemology, as well as teachers and pre-service teachers.

**Neil Hooley** is a Lecturer in the College of Education at Victoria University in Melbourne, Australia.

# New Directions in the Philosophy of Education Series
Series Editors
Michael A. Peters
*University of Waikato, New Zealand; University of Illinois, USA*

Gert Biesta
*Brunel University, UK*

This book series is devoted to the exploration of new directions in the philosophy of education. After the linguistic turn, the cultural turn, and the historical turn, where might we go? Does the future promise a digital turn with a greater return to connectionism, biology, and biopolitics based on new understandings of system theory and knowledge ecologies? Does it foreshadow a genuinely alternative radical global turn based on a new openness and interconnectedness? Does it leave humanism behind or will it reengage with the question of the human in new and unprecedented ways? How should philosophy of education reflect new forces of globalization? How can it become less Anglo-centric and develop a greater sensitivity to other traditions, languages, and forms of thinking and writing, including those that are not rooted in the canon of Western philosophy but in other traditions that share the 'love of wisdom' that characterizes the wide diversity within Western philosophy itself. Can this be done through a turn to intercultural philosophy? To indigenous forms of philosophy and philosophizing? Does it need a post-Wittgensteinian philosophy of education? A postpostmodern philosophy? Or should it perhaps leave the whole construction of 'post'-positions behind?

In addition to the question of the intellectual resources for the future of philosophy of education, what are the issues and concerns that philosophers of education should engage with? How should they position themselves? What is their specific contribution? What kind of intellectual and strategic alliances should they pursue? Should philosophy of education become more global, and if so, what would the shape of that be? Should it become more cosmopolitan or perhaps more decentred? Perhaps most importantly in the digital age, the time of the global knowledge economy that reprofiles education as privatized human capital and simultaneously in terms of an historic openness, is there a philosophy of education that grows out of education itself, out of the concerns for new forms of teaching, studying, learning and speaking that can provide comment on ethical and epistemological configurations of economics and politics of knowledge? Can and should this imply a reconnection with questions of democracy and justice?

This series comprises texts that explore, identify and articulate new directions in the philosophy of education. It aims to build bridges, both geographically and temporally: bridges across different traditions and practices and bridges towards a different future for philosophy of education.

In this series

**Education and Schmid's Art of Living**
Philosophical, Psychological and Educational Perspectives on Living a Good Life
*Christoph Teschers*

**Education and the Limits of Reason**
Reading Dostoevsky, Tolstoy and Nabokov
*Peter Roberts and Herner Saeverot*

**Radical Schooling for Democracy**
Engaging Philosophy of Education for the Public Good
*Neil Hooley*

# Radical Schooling for Democracy

Engaging Philosophy of Education for the Public Good

**Neil Hooley**

LONDON AND NEW YORK

First published 2018
by Routledge
2 Park Square, Milton Park, Abingdon, Oxon OX14 4RN

and by Routledge
711 Third Avenue, New York, NY 10017

*Routledge is an imprint of the Taylor & Francis Group, an informa business*

© 2018 Neil Hooley

The right of Neil Hooley to be identified as author of this work has been asserted by him in accordance with sections 77 and 78 of the Copyright, Designs and Patents Act 1988.

All rights reserved. No part of this book may be reprinted or reproduced or utilised in any form or by any electronic, mechanical, or other means, now known or hereafter invented, including photocopying and recording, or in any information storage or retrieval system, without permission in writing from the publishers.

*Trademark notice*: Product or corporate names may be trademarks or registered trademarks, and are used only for identification and explanation without intent to infringe.

*British Library Cataloguing-in-Publication Data*
A catalogue record for this book is available from the British Library

*Library of Congress Cataloging-in-Publication Data*
A catalog record for this book has been requested

ISBN: 978-1-138-64716-9 (hbk)
ISBN: 978-1-315-62720-5 (ebk)

Typeset in Times New Roman
by Apex CoVantage, LLC

Printed and bound in Great Britain by
TJ International Ltd, Padstow, Cornwall

# Contents

| | |
|---|---|
| *List of figures* | ix |
| *List of tables* | x |
| *About the author* | xi |
| *Preface* | xii |
| *Acknowledgements* | xvi |
| *Dedication by John Dewey* | xvii |
| *Poem* | xviii |

## PART I
## Thinking philosophically

1

### 1   Trends and tensions of philosophy and sociology

3

*Case 1: properties of the triangle  4*
*Case 2: knowing your students  5*
*Dewey, Vygotsky and philosophy  7*
*Durkheim, Habermas and sociology  10*
*Neoliberalism and the decline of epistemology  11*

### 2   Understandings of epistemology

16

*Historical location of epistemology  17*
*Centrality of human action  19*
*Mead, the social act and intersubjectivity  22*
*Epistemologies and neoliberalism  24*

### 3   Action theory and theorists

29

*Communication and the linguistic turn  30*
*Culture and conscientisation  32*
*Complexity and the physical and social worlds  34*
*Consciousness and quantum mechanics  36*
*Great community and the public sphere  38*

vi  *Contents*

**4   Creative democracy, ethics, power and control**                      42

*Creative democracy  43*
*Formation of ethical conduct  44*
*Power and control of curriculum  47*
*Generative themes for a cohesive education  49*

**Part I reflections**                                                     55

**PART II**
**Thinking educationally**                                                 57

**5   Education as philosophy of practice**                                59

*Philosophy 1: education as a knowledge discipline  61*
*Scenario 1: education as philosophy of practice*
    *(from a teacher's perspective)  63*
*Tensions and similarities  67*
*Exegesis: Jemma, education and pragmatism  69*
*Philosophy 2: religion, the sacred and profane  72*
*Scenario 2: religion (from the perspective of a secondary*
    *school student)  74*
*Exegesis 2: Emmet, culture and knowledge  76*
*Philosophy 3: conservatism, what is or should be  78*
*Scenario 3: conservatism (from the perspective of a working*
    *class mother)  78*
*Exegesis 3: Rydia, fractions and frictions  80*
*Philosophy 4: neoliberalism, capitalism personified  83*
*Scenario 4: neoliberalism (from the perspective*
    *of a middle manager)  83*
*Exegesis 4: Emile and the occasional dilemma of conscience  86*
*Philosophy 5: social democracy, in practice or in name  89*
*Scenario 5: social democracy (from the perspective*
    *of a trade union official)  90*
*Exegesis 5: democratic thought and deed  92*
*Philosophy 6: science, explanation or understanding  95*
*Scenario 6: science (from the perspective of an*
    *industrial chemist)  95*
*Exegesis 6: principles of the everyday and everyplace  98*
*Philosophy 7: Marxism, social class and social division  101*
*Scenario 7: Marxism (from the perspective of an artist)  101*

*Contents* vii

*Exegesis 7: aesthetics of matter and energy 104*
*Confirmations and conflicts across philosophies of practice 107*
*Investigating how, why and what we know 111*

**Part II reflections** 113

PART III
**Thinking democratically** 115

**6 Social class, equity and socio-economic positions** 117

*Social class in education 120*
*Feminism, pragmatism and equity in education 123*
*Socio-economic position and culture 127*

**7 Connecting with Indigenous education** 131

*Marginalised knowledge 132*
*Discursive learning 134*
*Funds of knowledge 138*
*Researching the bricolage 140*
*Conclusion: cultural change for recognition and respect 143*

**8 Appraising the practice turn in teacher education** 147

*Epistemology: the nature of knowledge and learning 150*
*Practice as progressive or conservative teaching 152*
*Scenario 1: mathematics 153*
*Scenario 2: science 153*
*Scenario 3: literature 154*
*Emerging arrangements of teacher education:*
  *core practices, clinical, praxis 155*
*Researching practice and teacher education 157*

**9 Critical schooling for all** 160

*Formation of critical life 161*
*Intersubjective praxis 161*
*Acting for what is right 163*
*Pragmatism and signature pedagogies 165*
*Significance of the model 172*
*Linked reason and emotion 173*

viii  *Contents*

*Radical action, knowledge, education, democracy  174*
*Epistemology  176*

**Part III reflections**                                                 178

*References*                                                             179
*Index*                                                                  188

# Figures

| | | |
|---|---|---|
| 0.1 | Relationship between education and other philosophies | xiii |
| 0.2 | Structural outline of radical schooling for democracy | xv |
| 4.1 | Three domains of human existence and education | 52 |
| 4.2 | Narrative exemplar process for philosophy of practice | 53 |
| 5.1 | Structure of Chapter 5 | 60 |
| 5.2 | Evolutionary development of gesture, lifeworld, dialogue | 106 |
| 7.1 | Model of discursive cultural knowledge formation | 144 |
| 9.1 | Three world's context of teacher education | 166 |
| 9.2 | Integrated process of praxis teacher education | 167 |

# Tables

| | | |
|---|---|---:|
| 1.1 | Summary comparison of knowledges, epistemology and social justice | 13 |
| 2.1 | Summary comparison of intersubjectivity, knowledges, epistemology and social justice | 25 |
| 4.1 | Generative themes for cohesive education | 51 |
| 5.1 | Distinguishing features of education as knowledge discipline | 62 |
| 5.2 | Characteristics of frames of practice | 67 |
| 5.3 | Characteristics of primary, secondary and tertiary frames | 68 |
| 5.4 | Intersection of political-democratic tensions | 89 |
| 5.5 | Intersection of political-democratic features of philosophies | 108 |
| 5.6 | Tensions and correlations between education and philosophies | 109 |
| 5.7 | Questions for education as philosophy of practice | 110 |
| 6.1 | Characteristics of bourgeois and proletarian viewpoints | 119 |
| 7.1 | Principles of discursive learning | 136 |
| 7.2 | Practitioner and community research protocol | 141 |
| 9.1 | Educational virtues of practice and application (for discussion) | 164 |
| 9.2 | Signature pedagogies of praxis teacher education | 170 |

# About the author

Dr Neil Hooley is a lecturer in the College of Education, Victoria University Melbourne, Australia. He has interests in critical theory, critical pedagogy, participatory action research and pragmatic inquiry learning as they apply across all areas of knowledge and the curriculum in schools and universities. He has been involved in projects that investigate professional practice, community partnership and praxis learning for pre-service teacher education to pursue social justice and educational equity for all students. In addition, he has participated in projects concerning narrative inquiry as research methodology and curriculum construct in primary and secondary schools. Dr Hooley is committed to reconciliation between the Indigenous and non-Indigenous peoples of Australia and sees progressive educational reform as a step towards this end. He strongly supports partnerships between schools, communities and universities as democratic means of improving dignified social life and of learning from and theorising social and educational practice to challenge organisational structures and personal understandings.

# Preface

Formal schooling under the political and economic dictates of neoliberalism cannot meet the educational needs of the vast majority of families and their children. Strict induction into narrow European Enlightenment rationality of accepted and determined knowledge, scientific reason and autonomous human subjectivity detracts from the continuing construction of personal knowledge based on experience, reason that emerges from social associations and subjectivities that are fashioned by histories that are both local and global. Schooling that presupposes a fixed, specified and technical rationality will necessarily exclude vast numbers of teachers and children from investigating and assembling their own perceptions of the social and physical worlds, over time, as their direct experience and personal comprehensions become more complex. This does not degrade the significance of Enlightenment achievements across a range of understandings, but it suggests that human insight rather than being imposed evolves from the internal characteristics of intellectual action and change within the external conditions of social action and change. While accepting the trustworthiness of the existence of the water molecule, all citizens will come to their own conceptions of its reality. *Radical Schooling for Democracy* therefore explores the new forms of schooling that are required to enable the construction of communicative and discursive rationalities of teachers and children that respect and bring together tentative discernments and possibilities in comparison and interaction with the understandings of others. Chapters in Part I provide a critical summary of philosophical, sociological and epistemological debates regarding the formation of identity and selfhood. Particular attention is given to social action as the basis of all learning. A number of theorists who generally support a 'theory of action' is considered ranging from Aristotle, Marx, Dewey and Freire to Habermas. From this analysis, Part II details the curriculum, pedagogical, assessment and research constructs of schooling such that a coherent and integrated model of education as an attribute of being human can be articulated, rather than being seen as a disparate derivative from other disciplines. In this way, a dialectical relationship is established between philosophy and education, each being knowledge disciplines and practices in their own right and informing the other. In Part III, implications from this approach are discussed including exclusion and discrimination based on social class and race and a reconstruction of teacher education. It is concluded that the current neoliberal and

*Preface* xiii

dehumanising dominance of education must be demolished, in favour of radical schooling for democracy and the inherent satisfaction of significant learning for all citizens that it would bring

*Radical Schooling for Democracy* not only seeks to defend public schooling in the age of an inquisitive mature neoliberalism but also attempts to theorise public schooling as a coherent and intelligible philosophy of practice and of living in its own right. In this way, public schooling can articulate its own purpose, principles and practice and speak back to critics whose political and economic interests are private, individual and mercenary. This is very difficult to do at present, with schooling in many countries being fragmented and in the main lacking direction. This book therefore has identified six philosophies with which public education must contend and respond, not only for its own distinctiveness, robustness and consequent improvement but also in turn, to offer critique of the assailing philosophy itself. That is, it is not only necessary to have a deep understanding of, for example, neoliberalism and its criticisms but also to be able to debate neoliberalism on its own terms and to point out limitations and weaknesses that bring its arguments into question. To achieve this intention, *Radical Schooling for Democracy* outlines and examines the following six philosophies (Figure 0.1) as those with which the philosophy of education encountered through modern public schooling must engage: the philosophies of religion, conservatism, neoliberalism, social democracy, science and Marxism.

It is hoped that the major issues raised by discussion of these philosophies will enable the purpose and nature of modern public schooling as generally

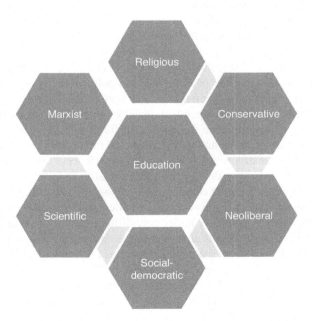

*Figure 0.1* Relationship between education and other philosophies

xiv *Preface*

understood around the world to be contrasted, defined, critiqued and defended. It is not proposed that a final, complete model of public schooling will emerge to be implemented across systems or schools, but that the writing will proceed as a narrative of ideas, reflections and practices that will inform and challenge progressive educational change that struggles for existence in very difficult political and economic conditions. Hopefully, the model will take shape as the journey and writing unfold, and the matrix of complicated ideas can be clarified. For example, it may be suggested that public education as expressed in schooling, teaching and learning should proceed democratically. If so, there is an immediate contradiction established between this principle and most, or in the minds of some, all of the six philosophies so declared. The question then becomes how resolution of this contradiction could occur, or if not, how education can secure what it believes to be a central principle and practice of its ontology.

There is a highly complicated relationship between the field of education and all other fields of human activity. Issues regarding moral outlook and ethical conduct should be central to all, but are often denied. Another set of factors essentially socio-economic in character must also be understood as infusing the debate. These factors include social class, racism, ethnicity, gender, disability, sexual orientation, geographical location, public policy formulation and resource allocation. It will be necessary, therefore, throughout the book to consider how teaching and learning might proceed in relation to such factors and realistically within significant economic and political institutions called schools. Formal education can be conceptualised as one aspect of a dominant economic system, existing within a complicated framework of bureaucratic regulation and procedure, aligned with and responding passively to changing political circumstances. Under these conditions, formal education will struggle to achieve some form of independence in its existence including the implementation of policies and strategies to best meet the educational needs of all families and students. Conversely, it is possible to conceive of formal education as one of a number of economic and political fields of human activity that exists in relation to all other fields in a constant process of interaction, tension and uncertainty. As a semi-independent, usually somewhat weak field, education will still come under influence from all other fields and in particular powerful economic imperatives, but it has an interrelational rather than a totally subjugated position within the matrix of historical human experience. Formal education then can attempt to shape its own destiny regarding social and educational progress and indeed piece together different counter narratives against prevailing trends. A field analysis of this type indicates how a range of alternative policies, procedures and practices can appear and survive under very difficult conditions and provide evidence that progressive change is always possible. Structuring education and public education in neoliberal times around the principles of human practice, community partnership and praxis experience is an example of this direction.

In keeping with its intended outcome of an integrated, holistic philosophy of practice, the book is structured accordingly in a narrative format. In broad terms, it asks questions like 'What can we know,' 'How can we know' and 'How can we live well, an intellectual and ethical life?' Part I is intended to outline some key principles drawn from philosophy and sociology that will form the basis of considering and modelling what a new approach to education will look like. Part II is not divided into chapters, but attempts to provide this coherent overview with all issues raised being connected. Part III then looks at some specific questions arising from a philosophy of this type that need to be dealt with separately at this time. Figure 0.2 shows this structural arrangement:

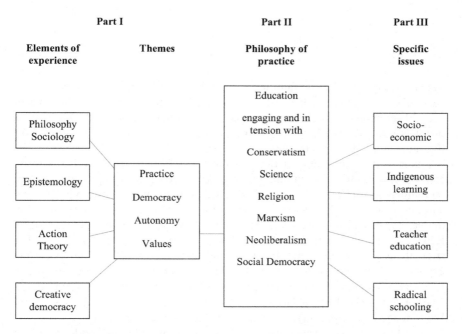

*Figure 0.2* Structural outline of radical schooling for democracy

# Acknowledgements

I acknowledge the Elders, families and forebears of the Indigenous peoples of Australia. I recognise that the land on which we live, meet and learn is the place of age-old ceremonies of celebration, initiation and renewal and that the Indigenous people's living culture has a unique role in the history and life of Australia. We live and learn together in the interests of peace and justice.

I express my warm appreciation to Aunty Lois Peeler, Aunty Melva Johnson and Mat Jakobi for their continuing friendship and collegiality in providing advice on Indigenous matters and discussions regarding Indigenous knowledge, learning and education generally. I am most grateful for the support, memorable discussion, mutual experience and cherished friendship of colleagues Marie Brennan, Tony Edwards, Sunny Gavran, Tony Kruger, Kerry Renwick and Jo Williams that has strengthened and enabled the social and educational perspectives and theorising expressed in this book. I also convey heartfelt gratitude for their advice and support over many years to esteemed colleagues Julie Arnold, Peter Burridge, David Jones, Claire Kelly, Brian Mundy, Greg Neal, Oksana Razoumova, Mark Selkrig, Mary Weaven and Lew Zipin. I am in personal and intellectual debt to all.

My life has been substantially enhanced by the theories and understandings of John Dewey and Paulo Freire. They encourage learning through personal and social action and respect the culture and experience that all humans bring to learning. Unfortunately, it is this very question that has proven too difficult for many schools around the world, especially in the face of highly conservative ideologies that exclude and discriminate. We continue the struggle for democratic and critical public education as a basic human right for all citizens.

*Neil Hooley*
*Melbourne*
*July 2016*

# Dedication

To John Dewey for his historical, social and educational scholarship and efforts in creating a better world through drawing on the best critical and communicative aspects of modern philosophy and modern science:

> The demand that philosophy should be *at* one with science is justified. But to be one with it is quite a different matter from being at one with it. Philosophy has to take account of scientific conclusions; it should not contain anything at variance with them as far as they are authentically scientific. It should utilise them positively. But this conception is entirely consistent with what has been said. For these conclusions, in their general trend and application, are an important part of the social beliefs with which philosophy is concerned. Yet philosophy takes them not as isolated, complete and final in themselves, but in the context of other beliefs, moral, political, religious, economic and aesthetic. Indeed, the apparent conflict that exists between some conclusions of science and some of the more cherished non-scientific beliefs sets one of the most urgent problems of present philosophising. To hold that the conflict must be resolved exclusively in terms of scientific beliefs is as one sided as it is to hold that it must be resolved in terms of traditional religious beliefs. For neither of these beliefs exhausts the field of experience.
>
> (Dewey, 2012, p. 16)

# Poem

*Aristotle ponders a lunar event*

Disturbance crosscuts the mind unsettling the orthodox
contraries jostling for position amidst confusions
with anxiety undermining the mission for certainty
yet clarity seemingly appears on a moonlit night
a cosmic pearl encased in awe and imagination
before the earth observes a curtain being drawn
dramatic scenes from history being witnessed above
interpreted with whatever is available and sensible
then darkness as silver brilliance is extinguished
nothing but the sounds of stillness and distant crickets
but transformation reversed as the circle re-emerges
light flooding again the nightscape establishing the known;
at his window Aristotle turns inward to human experience
puzzled by an orange tinge but seizing a contemplative moment
considers anew the exercise of human virtue as meaning
representations of eternity illuminate his mind and our own
while retinues of possibility form and enact the good and noble.

Note: all poems in this book, including *Aristotle ponders a lunar event* here and at
the head of chapters, are the work of the author, Neil Hooley. They are intended to
connect with one of the main themes of each chapter and to illustrate the integrated
knowledge and creative human thinking. Like all art, the poems exist in the eye of
the beholder and are designed to challenge interpretation and meaning.

# Part I

# Thinking philosophically

Coming to an understanding of our existence and its purpose, what is reality, where do our values and beliefs come from and how do we ever know anything are amongst the great questions that have puzzled humans forever. It is questions like these that we would expect to find underpinning all formal education as students engage key ideas and practices that frame social life. Unfortunately, this is often not the case as, even within broadly democratic societies, the dominance of capitalism and neoliberalism skews learning, knowledge and relationships towards the narrow and constrained. In setting out to immerse ourselves in the journey of knowing, Part I is intended to outline some necessary principles and debates drawn from philosophy and sociology that will form the basis of considering and modelling what a new approach to education will look like, an approach that is inherently philosophical in character. It is not intended that the theorists, debates and principles encountered will be fully elaborated, but that readers will pursue their interests through other readings and discussions as they wish with colleagues, family and friends. Part I, and the book itself, is therefore more of an overall map of our intellectual voyage of discovery, with each destination along the way demanding a more thorough stay and investigation. We will meet different philosophers and sociologists, delve into our understandings of knowledge and epistemology, consider the place of action in our lives and learning and be challenged by the contours of how to live ethically and well. Part I establishes a holistic basis of thinking about how the great ideas and unanswerable questions, the contests of philosophy and sociology that continue to inspire and provoke can take us over the horizon to new understandings of more substantial and radical schooling for all.

# 1 Trends and tensions of philosophy and sociology

> Shards of early morning brilliance
> irradiate eager layers of purple
> reaching out, speaking out
> as new energies warm and activate
> hidden forces within the bush rose
> transitioning at the dawn of spring.

As a general practice of inquiry, philosophy investigates problems and issues of existence and authenticity involving logic, ethics, aesthetics, metaphysics, ontology and epistemology. It poses questions, challenges orthodox viewpoints, encourages systematic argument and discussion and clarifies meanings. It continues to ponder questions regarding 'What does it mean to be human?,' 'How do we live well?' and 'What can we know?' In relation to education specifically, philosophy asks 'What is the purpose of schooling?,' 'What is the relationship between teaching and learning?' and 'What are the meaningful outcomes of learning for each person?' Sociology is a much younger field of inquiry than philosophy concerned with a study of society and of social organisation and practice. It conducts interpretive and empirical studies of social class, race, ethnicity, gender, disability, economics and politics and analyses the connections between social organisation and group or individual agency. Philosophy and sociology can merely describe situations, or propose approaches that will implement change for social improvement. In summarising some of the main historical trends in philosophy and sociology, this chapter distils key features that impact educational policy and practice today and those that support a 'theory of action' on which schooling can be based. It builds on the notion of Pring (2005, p. 28) regarding the importance of dialogue 'not simply of the logical structure of the subject matter to be learnt but also the variety of experience to be shared and made sense of.' Claims are detailed regarding human action and the 'social act' as being essential for all learning.

At the very beginning of his famous book, *Philosophy and the Mirror of Nature*, Rorty (1979/2009, p. 3) notes as one view that philosophers set about discussing enduring questions and problems regarding knowledge, the mind, the relationship

4   *Trends and tensions*

between humans and between humans and other objects of the universe. He continues that in very broad terms:

> Philosophy as a discipline thus sees itself as the attempt to underwrite or debunk claims to knowledge made by science, morality, art, or religion. It purports to do this on the basis of its special understanding of the nature of knowledge and of mind. Philosophy can be foundational in respect to the rest of culture because culture is the assemblage of claims to knowledge and philosophy adjudicates such claims.

This task continues to be very difficult and different approaches have been attempted over many centuries. Questions regarding theories of knowledge and of epistemology will be taken up in more detail in Chapter 2, especially from the point of view of the educator. At this point, we content ourselves with considering the notion that philosophy provides a framework by which to view, understand and critique other viewpoints so that what we think and value and more importantly enact, can be defended. Because there are different philosophical views of the social and physical worlds, choices must be made between them depending on a world view or paradigm that exists for each participant. Where these world views come from depends on the political and economic conditions of the times, for example, depending on whether slavery or serfdom is preferred, whether equity or elitism is dominant, whether public or private holds sway. As Rorty (1982/2011) also contends, philosophy acts as a framework for the consideration of the knowledge claims of culture, indicating that while culture arises from the totality of social activities, philosophy provides the strategies for evaluating cultural formats and their appropriateness. This demonstrates an essential difference between philosophy and sociology, although it may be more accurate to suggest the essential difference between *progressive* philosophy and *conservative* sociology. It is not required of sociology that programs of action arise from description, only that sufficient detail and analysis are provided to enable action if thought necessary. Political parties commission surveys regarding voting patterns of different communities and social groupings, but what to do about the trends so exposed is up to political strategists, not the pollsters. Progressive sociologists may of course see it as their obligation to provide action scenarios drawn from their description. Teachers and educators are always in the position of making their own professional decisions regarding how to combine philosophical and sociological research, reports and opinion in the best interests of their students and whether to place more emphasis on one or the other. Such decisions are collective and individual as experience accumulates and what it means to be an active, independent member of the profession matures.

## Case 1: properties of the triangle

Tim was feeling just a little anxious. He thought he had measured the angles correctly, or as best he could, but it was difficult using these large wooden instruments and with triangles of different sizes marked out with tape on the floor. It was awkward trying to line them up. He checked the results with Jake and they agreed

*Trends and tensions*  5

to pass on their readings to the next team who was compiling a table for each triangle on the whiteboard. As the results came in, another team was calculating the length of sides using a formula from the book. Jake and Tim generally liked their mathematics classes although they were finding some of the Year 9 topics much more difficult than last year. Their new teacher also got them involved in activities and projects that sometimes didn't make a lot of sense to them, but Mr Ciccone said he wasn't too worried about that, 'Things will work out in the end,' he always said with a laugh. It wasn't too much bother for Bluey Thompson either, who saw crawling around on the floor pretending to measure angles as a good way to get out of doing real maths. Even with the rough measures they were taking, Tim and Jake began to see a pattern emerge on the board as the lengths of the sides of the triangles that were being calculated were about the same as what had been measured with their metre rule. 'Well, what do you know about that,' interrupted Mr Ciccone, seeing them looking at the column of figures on the board, 'it looks like the equations we are using gives a rough approximation to the triangles on the floor. I wonder why that happens and how we could check?' He paused for a second before continuing seeing that he had their attention. 'Don't you think it's amazing that mathematicians centuries ago were able to work this out, to describe the universe in this way, triangles are everywhere after all?' As Mr Ciccone wandered off, Jake and Tim set about redoing their measurements. 'Why don't we map out some new triangles,' said Tim, tape and scissors in hand. 'It mightn't work for bigger and smaller ones.'

## Case 2: knowing your students

As a new teacher, Caitlyn was puzzled by the staff meetings she had been attending. When Giulio commented with some frustration the other day that his Year 9 classes were having trouble with trigonometry even after he 'had told them' a number of times how to use the correct function, she had heard the responses before. 'They seem to have little interest in equations,' noted Julia, 'and just want to plug in the numbers to get an answer.' Maria, who always took the side of the students, thought that the problem had something to do with the background of their parents who also may not have continued with formal mathematics in school or later for very long. 'I was reading the other night that the latest test results seem to show, again, that the children of families with lower income do not do as well and that schools cannot compensate for this, at least to any great extent.' 'Yes, I know that's what's usually said, but it's not the full story,' continued Giulio with recognisable agitation in his voice, 'I think that I explain equations quite well.' With her limited experience, Caitlyn wasn't going to get into this debate too early, as she couldn't quite understand the connection between family background and reluctance with school mathematics, there seemed to be pieces of the puzzle missing. If mathematics is interesting then all children should be interested, she thought. Just as she was formulating a question in her mind, Nick remarked quietly that he had seen some engagement last week: 'I think they got involved when they could investigate the relationship between angle and length of side for themselves, open it up and let them go for it, the answers will take care of themselves in time.'

## 6  *Trends and tensions*

Caitlyn appreciated Nick's approach, although she worried about some students in her classes who couldn't afford to go on camps or excursions and probably didn't have too many books at home as well. It will be difficult for school mathematics to find a place amongst those distractions.

In Case 1, Tim and Jake are initially a little confused as to why they have been asked by their teacher to measure the angles and lengths of the sides of triangles marked out on the floor, when they realise that it can't be done too accurately. However, they are prepared to try and then consider the results from both direct measurement and calculation as recorded by other teams in their Year 9 class. They are interested to see that a pattern does emerge when there is a rough correlation between both sets of readings and results. After discussion and with the encouragement of their teacher, they set about redoing their measurements not only with the original set of triangles but with others of markedly different dimensions. While doing so, they continue to chat about what Mr Ciccone meant when he mentioned the place of triangles in the universe generally, not only on their classroom floor. On the other hand, Caitlyn, as a new teacher in Case 2, struggles to participate in a staff debate regarding the socio-economic background of students because she feels that she lacks the experience and research data and analysis to contribute at this stage. Her colleagues seem to agree that many students are not suited to mathematics although there is little detail forthcoming to support this view. In what seems to be a minority opinion, Nick Ciccone from Case 1 does note quietly that when given the opportunity to actively investigate mathematical ideas, students do become involved and even take up their own questions. In spite of this evidence, Caitlyn is concerned that the shortage of family resources will prevent many of her students from gaining valuable personal experience including, she assumes, little reading at home and that this will impact their participation and therefore achievement at school. Regardless of these important social factors in their lives, Caitlyn thinks that while mathematics can be abstract and difficult, it is also inherently interesting and useful and that she should be able to gain the attention of all students in her class. This is why she became a teacher, after all.

In each of the cases noted earlier, there is a mixture of philosophical and sociological reasoning and/or practices at work, although to different extents. There seems to be a clear philosophy of 'learning by doing' in Case 1, as students set about developing their own ideas of triangles (and no doubt other geometrical shapes in due course) from their direct engagement with them. Correct answers do not seem to be important at this stage, as students are able to check their readings and pursue other avenues of investigation as they think about accuracy, equipment and alternative explanation of results. We are unaware of the socio-economic background of the students, but the pedagogical principle being adopted seems to be one of experiment and activity for all students who have found themselves in that particular class at that particular time. Pedagogy does not feature strongly in Case 2, where negative conjectures about family background appear to be dominant amongst the staff. This is primarily a sociological view, where characteristics of certain groups of students can be ascribed and applied to others from similar groups. This has been noticeable over recent years with connections being drawn between family income and test results, even though as Caitlyn muses, it makes little sense to assume that some children are interested in flowers and others not because of household resources. The philosophical and the sociological cannot be entirely separated of course in any class and the teachers and students noted in these cases will be impacted by both. It may be that the essential aspect of this question is settled by what each school and teacher can ultimately do in designing their programs and pedagogies and what happens when groups of students and teachers get together to try and understand the confusions and delights of their worlds.

## Dewey, Vygotsky and philosophy

In very general terms, the two grand traditions of human learning concern knowledge being held by experts or authorities that can then be passed on to others, or knowledge arising from human action as we interact with the social and physical worlds. This is the division between traditional/conservative and progressive/radical philosophies of knowledge, indeed between philosophies of what it means to be human. Of themselves, both of these traditions do not necessarily have to explain what knowledge is, or how it is obtained. For these matters, we must turn to the branch of philosophy known as epistemology (Audi, 2011) for more detailed explanations. It is certainly the case that modern schooling pays little attention to epistemology concerning the philosophical understanding of knowledge and what it means to know, placing more emphasis on the political and economic basis of education and on the measurement of outcomes. There is also a distinction that must be made between how a particular philosophical view conceptualises knowledge and human processes undertaken to engage with or make sense of that knowledge. This depends on the agreed purposes of formal schooling, for example, and whether or not importance rests with the understanding and learning of children, or with the replication of slices of facts and information. It may be that a particular child or groups of children come to appreciate the beauty of the universe and of school mathematics though a range of investigations over time concerning the location and purpose of geometrical shapes in nature. Such investigations may involve calculations regarding the area of circles, triangles and rectangles, but they may not, relying instead on the connections that can be noticed between the shapes of petals and leaves on plants and the feelings generated within each child. Under these circumstances, learning involves what each child comes to know about the physical world and how they can discuss this with other children and adults, rather than obtaining a correct answer from a calculation. Whether this makes all knowledge relative, generalised knowledge unlikely, or knowledge that exists for its own sake beyond personal experience impossible, is at the heart of epistemology and of how the school curriculum is hypothesised.

Questions regarding the nature of knowledge have been highly contested throughout the modern era. Central to this argument is whether there are philosophical differences between what might be called 'everyday' or 'concrete' knowledge (the way things are) and 'scientific' or 'abstract' knowledge (the way things

## 8  *Trends and tensions*

are thought to be). That is, when a family sets about discussing and deciding whether they should purchase a new car in relation to their other expenses and priorities, is the process fundamentally different to a research team working out how to undertake a particular experiment in the laboratory? In each case, the two groups will draw upon their prior knowledge, agree on the problems to be faced, consider alternative forms of action and agree on the preferred mode. Each group will be working with different experience and different ideas within different fields of practice, but the process appears to be quite similar. It is also difficult to argue that the ideas and practices of one field are always more complex or at a higher level than the ideas and practices of another, as this will need to be debated on a case-by-case basis. A group of construction workers installing large glass windows on the twentieth floor of a new building will need a more detailed knowledge of materials than a lab technician working with test tubes. If we are to take the key ideas and practices of each field as the point of comparison, then it is extremely difficult to correlate across fields, as each particular idea and practice will have its own history and culture that participants will have experienced. In his book *Bringing Knowledge Back In*, Young (2008) raises knowledge issues of this type and details how significant philosophers and sociologists have proceeded with such problems. While he agrees that the basis of knowledge is social, he also argues that knowledge is realist, existing in its own right. He draws a distinction between knowledge and 'common sense.' His discussion opens up a number of provocative avenues for investigation that will be taken up throughout this book, although more attention could have been given to the detailed nature of epistemology. This issue is discussed further next.

Dewey's contribution to philosophy generally and to the philosophy of education is beyond peer. He took the key principles of American Pragmatism and applied them to education in such a way that they envisioned a much more radical view of education and of schooling than existed at the time in Europe and the United States of America, shifting the understanding of schooling from a traditional to a progressive paradigm. His book *Democracy and Education* (Dewey, 1916) still endures today as a major international and historical work that theorises education and schooling and guides contemporary policy and practice change for the participation of all students regardless of socio-economic background. His work will be discussed and referenced throughout forthcoming chapters. At this point, however, let us consider Dewey's notion of *experience*. In recounting a famous story regarding a later manuscript that had been lost for a number of years and not found until long after Dewey's death, Deen (2012, pp. xviii–xix) notes,

> It is well known that Dewey came to question the use of the term *experience* and hoped to replace it with *culture*. This was striking, given that it is hard to find a word closer to Dewey's heart than *experience*. It stands with *democracy, education and inquiry* to form Dewey's final vocabulary.

This is indeed a remarkable repositioning and re-understanding, but it reflects a concern that experience can be interpreted in a more isolated and relative way,

*Trends and tensions* 9

instead of arising from 'that complex whole which includes knowledge, belief, art, morals, customs' (Dewey, 1958, p. 40) that need to be analysed as the many parts of experience. The work of Freire (1972; Darder, 2013) in relation to culture and social change will be incorporated throughout the text and its impact on modern schooling around the world. In looking at experience as comprising the many aspects of culture, Dewey may be attempting to get away from the problem of *my* experience at that particular moment and location and instead, be encouraging an analysis of *our* experience in history and association. This is a significant educational principle for progressive educators, of accepting that the starting point of learning is our own particular experience, but that our understanding needs to take into account the views of others that have been formed from a historical and reflexive inquiry process. For radical educators then, Dewey's insights regarding experience, culture, inquiry, practice, democracy, education and learning will not only continue to form the basis of how they think about education and schooling but also must be interrogated for contemporary intent. While continuing to be totally relevant and challenging, these ideas were formed 100 years ago and many social and economic changes have taken place in the interim. Dewey was a strong supporter of modern science as a means of opening up conservative ideas and customs to critique and experiment, but how he would deal with current technologies and social media is of course, unknown. How Dewey's theories and indeed American Pragmatism itself copes with modern social and political questions must also be considered, that is are they located within a critical social theory? Those questions are up to us. Dewey's educational legacy demonstrates that a general 'philosophy of life' not only explains human learning emerging from our lifeworld of experience and culture but also that informal/concrete and formal/abstract theorising this process lays the groundwork for critical change and improvement, both personal and social.

In contrast to Dewey's sometimes perceived lack of an explicit social theory, Vygotsky (1987) grounded his work in the social theory of Marxism and the movement of Soviet society towards communism. It is therefore understandable that he should emphasise the connections between theory and practice and the relationship between practical activity and knowledge and more systematic or 'scientific' knowledge. Like Dewey, however, Vygotsky saw education in the broad sense of the concept as an essential social process where to be human is to learn and through learning to become active social agents of change. It is also understandable that Vygotsky should take other Marxist concepts and incorporate them into his view of education and learning. As Young (2008, p. 49) points out, Vygotsky was interested in dialectical materialism and how material sensation can be converted into conscious human thought. The notion of consciousness and dialectical materialism will be discussed in more detail later, but it is an important idea in the progressive understanding of thinking. The argument here is that current principles of modern science need to be applied to the material of human existence in a materialist concept of humanity, to guide consideration of additional features that are seen as metaphysical such as emotion, values, aspirations, aesthetics and the like. Whether or not material alone can give rise to these human features remains one of the most

10    *Trends and tensions*

contentious issues of philosophy. Vygotsky emphasised language and sociality as key aspects of learning and thinking, processes that impact markedly on how curriculum is viewed and arranged. In likening the processes of theory, practice and labour, Vygotsky is close to those of experience and inquiry as advocated by Dewey and provides a clear framework for curriculum and pedagogy in schools. His well-known concepts of 'zone of proximal development' and consequent scaffolding of ideas and concepts for children (and adults) remain practical advice for all teachers. Dewey, Vygotsky, Freire and other critical philosophers therefore constitute a view of learning and of humanity that emphasises human action and the resulting connections that can be made between language, thinking and meaning emerging from the discourses, reflections and new practices that are constructed.

## Durkheim, Habermas and sociology

Together with Karl Marx and Max Weber, the French theorist and writer Emile Durkheim (Lukes, 1985) is considered the father of modern sociology. As well as outlining the principles and methodology of a new field of study called sociology, he undertook major studies into institutions, religion, suicide and the sociology of knowledge. Durkheim proposed the notion of social facts as a means of studying society, defined as those influences that exist throughout society and impact on individual and group activity. He introduced the term 'collective consciousness' to indicate those values, beliefs and practices that are generally held by communities as being appropriate and which guide individual and group action. He was strongly interested in the sociology of knowledge and, as mentioned earlier, how more systematic modes of thought can be produced from everyday experience. The place of language in learning was central to Durkheim's thinking, seen as a 'representation collective' that brings together collective understanding arising from ideas, practices, beliefs, images that combined, cannot be produced by individuals acting or thinking alone. In this regard, Durkheim made his famous distinction between 'profane' and 'sacred' knowledge, the former coming from immediate everyday experience and the latter from what might be called a religious and collective understanding of events, concepts and beliefs that do not depend on observable facts. This continuing separation between common sense knowledge and more abstract appreciations remains unresolved in schooling today. It can be seen in, generally speaking, more activity-based approaches being adopted in primary schools compared with secondary schools and with more abstract outcomes being assumed in some subjects such as physics and mathematics compared with arts and humanities.

As a result of the spread of fascism in Europe in the 1930s and the tragedy of World War II, the German social theorist Jurgen Habermas (1981) set himself the task of developing a new understanding of human reason. In effect, a new critical understanding of modernity. He theorised a narrow, controlling, technical reason expressing the need to dominate nature and other humans as underpinning fascist thought. Technical rationality of this type needed to be replaced by a more democratic practical and emancipatory human interest. To move in this direction,

*Trends and tensions* 11

Habermas proposed his theory of communicative action (Habermas, 1984) that focused on the democratic use of language between participants. Instead of following a process of 'strategic action,' where actors attempt to win and impose their will on others, Habermas saw a process of 'communicative action,' where participants work through a series of 'validity claims' involving the normative rightness, sincerity and truthfulness of what is said in support of an argument or proposition. These claims can only be redeemed or accepted if the collective discourse can be conducted in such a way as to disclose plausibility and reasonability. As well as providing a somewhat idealised view of the modern world at the beginning of the neoliberal period that could be based on language and communicative reason and action (referred to as the 'linguistic turn' in philosophy), Habermas offered a view of knowledge production that could be applied to education and schooling. Rather than the curriculum setting out predetermined information and facts, students could consider important questions, ideas and practices communicatively, discussing and defending their perceptions and interpretations through the redeeming of validity claims. In this way, students come to value the views of their classmates and see knowledge appearing from their own observations and discussions, rather than being imposed from some external authority without good reason. Sociologists such as Durkheim, Habermas and Giddens have attempted to theorise society, its institutions and procedures, so that improvements to the human condition can be made on the basis of accurate and detailed understandings of sociality. As in all other fields, there are conservative and progressive means of approaching this task, an issue to which we now turn.

## Neoliberalism and the decline of epistemology

From the brief and preliminary discussion of some major theorists outlined earlier, it can be seen that there are significant differences and tensions still to be resolved between philosophy and sociology. To combat a pernicious neoliberalism, an important judgement needs to be made as to whether the age of reflection as the dominant paradigm in education is over, to be replaced by a reorientation towards philosophy as social practice, an investigation of the philosophy of knowledge. This is especially so where schooling and epistemology are concerned. In making his distinction between traditional and progressive schooling, Dewey highlighted a dualism that he sought to reconcile, but it remains one of the great problems in education today. The notion of bringing theory and practice together, or in the terms discussed earlier, common sense or experiential knowledge and knowledge abstracted from experience, has proven to be an impossible task, at least for mainstream schooling. It is unclear why this problem has continued to be so difficult, although the dominance of modern economic systems since the Industrial Revolution has made the construction of progressive, experiential models of teaching and learning challenging and problematic. Over the past 30 years, for example, capitalism has implemented an international form of itself that demands a market-driven economic system consisting of small government, privatised, individualised and corporate profit-driven, 'bottom-line' imperatives. This neoliberal ideology has

12 *Trends and tensions*

been extremely successful around the world, squeezing out the previous welfare state and Keynesian economic philosophy following World War II that emphasised the role of government in supporting the 'public good.'

Harvey (2010) has argued that capitalism requires constant crises to reproduce and strengthen itself through a rethinking and reapplication of its basic tenets and doctrine as the social, political and economic world changes and the rapacious necessity for profit and markets intensifies. While most countries continue to allocate considerable resources to public education, neoliberalism does not demand that a large proportion of the population needs to be well educated to support the national economy, given that most economies are now locked into global systems and relationships. In the larger dominant economies, however, there is high public expectation that the children of most families will have access to quality schooling and that high levels of literacy and numeracy are required. For these reasons, education has become a major area of contested debate around the world with international testing regimes giving rise to eagerly awaited statistical and comparative tables of nations rated each against the other. Under these prevalent conditions, sociological issues have tended to dominate education, with epistemological concerns taking a very minor role. That is, questions of access to education, equity of resource provision and accountability for outcomes have become political issues for conservative and progressive educators alike, often from similar perspectives. Any discussion of epistemology and schooling usually proceeds from a restricted view of skill acquisition, rather than constructing a broad and creative understanding of the world and oneself.

Exactly what a neoliberal epistemology looks like in primary or secondary schooling is unclear and is certainly not usually provided by committed neoliberals except in the most general of terms. This will be developed further next. A distinction here needs to be drawn with a classical conservative view of education that generally is sharp and pure, a reliance on slices of facts, information and knowledge that are known and considered as culturally and educationally significant, together with a passive, teacher-centred approach to teaching. As will be discussed later, this ideology has been most apparent in debates regarding literacy and numeracy. The neoliberal insistence on markets, privatisation, individualism and accountability is most obvious in relation to mass testing and examination schemes rather than the detail of epistemology itself. On the one hand, a more liberal approach to teaching and learning could involve an 'anything goes' approach with a recognition that all students are different and that some will achieve and some will not. This view might see a wide spread of test results being normal, especially if it is thought that most students are not capable of achieving and only a few having the natural talent to progress to more advanced studies. On the other hand, a liberal view of teaching and learning could involve the incorporation of numerous avenues to knowledge and many different teaching methods to cater for individual differences, including child-centred, active styles. This is consistent with the former point that a recognition of individualism means a recognition of different approaches and different outcomes. Under these conditions, learning is essentially a private matter and a lack of achievement and progress for many is accepted as the normal order of things. This view is easily seen at the university level in the wealthy countries and debates regarding procedures and standards of entry and the numbers of applicants who should be admitted to tertiary studies. The neoliberal approach therefore will not be overly concerned with the problem of connecting concrete and abstract understandings and any disconnects between philosophy and sociology assuming that this will happen for the most appropriate students in due course. In many economies there is a tension between neoliberal and conservative opinion regarding education and public policy is usually the result of an uneasy compromise between the two. Because of the emphasis on more systemic questions, neoliberal epistemology has probably received little attention from neoliberals themselves. A summary comparison of epistemologies and their relationship with educational social justice is shown in Table 1.1:

*Table 1.1* Summary comparison of knowledges, epistemology and social justice

| | *Progressive Epistemology* | *Conservative Epistemology* | *Neoliberal Epistemology* |
|---|---|---|---|
| Concrete, Everyday Knowledge | World-centred Emphasised Activity Small-group discussion Unknown outcomes | Information-centred Unimportant Passive reception Class discussion Known outcomes | Individual-centred Diverse Active/passive Individual considerations Varied outcomes |
| Abstract, Systematic Knowledge | Project-based Emergent Activity Small-group discussion Problematic outcomes | Teacher-based Predetermined Passive reception Class discussion Known outcomes | Student-based Disparate Active/passive Individual considerations Varied outcomes |
| Social Justice Impact | Establishes personal and social environments as areas of action, progress, change and betterment for all | Maintains personal and social hierarchies and relationships of influence and power for some | Rearranges personal and social hierarchies and relationships due to non-regulated individual capabilities |

When comparisons such as those indicated in Table 1.1 are made, we are going to the heart of teaching and learning and in effect, the meaning of our humanity, what it means to be broadly educated and what we should expect from a democratic education system. From the point of view of Greek philosophy (and a more extensive discussion later), Aristotle was deeply concerned with these issues and described three rationalities of intellectual virtues that can guide our deliberation, the virtues of techne, episteme and phronesis (Flyvbjerg, 2001). Techne is taken to be context-dependent, variable and is based upon an essentially instrumental rationality oriented towards technique or craft. Episteme is context-independent, invariable and

## 14  *Trends and tensions*

exhibits an analytical rationality that today would be oriented towards science. Phronesis is ethically framed rationality or disposition regarding what is good and appropriate; it is based on a system of values rather than rules and requires human judgements to be made (Birmingham, 2004). Praxis is the action arising from phronesis regarding values and intent (Feenberg, 2014). From an epistemological standpoint, we now need to link the general ideas of practice and praxis more directly with concepts of knowledge. Bernstein (2010) is useful here and in particular, his distinction between horizontal and vertical knowledge forms. According to Bernstein, vertical knowledge structures enable theorised understandings to develop through the combination of propositions into more generalised schema. He saw physics as a paradigm case in this regard. On the other hand, horizontal knowledge structures consist of a number of concepts or languages that do not so much combine into higher order or theorised thinking but create new languages and perceptions for new meaning. Sociology is an example of a horizontal knowledge form. Bernstein discussed how these structures are classified and partitioned from each other. Physics is strongly classified and separated from other knowledge, whereas literature is weakly classified and not so separated. Bernstein also noted that some structures have a stronger relationship externally, to worldly influence and can maintain a more stable existence. Considerations of knowledge of this type raise questions for teachers and teacher educators regarding how to provide different avenues for students to investigate various knowledges and how to assess learning as students grapple with different internal and external epistemological structures. A distinction must also be made between Bernstein's analysis of different forms of knowledge and how humans come to create and understand that knowledge.

This brief introductory discussion has suggested that there are differences between major theorists on some seminal ideas in philosophy and sociology. As noted in the first paragraph, philosophy can be seen as a general practice of inquiry that investigates problems and issues of existence. With this understanding, it poses questions, challenges orthodox viewpoints, encourages systematic argument and discussion and clarifies meanings. In relation to education specifically, philosophy inspects the purposes of schooling and the meaningful outcomes of learning for each person. According to Bradatan (2015, p. 6), however, philosophy can also be interpreted as a social practice, or 'an art of living' such that

> to embrace the notion of philosophy as a self-transformative practice is to make yourself fundamentally vulnerable. If a philosophy is genuine only to the extent that it is embodied in the one who practices it, then the philosopher is not unlike the tightrope walker performing without a safety net.

In recognising philosophy as a way of life, Bradatan contends that the philosopher must walk the tightrope of 'living well' in regards to 'speaking the truth' and does not surrender to either the demands of the world or of personal conscience in favour of reputation, security or protection. Bradatan notes that to 'speak without reservation' (Gk: *parrhesia*: free speech) is a dangerous occupation, particularly as the philosopher usually has no authority or status except by so doing. In contrast to this view of

*Trends and tensions*  15

the philosopher acting in the world in order to change it, there does not seem to be a similar task for the sociologist. In general terms, the role of the sociologist remains that of description and analysis only without any obligation to ensuing action for change and improvement. Sociologists can produce accurate, perceptive reports of social situations of course, together with appropriate recommendations, but these refer to the situation itself, not the sociologist her/himself. This is similar to the academic researcher in any field who may produce important research findings but be unchanged and unmoved by them as a person. For these reasons, Hooley (2015) has theorised a 'practice interface' that exists between the findings of sociology and the practices of epistemology that needs to act on such findings in schools. He goes further in submitting that the practice interface is necessary to break the 'cul-de-sac that the sociology of education has reached on social justice questions' (p. 190) on education and that a new 'reflexive sociology of education' is urgently required.

This distinction between philosophy and sociology – or more correctly between progressive and conservative philosophy and sociology – bears directly on the key idea raised earlier, that of the difference between forms of knowledge, the concrete/informal on the one hand and the abstract/formal on the other. This is the historical question of epistemology. It generates argument between the traditional and progressive and social constructivist and social realist views of knowledge and schooling, or as Young (2008) remarks, differences between 'knowledge of the powerful' and 'powerful knowledge.' This is a central argument for educators regarding curriculum and pedagogy during the era of mature neoliberalism and its impact on schooling, especially in the major economies where large expenditures are disbursed on public education for mainly ideological and reproductive purposes. Dewey and the pragmatists would argue that those who set about exploring learning, who respect their own experience and culture and who engage in inquiries of personal interest, are in the best position of becoming critical and responsible democratic citizens. Democratic learning involves taking into account the views of others, observing what happens when experiments are conducted, being aware of possibilities, checking results and using inchoate thoughts to plan and guide new investigations. Over time, general ideas based on this experience are accepted by communities as being appropriate guides for further action. In suggesting that 'powerful knowledge' exists almost independently of human intervention, the social realists miss the epistemological nature of learning and deny the role of each person in coming to their own understanding and meaning of the world. They disagree with the epistemological point that 'powerful knowledge' exists in the mind of each person and cannot be imposed or premanufactured. The process of education is pursued by each citizen in their own way throughout their entire life, although backgrounded and contextualised by social and physical environments. They act, reflect, think, communicate, contest and adapt as they see fit, to make sense of their surroundings. To support this purpose, formal education needs to develop as a democratic, independent, cohesive field of progressive practice in its own right, not fragmented or derived from other fields, robust and rigorous, capable of informing and being informed by all other domains of human endeavour. Conservative and neoliberal ideologies will resist mightily.

# 2 Understandings of epistemology

Truth a property of matter in contest with conversation
exploration and confluence integrates perception
bringing observation and explanation into alignment
liberating boundaries of established thought;
meanwhile children languish in cells of alienation
as the delicate bourgeois ponder echelon and sip tea.

A branch of philosophy that considers the nature of knowledge, how it is possible for humans to know and the processes of learning, is called epistemology. Questions that are essentially epistemological in character involve 'How do we understand the concepts of the different knowledge disciplines?,' 'How is it possible to abstract ideas from experience?' and 'How can we be more creative and expressive in our thinking?' An empirical view of epistemology suggests that we know the world through our experiences and senses, while a rationalist view contends that understanding arises from reason. Kant proposed that we know the world as we experience it because of the way the mind is structured and arranged. From a contemporary educational point of view, epistemology is sometimes taken to mean access to specified knowledge through systems of teaching and learning, perhaps restricted to privileged knowledge of the Enlightenment period. This view has been emphasised through the neoliberal era because of the importance given to the private, economic benefits of schooling and outcomes that advantage systems and not the interests of communities. Whether or not it is possible for humans to exist outside their own minds and to know the world accurately, or whether we are 'trapped' within the solipsism of current neurological structures has crucial epistemological implications for all education. A 'theory of action' (see the following section and Chapter 3) argues that this is the way humans learn because this is the way we are and that therefore, teaching and learning in schools should proceed from an action basis. In pursuing learning as a 'social act' (see the following section), this chapter discusses epistemology as being at the centre of all schooling, not as passive processes of transmitting predetermined facts and information but as active, uncertain processes of investigation, experimentation, reflection and abstraction of meaning. All humans of all backgrounds are involved in this continuing process of becoming human and of understanding themselves and the universe.

## Historical location of epistemology

Questions of epistemology have been central to philosophical debates for many centuries. To inquire into truth and knowledge requires understandings and practices of logic, metaphysics and axiology (ethics and aesthetics) such that there is an all-sided appreciation of what it means to experience and to know. In the twentieth century, Piaget identified himself as a 'genetic epistemologist' defined by Vuyk (1981, p. 36) as

> genetic epistemology is an interdisciplinary science studying the necessary and sufficient conditions that make knowledge – including animal and human knowledge (the latter from that of the new-born child to that of the scientist) – possible, as well as the historical development of knowledge from states of lesser validity to those of higher validity.

In the first instance, Piaget denotes this version of epistemology as being 'interdisciplinary' rather than isolated within a single discipline, as a 'science' that is concerned with truth and fundamental principles, as a study of the conditions or practices that enable knowledge, as well as the analysis of the historical context that supports the transformation of concrete (lower) forms to abstract (higher) forms of knowledge. This is an extensive definition that lays the basis of Piaget's view regarding constructivism as the primary human epistemology and his emphasis on learning occurring through action. His view of learning had a major impact on schooling across many countries in the 1960s and sat alongside the development of 'child-centred' and 'reflective' learning. Piaget's work grappled with the problem of mind-body dualism by which Kant, for example, had argued for two sites of reality, the phenomenal site of conscious experience and the noumenal site of reality external to the human. This issue remains a difficult philosophical problem today, where qualities or properties of objects such as colour and taste may not be considered aspects of the objects themselves, but are generated when the human mind or brain perceives those objects. As will be discussed in later chapters, the enigma of whether a 'mind' exists separately to the brain and therefore whether the nature of human consciousness is purely material or not, is still unresolved. It is a central question for schooling and learning and, like epistemology, receives little attention today due to the strong dominance of neoliberalism and economics.

In formal systems of education and schooling, it is sometimes held that epistemology means a somewhat restricted view of knowledge that is already known and can be passed on to students in linear fashion. This gives rise to a curriculum that features subject content knowledge and passive approaches to pedagogy such that knowledge is basically 'cognivist,' being passed from the head of the teacher to the head of the learner. This approach may have emerged following the end of World War II and the expansion of secondary education in the more wealthy countries. In the confusion of the purpose of mass secondary education, it may have been assumed that secondary schools emphasised abstract knowledge, rules and procedures in relation to the concrete knowledge of primary schools and that abstract knowledge was not formed through student activity, but could only be

18  *Understandings of epistemology*

made available by the teacher and textbook. It would not be possible for all students to conceptualise their own model of the atom, for example, as distinct from accepting the current model as developed by scientists and researchers. It may also be the case that the preparation of teachers does not include a study of philosophy generally and of epistemology in particular, so that the education profession is weak in these areas. Under such conditions, education can easily become fragmented without reference to shared explanatory schema and theories to guide program development. There is of course, a point at which the teacher can bring their personal understandings and subject knowledge into play to broaden and challenge student thinking in relation to accepted convention. Access to a wide range of resources to contextualise and challenge what students think at any particular time is also necessary. If the epistemological tradition of human action as indicated by Piaget and many others is adopted, however, teachers will encourage students to formulate their own ideas over time and to constantly assess what they think through discourse, experimentation and reflection. They will also critique their own epistemologies and pedagogies in relation to professional practice and adjust their teaching accordingly. Teaching of this type is not 'cognivist' in the passive, predetermined sense of the word, but is 'activist' where new understandings are generated by groups of people working together for mutual interest and learning.

In tackling the complicated problems of contemporary epistemology in schools, Kincheloe (2004) proposed the notion of 'critical complex epistemology.' As a critical scholar working in the tradition of Freire, Kincheloe (2004, p. 52) positions epistemology in its cultural – historical context and suggests a 'meta-epistemological perspective that grounds many of the categories of knowledges that teachers need to know.' He goes on to claim,

> In our meta-epistemological construction, the educational knowledge base involves the recognition of different types of knowledges of education including but not limited to empirical, experiential, normative, critical, ontological and reflective-synthetic domains.

Kincheloe adopts a more sociological approach to his educational theorising rather than delve more deeply into the philosophical issues noted earlier. However, his role over many years in exposing how 'all disciplinary knowledges are produced in discourses of power' (p. 58), for example, confronts all teachers to not see research and epistemology as arising from neutral and disinterested situations that can then be applied elsewhere to a range of different settings, but as being socially constructed like all knowledges. He notes in this regard, that 'the knowledge derived from practice about education is shaped by an epistemology significantly different from the one shaping propositional empirical knowledge' (p. 61). Kincheloe may be drawing on Greek philosophy here where phronesis/praxis and practical wisdom give rise to perspectives that are different to those of reason alone. It is not possible of course for teachers to resolve the yet to be resolved in philosophy, but it is possible for them to have an overview of the main issue involved and to take them into account when designing their programs and specific curriculum. As a working hypothesis for teachers at all levels of schooling for instance, philosophy could be thought of as 'social practice as acts of living and knowing' and, based on that account, epistemology could be envisaged as 'practitioner investigation of social practices that enable the construction of understanding from personal subjective experience.' Investigations of this type will be difficult for teachers to undertake within the confines of their work, but small groups of teachers working with an external critical friend could indeed gather appropriate data that will inform practitioner-based epistemology so defined. Long-term discussions with students and teachers will gradually produce narratives of practice and learning that will impact how epistemology is perceived and how knowledge is assembled. This process will take into account historical and socio-cultural factors as advocated by Piaget, Freire and Kincheloe.

Epistemology persists as a contested term in the field of philosophy. Descartes ensured his question would live throughout history when he asked, 'What propositions are worthy of belief?' In this way, Descartes underlined the criteria by which we judge what might be true and to consider what we think is true using these criteria. It will continue to be so as long as there is dispute regarding how humans perceive the external world and whether or not there is a mind-body dualism. Exactly how sensory perception is converted into knowledge of what is 'real' or external is unknown, let alone the conversion of these perceptions into 'conscious' thought. Descartes may have resolved this problem for himself by introducing the concept of 'soul' into the equation, but this has yet to be confirmed. Quine (1976) put forward the notion of 'naturalised' epistemology and argued that epistemology should adopt natural scientific methods. He attempted to move from a philosophical approach to an empirical process that may involve a different mix of each. In this regard, it is interesting to note the work of Kuhn (1962/2012) and his submission that theory change in modern science occurs through a process of 'paradigm shift.' Kuhn noted that scientists decide on whether a new paradigm is reasonable depends not only on data but how they think about what the data are saying from a varied range of social and political perspective and practice. On this view, science is not isolated from the economic, cultural and political trends that exist, but these influence how those involved in the field think about the nature of science and its directions. These considerations make epistemology a complex and difficult issue for teachers and educators and how they might include a broad understanding in their own paradigm of knowledge, teaching and learning. In practice terms, it probably means being comfortable with a small number of epistemological ideas and principles that are kept under review as experience accumulates. However, the place of human action in learning will be of central concern.

## Centrality of human action

In his seminal book, *The Structure of Social Action*, Parsons (1937/1968) set about the development of a 'theory of action' that brought together a number of different trends in sociology at the time, or what was called his 'convergence' theory. For his purposes of action theory, Parsons spoke of the 'unit act' (p. 43) involving the

20   *Understandings of epistemology*

properties of action systems without which they do not exist. He listed the properties of an 'act' as being the presence of an agent or actor, a future towards which the act is directed, a situation that is different to the intention of the act itself and a relationship between these properties. Features such as these are very similar to the viewpoints of other theorists who privilege human action in learning, including the American Pragmatists and Mead whose concept of the 'social act' will be discussed next. Further, Joas (1996, p. 8) has commented that the work of Parsons 'was an unprecedented attempt to bundle together in concentrated form historical, epistemological-methodological and substantive aspects of a theory of action.' According to Joas, Parsons also wanted to provide an alternative to the view of rational action provided by utilitarianism and to show how action theory could 'defend a *normative* concept of social order' (p. 14):

> If social order is to signify more than the mere factual order of an aggregation of actions and more than the temporary stabilisation of competition for resources and power, then this presumes that all actors share *common* orientations that are not subject to the individual actor's subjective calculations of utility, but on the contrary, are what make individual calculations of utility possible in the first place.

This determination shows that Parsons was making strong connections between how humans learn and broader social concerns regarding values and norms. His attention to better underpinnings of social order may have reflected the times in which he lived and political movements that were gaining alarming prominence in Europe and elsewhere. Was it possible to value learning and social existence for their own intrinsic good and the satisfaction they bring, rather than to covert 'utility' (or perhaps 'celebrity' in today's neoliberal world) as the point of departure of human endeavour? Action epistemology, knowledge and learning have a key role whichever interpretation is grasped.

Supporting the grand philosophical tradition of human understanding and learning emerging from social experience rather than from imposed external authority necessitates consideration of action theory and specifically, American Pragmatism. Beginning with the work of Peirce and James in the late nineteenth century, pragmatism sought to break with Cartesianism in terms of distinctions that were made between mind and body, mental and physical, experience and thought, subject and object. For instance, pragmatism did not support the idea that there was a predetermined foundation or certainty to human existence, but that direction, purpose and ethics/values arose from human action over long periods of time. A key feature of this aspect of pragmatism is that it is possible for humans to be 'fallible and anti-sceptical' at the same time. That is, while recognising that humans make mistakes, it is still possible to have knowledge and justified beliefs. Following Peirce and James, Dewey became well known throughout the world in the twentieth century as the major proponent of pragmatism and his writings and critique of traditional education from a pragmatic viewpoint continue to influence educational policy and practice today. There are strong connections between

*Understandings of epistemology* 21

the praxis model of teacher education outlined in this book and pragmatism. In particular, the emphasis on continuing movement and change that leads to the transformation of ideas and practices, the dialectical integration of all knowledge and learning as such change occurs and the blurring of any distinction between subject and object through personal and community inquiry. These concepts assist the notion of education in its broadest sense being concerned with human 'subjec-tification' as all citizens seek to expand their practice of becoming fully human. In breaking with Continental philosophy, American Pragmatism was understandably not fully appreciated in Europe and elsewhere until more recent times, perhaps also because of the dominance of analytic philosophy. The writing of Dewey and that of other pragmatic and critical theorists continues to provide a strong framework for the development of more radical and progressive approaches to schooling, teaching and learning.

As the name implies, Cultural-Historical Activity Theory (CHAT) attempts to position human learning through action and activity within its cultural and histori-cal context. It is another way of looking at the theory-practice connection as the basis of the mind-body dualism and the development of human consciousness. It emerged from the work of Vygotsky who, as mentioned earlier, was considering the nature of conservative psychology and in particular behaviourism, following the Russian Revolution in 1917. One of the key ideas of Vygotsky was that of 'cul-tural mediation' that argued the subject-object relationship was always mediated by the social context in which it was situated. This approach has been extended since Vygotsky's time to include the detail and dialectical relationship of rules, community and division of labour. In his reporting of a CHAT project regarding teacher education in England, Ellis (2011, p. 192) notes,

> In presenting what I believe is the positive case for CHAT-informed interven-tions in stimulating teachers' professional creativity, at points I have briefly contrasted CHAT designs with action research approaches to elaborate on the distinctiveness of CHAT's way of thinking about practice. This distinctive-ness, as many have argued, arises out of its critique of the dualism between mind and action. Specifically, I have identified knowledge and history in rela-tion to practice as key, generative, conceptual 'where to tools.'
>
> (Engestrom, 2007)

In attempting to bring together the concepts of culture, history and human activity or practice, CHAT accepts the challenge of Dewey and others in reconciling mind and body and in respecting the capabilities of all humans to act, think and under-stand. A particular form of research known as the 'Change Laboratory' has been implemented to pursue intervention in activity systems to research the conditions of change and to improve the work of participants and collaborative researchers. In general then, human action occupies a significant position in epistemology and our understanding of how humans learn and engage their subjectivities. It means therefore that formal schooling and curriculum that denies human activity and practice will be sterile and corrupt.

## 22 *Understandings of epistemology*

## Mead, the social act and intersubjectivity

While it is not generally recognised or highlighted that John Dewey placed emphasis on human communication and language in learning, his lesser-known colleague George Herbert Mead highlighted the 'social and intersubjective act' of learning (Biesta, 1998). Mead argued that learning is always social and intersubjective as people come together in their attempts to understand each other and worldly phenomena. The principle of intersubjectivity locates learning as taking place between instead of within individual subjects (or in addition to) as they explore different concepts of meaning and attempt to reach shared understanding. This process and conversation does not occur in a vacuum, but is contextualised by the lived experience and practices of participants that they bring. In theorising that teaching is 'intersubjective praxis' therefore, we are accepting that learning environments should enable all participants to consider issues of their interest that of necessity will draw upon background personal and community culture and will involve fertile language situations of conversation, description, initiative and creativity. There is thus a combination of experience, experimentation and interest as current ideas and practices are transformed into the new.

Consideration of subjectivity and intersubjectivity is an important concern in relation to the dominance of neoliberalism, socially and in education. A central economic imperative of capitalism and neoliberalism is the abstraction of major characteristics of humanness, followed by their quantification and finally their allocation of certain value to the production line. In this way, the human workforce is 'objectified' as mere objects of production, devoid of all aspects of compassionate humanity. This process of reification leads to alienation not only from the outputs of production but also from what it means to be human itself. Formal education has a key role in reversing this process, to counter dehumanising objectification and to replace it with 'subjectification.' This latter process will need to emphasise respect for the autonomous action of all persons, the culture, character and knowledgeability of people from all backgrounds, the need for discursive community environments for the development of views and practices and the establishment and consolidation of democratic public spheres for mature and non-coercive free assemblies and debate. Broad subjectification principles of this type then need to be adjusted as need be for application in educational institutions and public schools at all levels, such that the main purpose of schooling becomes the subjectification impulse. One way of thinking about this process is to concentrate on the human subject in terms of 'Who I am,' although this can overly psychologise the subject and bring identity politics into play. Post-structuralism in particular has influenced the ascendancy of feminism and ethnicities in comparison to social class as the major sociological focus of analysis. In contrast, the concept of 'How I am' (Biesta, 2013) links strongly to pragmatism and practice and the ways in which social action is taken to construct the selfhood and lifeworld. The formation of subjectification therefore builds on the notion of 'I think, therefore I am' (action), rather than 'I am, therefore I think' (existence).

Biesta (1998) has written that American Pragmatism advanced a philosophical view of human consciousness that was collective, intersubjective and between

*Understandings of epistemology*   23

participants, rather than individual and dependent on the subjectivity of or within each person. He makes the strong statement, 'At stake is the claim that intersubjectivity precedes subjectivity and is constitutive of it' (p. 74). There is an important question here for education and teaching. If the development of subjectivity occurs between those undertaking a particular activity, then it would seem that group work is vital for all learning and that action must occur first. While this is a chicken and egg argument, it means that students need to work within continuing cycles of activity and reflection with other classmates as they explore what they want to know. It may then occur that at those moments when observations are being made, when problems are being discussed, when refinements are being made, that each member of a group comes to a new understanding, or consciousness, of the issue being investigated. At this point, at this exact moment, the notion of teaching and learning disappears and all participants involved realise a new consciousness intersubjectively. These new insights, ideas and concepts will be different for each person in the group and will emerge from current personal experience and conscious understanding. A group of people considering the electron, for example, may stumble across the metaphor of a football tumbling in air and be able to relate that to electron spin. It is possible that each person will refine his or her understanding of the electron to a different extent. Exactly how this happens in the human organism is unknown, but the notion of the expression of different social acts becoming aligned as experience proceeds can be imagined. Considering the question of intersubjectivity in this way has important consequences for formal education and teaching generally. If human consciousness arises from interactions between participants and builds on what already exists with individuals, then it follows that teaching and learning in schools should involve groups of students and teachers working together on projects that they find mutually interesting. It also means that at a certain point of an investigation and because of the activity and discourses that have been flowing, that each participant may begin to refine their thoughts and reach a new threshold of understanding. For example, at a particular moment of a science activity, a metaphor may be used by any member of the group to relate a football tumbling through the air to the spin of an electron. At that exact point of discussion and experiment, for some individual reason, each participant may think about the electron differently, as a result of their personal intersubjective experience, the use of metaphor in this case. It is possible of course that such thinking could occur individually when sitting alone reading a book, or when going for a walk in the early morning, but this will have also depended on previous experience in combination with others or alone. If human experience occurs in continuous cycles of practice, it is impossible to disentangle the collective from the individual. In his discussion of such matters, Biesta (p. 75) comments,

> The paradigm shift from consciousness to intersubjectivity will have crucial implications both for the way in which we understand human beings and their mutual interactions and for the way in which we conceive of knowledge, rationality and morality.

## 24    *Understandings of epistemology*

Whether the notion of intersubjectivity has provided a different way of considering human consciousness may not, as yet, been resolved. That is, whether intersubjective experience produces something else that we call 'consciousness' or is consciousness in itself, remains a major topic of contestation in philosophy and neuroscience. It is certainly true that to take the issue of intersubjectivity seriously, provides new and challenging ways of apprehending 'knowledge, rationality and morality' and what it means to be human. Further discussion in the following section will link the ideas of phronesis/praxis and intersubjectivity to suggest a new intersubjective praxis model of teacher education to combat the ravages of neoliberalism socially and educationally.

### Epistemologies and neoliberalism

It is difficult to delineate exactly the major components of neoliberal education, especially at the level of schooling. On the other hand, the general policy settings of neoliberalism are quite clear. It could be taken that the role of the state is minimal in provision and in planning, but beyond that, whether or not a random market place or smorgasbord of ideas should constitute the curriculum is vague. At some point, the neoliberal view will probably emphasise the 'human capital' role of secondary schooling in particular and the need for schools to explicitly serve the economy, but this is usually the case under various forms of capitalism. Whether or not the purpose of schooling is to prepare students for work, to prepare students for ongoing study or to be concerned with personal growth through a broad general education, are questions for any economic system. Table 2.1 indicates that neoliberal education in terms of epistemology will most likely support a non-regulatory approach where economic outcomes rather than personal learning are given top priority. In stark contrast, the notion of intersubjectivity provides a philosophical counter to the impersonal economic and human capital argument. Mead's contribution to the concept of intersubjective consciousness in particular draws attention to the 'social act,' described as follows (Mead, 1962, p. 7, Footnote 7):

> A social act may be defined as one in which the occasion or stimulus which sets free an impulse is found in the character or conduct of a living form that belongs to the proper environment of the living form whose impulse it is. I wish however to restrict the social act to the class of acts which involve the co-operation of more than one individual and whose object as defined by the act, in the sense of Bergson, is a social object.

Through theorising the process of acting in the social world and the objective of acting as being 'found in the life-process of the group' rather than in individual activity, Mead developed the concept of the 'generalised other.' With this impression, each person comes to understand how their own views are formed, how others will respond to those views and becomes conscious or aware of selfhood and personality. Social acts allow different perspectives to be experienced, to be refined and to be changed as we encounter the diverse opinions and practices of

*Understandings of epistemology* 25

*Table 2.1* Summary comparison of intersubjectivity, knowledges, epistemology and social justice

| | *Progressive Epistemology* | *Conservative Epistemology* | *Neoliberal Epistemology* |
|---|---|---|---|
| Intersubjective Practice | Recognition that learning and consciousness arise from sociality or *interactions between* participants | Acceptance of learning and consciousness being individual subjectivity or *processes in* participants | Little interest in specific philosophy regarding learning, consciousness, values, norms, only *outcomes by* participants |
| Concrete, Everyday Knowledge | World-centred Emphasised Activity Small-group discussion Unknown outcomes | Information-centred Unimportant Passive reception Class discussion Known outcomes | Individual-centred Diverse Active/passive Individual considerations Varied outcomes |
| Abstract, Systematic Knowledge | Project-based Emergent Activity Small-group discussion Problematic outcomes | Teacher-based Predetermined Passive reception Class discussion Known outcomes | Student-based Disparate Active/passive Individual considerations Varied outcomes |
| Social Justice Impact | Establishes personal and social environments as areas of action, progress, change and betterment for all | Maintains personal and social hierarchies and relationships of influence and power for some | Rearranges personal and social hierarchies and relationships due to non-regulated individual capabilities |

those around us. Referred to in this way, Mead is able to link the past, present and future of participants through their action. Joas (1985/1997, p. 192) comments, 'Selfhood for Mead does not consist in immobilely remaining identical with oneself; rather it is the continuously active, reconstructive processing of occurrences and the planning of actions.' Based on these ideas, it is now possible to expand and detail Table 1.1 from Chapter 1 and how intersubjective educational practice can inform our understanding of epistemology (Table 2.1).

In relation to Table 2.1, let us consider a junior secondary mathematics class in a co-educational secondary school with class sizes of around 24 students and with the curriculum having a modest resource base. Four mathematics classes of 80 minutes each are available every week over a ten-week term, or a total of 40 weeks per year. While teachers work within an agreed curriculum, they have professional autonomy regarding how they organise their own classes. Each teacher has participated in developing student assessment tasks, some of which occur throughout the term, whilst others occur at the end of each term. It is common for each teacher

26    *Understandings of epistemology*

to work within their own preferred epistemological framework, although a range of different epistemologies can be discerned across each class at the discretion of each teacher and in relation to each mathematics topic.

- Progressive epistemology. It is usual for the class to be divided into four groups of six students each for every topic. The teacher encourages all students to outline their understanding of each area of mathematics they encounter through words, ideas and questions being written up on large posters that are displayed in the classroom. Each group discusses with the teacher various ways of investigating the topic and agrees on a way to proceed. This may involve interviewing other teachers, parents and more senior students, working outside to describe and make observations, excursions to relevant sites, gathering ideas from the Internet, drafting reports for presentation to the entire class. Conversation between students and teacher is encouraged. Because the teacher is more concerned with the emerging ideas of students than with specific subject content, assessment tasks are seen as work in progress and can offer new ideas and pathways to explore. Grading of student work is not done unless absolutely necessary and can be incorporated into descriptions or narratives of student progress.
- Conservative epistemology. Tables in this class are usually arranged in rows, or in a 'U' shape that allows the teacher to walk around the room quickly and review the entire class. Topic content is specified by the teacher and can be found in either books or the Internet where tablet devices are allowed. It is generally the case that outcomes for each lesson are listed and the teacher sets regular homework accordingly. Some quiet discussion amongst students is allowed, but it is expected that students will work on their own on specified examples from texts unless problems are met. Activities and excursions are generally not required as valued content is known. Importance is placed on preparing for and undertaking tests as these show what has been learned during the allotted time. Student work is graded and posted on lists in the classroom so that all students can see the achievements of others.
- Neoliberal epistemology. Provided that students are working towards the learning outcomes set by the mathematics staff, or perhaps by external authority, the teacher in this class does not necessary follow one approach or another. It is assumed that different students will have different mathematics abilities and that therefore a range of outcomes will be the natural order, some students will do well and others not. Students can work as groups or individuals and can use whatever resources are available including books, Internet and project materials. Generally, the teacher co-ordinates such work so that students are always aware of the specified outcomes for which they should be striving. It is therefore known by students that although they have a certain latitude in deciding how they go about their mathematics, their test results are important in showing what they have achieved and future options that may be available to them. Those that do not do well can always try again.

*Understandings of epistemology*   27

There is a very general indication given in these three scenarios as to how epistemology exists in many school classrooms around the world. Like everything else that teachers do, their implicit and explicit actions fit within an epistemological structure that will influence the learning of students in one direction or another. For the progressive educator noted earlier, learning emerges from the sociality of communities, schools and classrooms, where groups of people interact and participate in important projects that have meaning for their lives. Such meaning may involve the beauty of a rainbow, the impressions of a painting, the rhythm of a poem or the sadness of a story. The beginning point for such investigation and therefore for epistemology is the culture and language of the people concerned and how key aspects of this experience can also be located in other fields and then more generally. On the other hand, the conservative teacher accepts that truths are known and can be transmitted to those who do not know. Time need not be wasted in trying to find multiple pathways to entry, but merely restate what is known for adoption. Significance and meaning can be relayed rather than be explored and constructed by group experiment and discourse. However, it is difficult to define neoliberal epistemology arising as it does from a reliance on market forces and a belief that not all can achieve, some will grow and become strong, while others will wither and become bankrupt. A neoliberal epistemology that is true to these principles will most likely adopt a non-regulatory or laissez-faire approach to schooling, teaching and learning, where neither conservative or liberal achievement is paramount, but the fact that some will be at the upper end and others at the lower, probably across a wide range. This will be difficult to establish for public policy, particularly in societies where there are community expectations of schooling being of benefit to most citizens, but trends can be put in place to move in this direction. Various types of schooling can be seen around the world for this intent including voucher systems, free schools with little or no regulation, charter schools with limited social responsibility for curriculum and forms of private schooling that caters for different religious, economic and cultural communities and aspirations.

Epistemology goes to the heart of what it means to be human, where knowledge comes from and how we learn. It is very much tied up with the political and economic forces of the day, and as such it can distort the understanding of ourselves and of others. It impacts how we view our hopes and aspirations for a better world. Dewey, for example, in this discussion of the public, noted the difficulties of what he termed a Great Society being transformed into a Great Community. He noted trends in philosophy that focused on the individual and the ability of each person to make appropriate decisions, to evaluate results and to respond with new actions. In pointing out that these assumptions often proved illusory, Dewey (1927, p. 158) remarks,

> But current philosophy held that ideas and knowledge were functions of a mind or consciousness which originated in individuals by means of isolated contact with objects. But in fact, knowledge is a function of association and communication, it depends upon traditions, upon tools and methods socially

## 28   *Understandings of epistemology*

transmitted, developed and sanctioned. Faculties of effective observation, reflection and desire are habits acquired under the influence of the culture and institutions of society, not ready-made inherent powers.

What Dewey has alerted us to here in our discussion of epistemology, is that not only do the three forms of epistemology discussed earlier exist, but they are in relationship with each other depending on the social conditions that prevail. These conditions extend across society and within particular institutions and are supported or contested on the basis of the habits that all participants reveal. In addition, as noted earlier, it could be suggested that the strength of neoliberal economics has not generated a similarly strong neoliberal epistemology that is in apparent contradiction with the social purpose of schooling and the still-prevalent progressive and conservative approaches around the world. That is, neoliberalism has markedly influenced the funding and accountability mechanisms of schooling, but has not completely colonised current habits of epistemology themselves. This is a significant point in educational planning and strategy for progressive and democratic educators given that Dewey (1927, p. 159) quotes James in his view that 'Habit is the enormous flywheel of society; its most precious, conservative influence.' Old habits it seems diehard and there is substantial resistance to neoliberal approaches to education and schooling around the world. Neoliberal epistemology is weak and unstable. Dewey's 'search for the Great Community' can continue through the efforts of teachers, students and local communities everywhere. This does not mean 'more of the same,' but a dramatic reconceptualisation of what schooling is all about for the vast majority of citizens, to construct and reconstruct education and through this social and epistemological experience, to construct and reconstruct our own consciousness of the world.

# 3 Action theory and theorists

Economic dependence lies festering on the mind
of the living, but establishes a consciousness
linking histories, a common knowledge of practice
that offers an emergent view and understanding,
within the shell of the apparently indestructible
a teacher stirs and prepares to put the learning first.

Many attempts throughout the centuries have been made at navigating the two great traditions of learning – that is, through accepting the truths and perceptions of others (a priori) or through constructing our own understanding from personal experience (a posteriori). From a 'theory of action' viewpoint, Greek philosophy continues to influence thinking with Aristotle's 'practical wisdom' of phronesis and praxis a common thread. Marx emphasised the role of labour in forming our view of the world and how the combination of theory and practice that subsequently arose was central to learning. Dewey and Mead as colleagues understood the social role of learning and how communication and participation were essential acts in the inquiry process. Democratic dialogue was a key component of Freire's cultural approach to education, while Arendt highlighted the notion of the 'active life' in becoming human. The 1980s saw critical sociological and epistemological work undertaken by Habermas, Giddens and Bourdieu as they sought to consolidate previous theories. Habermas developed his approach to 'communicative action,' Giddens his view of structuration and Bourdieu wrote of the reflexive action between habitus and field. While there are differences of emphasis between these major theorists, their intent is to establish and strengthen a 'theory of action,' or indeed a 'theory of humanity,' that privileges the lives and activities of ordinary people and the view that learning emerges from our reflexive interactions with the social and physical worlds, rather than having meaning imposed. This view sees connections between ontology and epistemology, but ensures that the 'active life' retains its centrality. The common theorising summarised in this chapter provides guidance for the policy and practice of education and how teaching and learning for human purpose can be arranged. It proposes that a strong theoretical basis exists for establishing forms of human action at all levels of education, in contrast to conservative ideologies that attempt to constrict learning to the narrow and conformist.

## 30  *Action theory and theorists*

### Communication and the linguistic turn

Dewey and his extensive catalogue demands careful reading and rereading to appreciate the scope of his insight and the way in which he connects rather than separates understandings and ideas. In his groundbreaking work *Experience and Nature*, he sets out to discuss how human experience penetrates into the very nature of nature itself and that 'experience is *of* as well as *in* nature. It is not experience that is experienced, but nature – stones, plants, animals, diseases, health, temperature, electricity and so on' (Dewey, 1958, p. 4a). As mentioned previously, Dewey was compellingly influenced by developments in modern science that he witnessed around him at the time and what he saw as the opening up of knowledge, including the empirical and philosophical to the citizenry in democratic ways unknown before. His *Experience and Nature* (1925) and *Logic: The theory of inquiry* (1938) locates Dewey's thinking on the principles and direction of philosophy and connects with debates regarding the 'linguistic turn' in that field. He cannot be more definite when he writes (Dewey, 1958, p. 166),

> Of all affairs, communication is the most wonderful. That things should be able to pass from the plane of external pushing and pulling to that of revealing themselves to man and thereby to themselves and that the fruit of communication should be participation, sharing, is a wonder by the side of which transubstantiation pales.

In this somewhat astounding passage, where communication is denoted as the 'most wonderful' of all human activities, Dewey proposes that the isthmus between existence and essence is that of communication, language and discourse. In the example of experience given earlier of 'stones, plants, animals, diseases, health, temperature, electricity,' meaning of each occurs though communication and language where each object is named in relation to its specific characteristics, thereby establishing an agreed convention. A stone may be broadly named as 'a hard, non-metallic substance found throughout the universe and forming part of the solid matter of planets,' enabling conversation to occur between participants in describing and understanding their experiences, *of* and *in* nature. But Dewey goes even further. He startles and provokes by stating (Dewey, 1958, p. 202),

> Communication is consummatory as well as instrumental. It is a means of establishing co-operation, domination and order. Shared experience is the greatest of human goods. In communication, such conjunction and contact as is characteristic of animals become endearments capable infinite idealisation; they become symbols of the very culmination of nature.

It is unlikely that Dewey has made a more dramatic statement in all his writing than 'Shared experience is the greatest of human goods.' Although Dewey's following explanation is not totally clear, the statement exposes the heart of what

*Action theory and theorists*  31

it means to be human and lifts us from the daily grind of social existence to recognise the significance of ordinary lives. He points out that all the objects of communication and therefore language are worthy of respect and consideration because they provide the means by which we construct our lives and they are constitutive of ends because they enable imagination of what might be. In an extensive footnote to this particular discussion, Dewey (1958, pp. 205–207) raises issues regarding the detail of language including his view that 'language is primarily a mode of action used for the sake of influencing the conduct of others in connection with the speaker.'

In 1981, the German social theorist, Jurgen Habermas published his famous *Theory of Communicative Action*. At the very beginning of Volume 2, he notes that, following Weber and from a Marxist perception, 'the rationalisation of society was always thought of as a reification of *consciousness*' (Habermas, 1981/1987, p. 1, original emphasis). In this way, he attempts to theorise a communicative rationality for society that does not depend on human consciousness as individual a priori, but where social rationalisation arises from the language, communication and actions of social solidarity. Neoliberalism is a good example of economic rationalisation dominating the views, traditions and understandings of communities and imposing on the population a purposive rather than communicative rationality. In explaining communicative action, Habermas developed the notion of *lifeworld* 'as the horizon within which communicative actions are *always already* moving' (p. 119). He went on (p. 120) to detail,

> In fact, communicative utterances are always embedded in various world relations at the same time. Communicative action relies on a co-operative process of interpretation in which participants relate simultaneously to something in the objective, the social and the subjective worlds, even when they *thematically stress only one* of the three components in their utterances. Speaker and hearer use the reference system of the three worlds as an interpretive framework within which they work out their common situation definitions.

It is possible to consider two markedly different scenarios in which communicative action may operate. In the first, participants have a mutual concern to understand and to resolve, without ego, power or status being involved. In this respect, they are able to consider each utterance with the subjective, objective and social worlds as reference. In the second, the intention is somewhat or slightly purposive, with a consideration of the three worlds assisting how to win a point of view even amongst friends. A family discussion regarding whether to go to the zoo or the beach can be conducted in the general interests of all members for the family good. It may not be known, however, that, because of recent experience, a particular person may have a deeply personal or selfish reason for supporting one venue compared with another. In a professional environment such as a staff meeting of teachers, there will be many factors at play for each participant influencing how they respond. A discussion of literacy and approaches to teaching will draw heavily from progressive and conservative perspectives and the notion of truthfulness,

## 32  *Action theory and theorists*

sincerity and accuracy will be difficult to sustain. Under these conditions, the interaction of lifeworld, personal history of inquiry and consciousness will be a powerful mix of imperatives governing action. The linguistic turn to communication, language and discourse advocated by Habermas is therefore layered with idealism that is difficult to achieve in social practice. Regardless of this defect, his attempt to shift from a bureaucratic, economic and technical rationality that reifies what it means to be human, where ideology is violent and cruel, has many features to guide a more democratic and compassionate society today.

## Culture and conscientisation

Writing from a broadly Marxist tradition, Raymond Williams famously stated that 'culture is ordinary, in every society and in every mind' and that (Williams, 1989, p. 4)

> a culture has two aspects: the known meanings and directions, which its members are trained to; the new observations and meanings, which are offered and tested. These are the ordinary processes of human societies and human minds and we see through them the nature of a culture: that it is always traditional and creative; that it is both the most ordinary common meanings and the finest individual meanings.

Williams significantly sees culture as 'everything,' as a way of life that is ordinary or one that is encountered every day, but one that involves meaning that is both individual and collective, traditional and creative, fixed yet dynamic. A culture of this type is relational with other key ideas in society such as learning, art, democracy, transformation and is not restricted to the realm of wealth and privilege. It also does not have a religious imperative. The connection between culture and meaning intimately links this understanding with epistemology regarding how meaning is approached by individuals, groups and communities.

The British critic, poet and educator Matthew Arnold (1932, p. 69) spoke of culture from a religious framework as humans pursuing 'perfection' and 'sweetness and light.' This is a concept of culture concerned with pure knowledge and understanding, not only in a scientific sense, but in the moral sense of doing good as well. When this is occurring for as many people as possible, humanity experiences 'happy moments' and

> how those are the marking epochs of a people's life, how those are the flowering times for literature and art and all the creative power of genius, when there is a national glow of life and thought, when the whole of society is in the fullest measure permeated by thought, sensible to beauty, intelligent and alive.

These are inspirational words from Williams and Arnold. They conceive of culture as being a major construct of our humanity, present in and comprising our 'ordinary,' everyday and everything experience where judgements and decisions

*Action theory and theorists* 33

are required for living. This approach connects closely with the notion of life-world described earlier by Habermas, as well as the links between experience and culture noted earlier by Dewey. There is also a common theme here with the understandings of Freire. In describing what he termed 'conscientisation' (Freire, 1972, p. p. 51), Freire argues that humans exist both *in* and *with* the world. This means that human consciousness emerges when citizens recognise that they are not only part of the totality of existence that includes the social and physical worlds, but that they interact with all aspects of existence as part of a continuing process of change and transformation. That is, in identifying their objects of interest and concern, humans undertake an ongoing dialectical process of subjectification and objectification as they engage experience, thoughts, concepts, responses and as a result, redefine what they think, value and authenticate, a process of active human-isation. Freire (1972, p. 61 p. 51, footnote 2) saw this as conscientisation, or the means by which humans 'not as recipients, but as knowing subjects, achieve a deepening awareness both of the socio-cultural reality which shapes their lives and of their capacity to transform that reality.' In seeing conscientisation as criti-cal consciousness and critical awareness, Freire described a social, cultural and experiential process of moving from what he called a 'semi-intransitive' state to a popular or 'naïve transitive' consciousness and finally critical consciousness. While not a linear, or necessarily prolonged progression, Freire contended that our understandings are directly related to our social being, initially dominated by closed structures and concrete reality but, as experience of transformation grows, moving to a deeper comprehension of generalised conditions outside of the per-sonal and individual. He pointed out that this is a historic journey for all society and peoples and that contradictory themes and contradictory positions will emerge along the way. Unless handled sensitively and wisely, the themes themselves can become 'mythologised' leading to irrationality and sectarianism. He further noted (Freire, 1970/2000, p. 102),

> This climate threatens to drain the themes of their deeper significance and to deprive them of their characteristically dynamic aspect. In such a situation, myth-making irrationality itself becomes a fundamental theme. Its opposing theme, the critical and dynamic view of the world, strives to unveil reality, mask its mythicisation and achieve a full realisation of the human task: the permanent transformation of reality in favour of the liberation of people.

All philosophy has to deal with fundamental questions such as the nature of reality and where it originates. From an epistemological viewpoint, this necessitates the question of what and how humans can know. Taking Freire's view of 'striving to unveil reality,' the sections that follow give some specific examples of how science and the human sciences continue to probe what it means to be human, the material-ist relationship between mind and matter and how we come to understand. These sections are clearly historical work in progress but bear directly on how formal education in every classroom, at every level, needs to confront rather than deny the flora and fauna of existence.

## Complexity and the physical and social worlds

Originating from a number of scientific knowledge disciplines during the past 20 years or so, complexity theory draws upon notions of chaos, complexity, information, non-linearity and dynamic systems theory. It concerns complex, adaptive and emergent matter or objects that are close to chaos but are ordered at the same time. In relating complexity to education and knowledge, Osberg, Biesta and Cilliers (2008, p. 204), comment,

> Our interest is primarily in articulating an epistemology that helps us think about knowledge, representation, education and the world that does not result in, or seek, closure. To put it differently, we are trying to articulate a different ethic or 'way of being' in education, that is less concerned with representing the real than it is with living it out in different ways.

To consider knowledge as always being emergent or not final raises very serious ethical questions that will be taken up later. However, if human becoming is an ongoing process from birth to death and involves constant interaction with the objects of human interaction and understanding, then whether or not we appreciate those objects accurately at a particular time can be contested. This is a serious issue for formal teaching and learning. It certainly casts doubt on traditional assessment and testing regimes. Complexity then applied to material and to systems challenges who we are as humans regardless of the evidence that we do have some understanding of the social and physical universe through a combination of experiment, theorising and discourse. We now turn to a more detailed discussion of this idea from a physical point of view.

Modern science and particularly cosmology are grappling strenuously with the problem of complexity. It involves systems that are formed abruptly and therefore making them difficult to mathematically model, usually having a large number of components, are open to the environment rather than closed and are non-linear. In a classical sense, such properties or experimental results could often be overlooked or discarded rather than being seen as essential properties of irregularity. Access to computer modelling over recent times has provided added impetus to these ideas and further enables the physical and social sciences to be mutually supportive rather than automatically counter distinctive. Initially, complex systems were considered as a collection of simple systems and reducible to simple and analysable parts. It is now thought that severing the connections between parts destroys the overall nature of the system. In a non-linear arrangement, small inputs can lead to large, unpredictable results, in a way that the current, linear laws of physics cannot accommodate. Complex phenomena can include the catastrophic, the chaotic, the paradox and the emergent, where new properties arise after a threshold has been breached. Today, examples of complexity are found in both the social and physical sciences including economics, meteorology, biology and neurology.

While matter and energy are considered the basic building blocks of the universe, work during the mid-twentieth century particularly with the discovery of the double helix structure of DNA, prompted the concept of information as a third aspect and more latterly with research on complexity, human consciousness is being investigated as a fourth. This field is of course, highly contentious, but the idea that consciousness is made possible as a function of physical and molecular complexity and emerges after a complex threshold has been passed, means that the universe is not predetermined clockwork fashion, but is rather predisposed to the formation of consciousness. Thus the idea that the universe is 'teeming with consciousness' somewhat like a super saturated solution ready to crystallise with extra-terrestrial intelligence at any moment, may yet prove to be one of the great defining philosophical ideas of the modern era. Here again, science challenges religion for explanation, superstition and myth versus fact and experiment.

Allied to this thinking in science is the concept of 'dissipative structures' that exist under conditions far from equilibrium and in symbiosis with their environment. Structures such as this exist in two configurations – that is, when close to equilibrium their order tends to be destroyed but when far from equilibrium order can be established with the creation of new structures and characteristics. The heating of a liquid from below with the resultant convection and conduction effects, is an example of a dissipative structure. Isolated systems, on the other hand, such as crystals exist at equilibrium. The conceptual similarities between the ideas of complexity, dissipative structures and experiential learning, are very close and connect the characteristics of the human organism with the operation of the universe generally. The emergence of an overall pattern of a jig saw puzzle long before all the pieces are in place, the formation of black holes, points of singularity and big bangs as the creative formation of the universe, new characteristics of consciousness and morality occurring because of the arrangements of matter, energy and information, all contribute to our understanding of how thinking and learning might similarly occur in the human brain.

A model of learning based on these analogies, suggests points of singularity or idea structures that contain essential component parts which, for some reason as experience is accumulated, change, expand, transform with a rush of what we call imagination, speculation, confusion, enlightenment and construction. This can be viewed in physical terms as controlled or uncontrolled, uncertain and unpredictable, non-linear and irregular, to be feared or encouraged. It certainly does not conform with the 'filing cabinet' or 'empty vessel' view of learning, where known information is stored in neat arrangements, ready to be found when required. Structures of the brain may not be ordered in alphabetical draws as in a filing cabinet, but be multilayered, interconnected and highly complex networks whose information and detail can be found, retrieved and translated at the speed of light. Sometimes this process may involve some slippage where similar, yet to be completed, or linked structures are mistaken for others, thereby prompting a 'why did I think of that' response? On other occasions, a 'Why didn't I think of that?' comment may be more significant. Perhaps a 'critical mass' of experience, inquiry and social practice needs to be reached before a certain degree of complexity of thought can be achieved, permitting another cognitive leap into a new consciousness of

36  *Action theory and theorists*

known-unknown to be taken. This is in accord with the cycles of 'thesis, antithesis, synthesis,' 'perception, conception, perception' and 'assimilation, accommodation, equilibration' familiar to both sociology and epistemology.

## Consciousness and quantum mechanics

Human consciousness is difficult to define and it has been called the 'hard problem' (Chalmers, 2003) of philosophy that has not been resolved. On the other hand, each person has his or her own direct experience of what is called consciousness, a feeling of knowing and understanding that comes from personal engagement with an idea, practice or object. Exactly why it is difficult to think about the nature of consciousness is also challenging to apprehend, except perhaps it is difficult for consciousness to think about itself in what amounts to a never-ending recursive process. It is a crucial question for education and learning, however, especially in the neoliberal age where assumptions and correlations are made between high stakes testing and the capabilities of students and their socio-economic background. Can our understanding of consciousness make these connections to be made, or indeed, make them invalid? A starting point for attempting to understand consciousness could be the material from which humans are made and in particular, the brain. Our best understanding of this material to date comes from the insights of modern science provided by physics, chemistry, biology and mathematics.

On a macro scale, classical physics provides a model of how the material of the universe was formed, its properties and interactions between different forms of that material – that is, interactions between matter and energy. On a micro scale, quantum mechanics develops understandings of the sub-atomic universe such that micro particles have properties of both particle and wave simultaneously, the puzzling concept of wave-particle duality. Electrons, for example, are seen to inhabit a probabilistic wave-particle orbit around the nucleus of an atom rather than a fixed orbit that is deterministic. An important feature of quantum mechanics is that the wave function or many states of a system can collapse into a single eigenstate by measurement or observation of that system. By this mechanism, measurement transforms the wave function into a particular state at that moment and is in accord with the Copenhagen interpretation. It is generally thought that this clarification of quantum mechanics was developed by Niels Bohr and Werner Heisenberg during 1925–27 at the Copenhagen Institute for Theoretical Physics, established by Bohr. Under this interpretation, quantum mechanics can only anticipate the probabilities or likelihood that measurements or observations will produce certain outcomes; the set of probabilities is reduced to only one of the possible values at the instant of measurement. It is understood that immediately after measurement, the wave function reforms with different probability parameters.

According to Chalmers (2003),

> The hard problem of consciousness is the problem of experience. Human beings have subjective experience: there is something it is like to be them. We can say that a being is conscious in this sense – or is phenomenally conscious,

as it is sometimes put – when there is something it is like to be that being. A mental state is conscious when there is something it is like to be in that state.

It is difficult to describe 'subjective experience' in terms of a mental state such that 'there is something it is like to be them.' I am aware of the love I feel for my mother, but how and where this feeling has been generated in my being and forms part of my continuing awareness of the world is decidedly imprecise. Perhaps a small amount of chemical released by the brain and initiating a slight alteration in stomach juices or muscle contractions causes the sensation, in the same way that emotion of various types is generated. A materialist approach to this problem will only refer to physical processes, whereas a non-materialist view will need to suggest something other than physical systems at work. This later view could involve a mind separate from the brain, for example. Stapp (2009) draws a distinction between mental and physical processes whereby there is some connection between the values and beliefs that we hold and these influence complicated physical processes occurring in the brain. Dennett (2003) proposes that there is nothing 'magical' about the 'hard problem' of consciousness and that when all the separate components that go to make up consciousness are understood (the 'easy' problems); then the process as a whole will be explicable. Penrose (2009) has suggested that quantum events, entanglements or oscillations could take place in cytoskeletons and microtubules giving rise to human consciousness. Theorising such as this indicates that widely divergent views still exist regarding human consciousness and that describing its 'feeling' or 'awareness' remain as aloof as ever. It may, however, be possible to draft a broadly descriptive model of consciousness that combines classical and quantum physics, as well as epistemological and ontological concerns to guide apprehensions of learning. Detail of processes will come later as research unfolds.

A model of consciousness can be considered in broadly descriptive terms involving both scientific and philosophical issues without necessarily answering all questions or answering all questions completely. It is not a neutral undertaking, but occurs within the dominant political-economic conditions of the times. It will therefore demand adherence to a set of criteria that outline a particular philosophy of living. In the first instance, the model should adopt an integrated 'mind-body' outlook that respects the capabilities of all humans regardless of background. It is social being that determines consciousness, not an isolated, individual consciousness that determines social being and capability. That is, a 'progressive' rather than 'deficit' view of humanity will be required. From a materialist perspective where it is not necessary to imagine anything else except matter and energy as constituting the basic materials of the universe, it is possible to create an understanding of consciousness from these alone. Understandings drawn from classical and quantum mechanics can form the basis of a model of consciousness, in the same way that understandings emerging from the model of the atom have informed how we think about and act with all concepts of physical phenomena. This means a combination of classical and quantum mechanics as currently understood acting together such that consciousness is central to what

## 38   *Action theory and theorists*

it means to be human, arising from social experience and causing sensations or mental states of awareness for each person.

It may be that sensations of conscious awareness are a function of molecular complexity involving primarily carbon but in association and relationship with a range of other atoms and molecules. Once a certain threshold of complexity has been reached, the brain may act as a unified quantum mechanical system – or appear to be acting as a unified quantum mechanical system – generating an infinite and continuing number of wave configurations collapsing and reforming as an infinite and dense array of observations and measurements are made. With this conceptual understanding, consciousness or being aware of and guided by one's social and cultural experience, is at the core of being human and is present at all times, from birth to death. Thoughts and ideas emerge from each particular and unique consciousness as social acts of advice, observation, comparison, inspection, interpretation and communication occur, that is as wave functions are transformed into single states, immediately giving rise to new wave formations. Classical mechanics can take care of questions of electromagnetism and pathways, transfer of ions their speed and concentration, structure and connections of materials, while quantum mechanics in dialectical relationship, enables the fine grain detail of where ideas (envisaged as single state 'particles' of matter and energy) come from. Wave and particle are dialectical, dependent on each other, in constant motion and transformation as subjectivity accrues. Whether or not consciousness is universal, a fundamental property of the universe itself similar to matter and energy, or is particular to degrees of complexity involving large numbers of certain combinations of atoms and molecules in humans, is a question that does not need to be answered at this time. Rather, it can be proposed that consciousness is universal to humans, the evolutionary species-being, sentient, cognitive, responsive to continuing social acts arising from integrated cultural and communicative formation. Dialectical materialist consciousness then becomes the basis for all learning for all humans, making the social and physical worlds accessible and knowable for everyone without discrimination.

## Great community and the public sphere

In Chapter 4, we shall outline in more detail the connections between democracy, education and epistemology. At this point, however, we shall raise some issues regarding specific aspects of democracy and how they relate to communities generally. To begin, the broad parameters of democracy are outlined next (Hooley, 2009, p. 24), indicating that democratic forms of social life should not be idealised or considered in simplistic, unidimensional terms:

- economic, cultural and employment arrangements that set up horizontal rather than vertical processes of authority, responsibility and relationship as the basis of autonomy, reciprocity and personal dignity;
- resource allocation that meets the needs of all people within an appropriate framework of principle and enhancement;

- decision-making structures that are inclusive, participatory, persuasive and consensual and that are intended to support the interests of the entire group;
- aspirations that include social progress and change in all fields rather than the status quo for the purposes of improvement;
- approaches to the quality, equity and meaning of daily life that are holistic and integrated regarding work, family, culture, learning, political and recreational activity;
- theories of society and theories of practice that emphasise the continuing unfolding of history, the role of citizens as agents of change, the unity of practice and theory in all phenomena, a compassionate science and technology, protection of the natural environment and critical and participatory processes of investigation; and
- consideration of the relationship between public and private interest.

These parameters attempt to deal with the main pressures of neoliberalism and globalisation, those of economic, political, knowledge, technology and ideology critique. They are applicable for all societies and for all citizens Indigenous and non-Indigenous. Their scope is much broader than liberal and representative parliamentary democracy as witnessed by the Westminster system, for example. An integrated matrix of intersection and interaction needs to guide transformative action between all the issues concerned as the development of democratic process occurs. As a central theme in his work, Dewey was concerned with the basis of democratic life and how it could be established and thrive in the nascent American republic. In his book, *The Public and its Problems* (Dewey, 1927, p. 142), he argues that local community is the locus of democratic process where resident people can participate, inquire and express their hope and problems in communion. Dewey expands his statement noted earlier regarding 'shared experience is the greatest of human goods,' to the view that

> without such communication the public will remain shadowy and formless, seeking spasmodically for itself, but seizing and holding its shadow rather than its substance. Until the Great Society is converted into a Great Community, the public will remain in eclipse. Communication can alone create a great community.

In this extract, Dewey is expressing the hope that broad ranging associations within the general public can result in a democratic community, not only involving democratic forms of government at different levels but also embracing all citizens through its organisations such as school, family, church, political and social institutions. We learn to be human through this process of engagement with others and through grappling with the ups and downs of interaction. Based on his concept of pragmatism (Pihlstrom, 2015), one would expect that action will play an important part in Dewey's concept of communication and community and he states that a public comes into existence by participants acting on important events that have serious consequences. Again, there are very close connections

40    *Action theory and theorists*

being drawn between social causations and human learning whereby we need to learn about society and ourselves in the process of observing, reflecting, evaluating and transforming social reality so that problems and interests can be resolved. He reveals that 'association itself is physical and organic, while communal life is moral, that is emotionally, intellectually, consciously sustained' (p. 151), making a strong distinction between public and private fellowship. This is a central aspect of consideration regarding ethical and moral conduct and how these human characteristics arise (see Chapter 4). For education, it means that ethical and moral understandings do not need to be taught, but they need to be lived as an integrated facet of knowledge and curriculum.

In a similar communitarian vein to Dewey, Habermas (1992) proposed that there exists in society forms of democratic association where citizens meet and discuss issues of community importance. These associations are not recognised as formal decision-making structures in the sense of parliaments or local government, but provide avenues for the development of informal and reasoned opinion amongst the general population. It may be of course that such association does not agree with the decisions of formal bodies and, in some circumstances, encourages debate that might otherwise be difficult or illegal. Habermas spoke of the coffee houses of London and Paris of the 1600s as places where such democratic conversations could occur. Indeed this may still be the case today with renewed emphasis on barista culture in many cities and towns of the world. Today, we could also point towards trade unions, local neighbourhood groups, environmental organisations, women's groups and schools and universities as being emblematic of public spheres. In this regard, Eriksen and Weigard (2003, p. 179) note, 'The term public sphere signifies that equal citizens assemble into a public and set their own agenda through open communication. What characterises this public sphere is that it is power free, secular and rational.' Fraser (1992) raised concerns regarding this viewpoint, in that some participants such as women and disenfranchised groups could still be excluded from discussion and may need to form their own public spheres. In this regard, Kemmis (2001, p. 24) advocated the notion of 'many public spheres, constituted as networks of communication.' In accord with Habermas, Kemmis and McTaggart (2005, pp. 584–591) described public spheres as having ten characteristics as follows:

- constituted as actual networks of communication among actual participants;
- self-constituted, relatively autonomous and voluntary;
- exist in response to legitimation deficits within current political practices;
- constituted for communicative action and public discourse;
- aim to be inclusive;
- involve communication in ordinary language;
- presuppose communicative freedom;
- communicative power generated through respect of participants;
- indirect impact on public systems; and
- arise in association with social networks.

These characteristics of public spheres accentuate language, discourse and communication, non-coercive dialogue and the independence and autonomy of conduct. If applied to formal education, democratic public spheres of this type are intimately linked to the broader social trends that surround and influence education generally. Educational issues cannot be isolated from the broader society as a whole or be resolved in a manner disconnected from the socio-economic environment. In a more formal sense, the public sphere consists of a number of discourses that enable communication to be grounded in an informal baseline of experience and culture and to arrive at viewpoints that are defensible and realistic for participants. From this discussion, the concept of the Great Community as envisaged by Dewey connects closely to the later work of Freire and Habermas regarding the critical role of democratic social action, the place of culture and experience in communication between participants and the organisational concept of public sphere that brings citizens together for discussion of mutual interest. These ideas if appropriate, should also infuse public education as the basis of a 'great community,' one that is democratic in all associations, is compassionate and egalitarian regarding all citizens regardless of background and recognises the personal, community and historical transformations that occur everywhere. In a 'great community,' citizens will need to experience the pursuit of knowledge and the dignity of knowing and imagining, of challenging the orthodox and conventional. Communities will share their combined understandings when investigating and changing practices for the public good. An integrated, balanced and holistic approach to community, education and learning identifies the historic and humanistic disposition of being human and of human being as a doing and knowing subject.

# 4 Creative democracy, ethics, power and control

A gentle breeze disturbs the branches
and a myriad of creative synapses
contributing to the mood and aura
of encountering the extraordinary
connect and network the imagination
unknown amongst the asphalt and grime.

At this point, we bring together a number of major epistemological themes that have been discussed in previous chapters and which will form the basis of conceptualising a coherent model of education that will be outlined in Chapters 5–8. For example, in constructing a 'theory of action' for learning whether formal or informal, the concept of 'social act' can be thought of as 'human action that arises from situations of interest and meaning to pursue further understanding.' Action and communication occur within a social context of meanings and practices, and occur as either groups or individuals confront various situations for resolution. This proceeds in vigorous debate at a town hall council meeting, or in reading a book on the riverbank. Modern schooling, however, has not been established to maximise learning through action and communication amongst participants, but to enforce the views and imperatives of dominant economic sectors. A significant contradiction exists between the aspirations of the vast majority of people and those who control resources, policy and what is socially valued. Contradictions that frustrate knowledge and satisfaction produce high levels of alienation within society and within schools where teachers, students and their families alike often realise that they are not required to know thoughtfully or investigate the world profoundly. Consequently processes of inquiry, action and communication must be included in education programs whatever the topic and wherever possible. This chapter proposes that power and control of education and schooling need to be relocated from the minority to the majority of learners of all ages and socio-cultural backgrounds, such that personal interest and meaning can establish and guide all investigations, generating new reflections, problems and possibilities in an open-ended manner. Established knowledge remains as a respected and important network of practices, ideas and traditions within

*Creative democracy* 43

which new understandings are created. New concepts emerge as current issues are worked through and resolved identifying central concerns. In this way, there is a dialectical relationship between old and new knowledge, as the old provides a basis for thinking about problems and the new generates perspectives that have not been encountered before. Current and old knowledge is therefore subject to change, in the same way that new knowledge justifies its position in relation to accepted understandings.

## Creative democracy

In a speech delivered on his eightieth birthday, John Dewey summarised his view of what he called 'creative democracy,' emphasising again that democracy is not merely a system of institutionalised permission, but internal understandings and actions of all citizens. Within the context of international events such as war and economic depression that had occurred prior to 1939, or were predicted, Dewey's remarks offered a counter point to restriction and imposition and instead, argued for an extensive and compassionate human experience available to all. He proposed that 'At the present time, the frontier is moral, not physical. The period of free lands that seemed boundless in extent has vanished. Unused resources are now human rather than material' (Dewey, 1939). He demonstrated his commitment to the capability of ordinary people to conduct their own and community lives in sensible and judicious ways by going on to write,

> Democracy is a way of personal life controlled not merely by faith in human nature in general but by faith in the capacity of human beings for intelligent judgment and action if proper conditions are furnished. I have been accused more than once and from opposed quarters of an undue, a utopian, faith in the possibilities of intelligence and in education as a correlate of intelligence. At all events, I did not invent this faith. I acquired it from my surroundings as far as those surroundings were animated by the democratic spirit. For what is the faith of democracy in the role of consultation, of conference, of persuasion, of discussion, in formation of public opinion, which in the long run is self-corrective, except faith in the capacity of the intelligence of the common man to respond with common sense to the free play of facts and ideas which are secured by effective guarantees of free inquiry, free assembly and free communication?

In this segment, Dewey is outlining the pragmatist and essentially epistemological position that all people come to their understandings of the world through social action that brings them into contact with and the review of other actions and other perspectives. This is best done democratically, such that all experience is open, respected and subject to change without prejudice where the real is heard. At the centre of democratic process is ethical conduct, the practice and aspiration of living well, in the interests of others.

## 44 *Creative democracy*

## Formation of ethical conduct

We generally enjoyed camping. Not only did it get us into the calmness of the outdoors, but it took us away from all that commotion at the end of year, that was the plan. To be self-reliant as well we told ourselves. It encouraged the kids to think about other things around them, like the brightness of the stars at night, the sounds and silences of the bush, collapsing into bed exhausted at dusk and getting up with the early birds at dawn day after day. It also meant that we could argue that the entire family had given itself one big present to greet the new year, the chance to get away together, to explore what we thought and what was important to us all. Nothing else was required. This was often received with a rolling of the eyes, like the time we bought the tent, but they would be a year older next year and we could have the kitchen table talk again as different people. It was great to see Ali change and exhibit her growing personality of reason, fairness and humour. Even irony at her age: 'I can't wait to get home, I'm really missing the seven o'clock news,' she would declare with a straight face, knowing full well my ritual every night, 'I wonder what's happening?' 'We will just have to survive in grand isolation for a couple of weeks,' was my standard reply, 'the world will get on without us I'm sure.' But I had a nagging worry at the back of my mind, were we imposing this view onto the kids, of escaping one ideology of orthodoxy that seemed to grip many other families at this time and merely replacing it with another? In trying to free up their thinking so that they could compose their own minds, were we adding other clutter? As the moon began to rise and my thoughts turned to generations of humans having this same experience, Ali came bounding across the camping ground all excited and breathless: 'Mrs Thompson says I can watch a DVD with them in the van, it's a Disney about frozen lands or something, can I, please?' I loved her dearly, the future of the world depended on her and I had to trust her judgement in making her way. I sighed, the best laid plans, it would be tough going arguing for a total ban on all devices next year.

When a person attempts to act correctly, or may want to do what is right, they may find themselves acting differently for a range of reasons (Hare, 1989). The Greeks called this possibility *akrasia*, or acting against one's better judgement. Apart from a lack of rigour in our own appreciation of each virtue, it can often be the case that a number of factors are operating at once, each of which has to be taken into account. For example, if honesty is a virtue, it may be appropriate to not be totally honest with a particular person, if it is judged that such action may have an undesirable effect at that time either for that person or for others. It may be appropriate to wait for a more suitable occasion where total honesty will have more favourable outcomes. There are complicated judgements to be made here regarding the greater good that do not necessarily reflect a weakness of will, but judgements made on a social and political evaluation of the situation at hand. We can ask questions of ourselves about what is the right thing to do under particular circumstances, questions that involve ethical reasoning, or we can ask questions about what is the best way to live, involving practical reasoning about how we see life in general and what we do. Practical reasoning means an understanding of human virtue, a set of actions or excellences that indicate we care for and are committed to acting correctly and can judge appropriately how to put them into effect. Aristotle suggested that an end point of this process conducted over a lifetime of acting virtuously, would result in human 'flourishing,' or sometimes called well-being, happiness or eudaimonia (Wright and Pascoe, 2015). In this regard, happiness is not a fleeting moment or a specific mood or feeling that comes and goes, but is a long-term disposition based on living well. It would seem that each person needs to consider his or her own understanding of virtue and then how to live in accord with such understandings. In this way, each person can 'become good' through acting, that is become of excellent character, rather than merely 'know' what 'good' is about.

All people, including educators, teachers and parents, make ethical judgements every day about themselves in relation to children and young people in their care. If ethics is concerned with conduct that seeks to distinguish right and wrong behaviour, then it is essentially a field of human action taken with due regard to others. It is often a difficult field of action when adherence to a generally agreed set of principles may cut across specific interest of those involved. If democratic conduct (associated living where actions are reviewed by others) is taken as a significant human virtue, then this needs to be followed fully, rather than in part. In fact, it is not possible to be a little democratic whereby thinking, practice and discourse are approved for some (usually minority) aspects of a topic, but not for other (usually majority) aspects. For example, the science teacher may espouse a democratic approach to investigation and experiment, but not accept results that are at variance with the norm. The temperature of the boiling point of water must be measured as very close to 100 degrees Celsius by the Year 7 student, or be marked as incorrect. In this case, the teacher decides that outcomes are predetermined and that there is little if any scope for student originality and imagination within the parameters of the investigation. For many citizens, democracy is a difficult concept, not only because outcomes can be very uncertain, but because there is not a rigid hierarchy of authority and process; authority is internal rather than external. For educators, teachers and parents, a judgement must be made here about democracy as a virtue (certainly as an educational virtue) and that personal thinking and learning are the ultimate democratic acts, depending on the participant alone acting independently. What each person thinks and believes to be so is up to them and no-one else, that is their process of thinking as distinct from the outcomes of thinking. It cannot be any other way than each person making up their own mind, but this is navigated through the social, political and economic context within which they find themselves (Seddon, 2015). Each person has their own subjective experience that is peculiar to them precisely because of their personal experience continuously and ultimately fashioned by their personal philosophy and biology. Along with prudence, justice, courage and temperance, democratic action as ethical conduct is understood accordingly as a cardinal virtue in modern society.

All of these cardinal virtues can be debated, but justice both particular and general has a strong claim for the short-list. Rendering rights that are due to others must surely be central to a virtuous life, whether those rights concern the

## 46   *Creative democracy*

right to know, to speak, to act, to associate, to decide and include access to equal rights under the law, an independent judiciary. In countries like Australia, these are rights that are often ascribed to the Westminster system of government and to numerous national constitutions that also accept the necessity of a free press or forms of communication to hold elected and non-elected decision-makers to public account. Justice of this type would seem to be an important educational principle as well, given that a denial of the right to speak, to act, to decide will make learning except of the totally superficial type, almost impossible, a misnomer. The issue of justice presupposes that certain action has been taken for which appropriate justice can be practised. That is, there needs to be agreed social frameworks within which either 'right' or 'wrong' action can be judged. For example, certain action might be considered in bad taste, insulting or offensive, but is allowable. Commentary that is considered racist or sexist is seen as inappropriate, whereas vigorous public debate and criticism regarding social policy and the conduct of decision-makers is usually taken as a necessary aspect of democratic society. There is also the issue of intent, both good and bad, that must be interpreted and considered. Ensuring justice then, that the rights of others are duly protected and that the relationship between citizens and colleagues is democratic and equitable, is a mark of a responsible, compassionate and professional society. It brings other cardinal virtues such as prudence or practical wisdom into play. Character traits such as these need to be incorporated across all aspects of educational systems to ensure that policies are appropriate, that procedures are reasonable and that relationships are respectful in their adherence to due and agreed process. Quality depends on their presence.

It should be noted that deontologist, consequentialist and instrumentalist ethics will have different approaches to virtue ethics on this matter. However, it could be argued that from an Aristotelian point of view, ethics and politics are separate, one concerned with living well, the other with the workings of the nation (or city in Aristotle's time) state. On the basis of the close connections and dominance that we now see under mature neoliberalism between systems and lifeworlds, this separation is difficult to sustain; while systems may seek to dominate the lifeworld, it is more appropriate that each appraise and inform the other. How do political systems justify their authority as distinct from their power? If the purpose of the polity is to enable a flourishing humanity, then political processes at all levels must allow citizens to live an ethical, virtuous life. In this sense, organisational authority needs to support personal autonomy, self-reliance and professional sovereignty. In a public institution, where the purpose and direction is public, there is an ethical obligation of all participants to act in support of public attributes and be able to justify policies and actions in reference to a philosophical baseline for the public good. In addition to moral convictions, political principles are required that allow groups of people with different pluralist persuasions to reach consensus for mutual benefit. This means a respected and vigorous two-way critique and scrutiny of the web of relationships between system and lifeworld, between politics and ethics, between personal and professional conduct. Without ethical bearing, we are lost.

## Power and control of curriculum

In previous times, those immediately following World War II, for example, it was possible to relatively easily identify those who had control or influence over the school curriculum in the English speaking countries. Most students attended primary school only where the emphasis was on reading, writing and arithmetic supported by a syllabus and materials often compiled and distributed by a state education department. As more students began to stay at school longer, it became necessary to distinguish between the purpose of primary and secondary schooling and, as late as 1967, the Plowden Report (UK, 1967) generated considerable controversy in suggesting a Piagetian 'child-centred' curriculum for primary schools. This left the purpose of the early years of secondary schooling a little unclear, a situation that remains frustratingly common. During this time, universities were often responsible for setting examinations for the senior years of secondary schooling and thereby controlling tertiary entrance. To this day, some countries still set examinations from England for their students. As teachers became more professional in many countries and demanded a greater say over the curriculum they taught, many nation states established independent boards to oversee curriculum while schools and teachers were accorded responsibility for their programs of study and assessment procedures. This is now a familiar process, with departments of education providing supportive materials and all but the final years of secondary schooling having exams set internally. Universities may still have representatives on somewhat independent curriculum boards established by governments and exercise influence in both content and assessment. From an Australian and critical perspective, Teese (2000/2013, pp. 246–247) comments,

> Control over the curriculum hinges on the ability of the top universities to dominate their field and as a consequence to expand both their institutional and their academic autonomy. Relative prestige gives them access to bureaucratic and political power, while at the same time, limiting the direct involvement of government in academic affairs. It enables them to enforce the authority they claim on academic grounds against contending claims from schools, teacher unions, subject associations, or by other universities lower down in the hierarchy – or indeed by all of these forces together.

It is significant to note that Teese points to a hierarchy of influence for universities and that, as the tertiary education sector has expanded, only some university staff and faculties have managed to maintain their position of esteem. Within universities themselves, program content and student assessment are usually in the hands of academic boards with elected staff positions. Budgets and course profiles are usually controlled by university councils or senates which react to financial trends and political advice in their budget settings. According to Exley and Ball (2014), however, neoliberalism now operates on a messy network of association and fraternity, rather than the clear lines of demarcation of the recent past. Networks involve international think tanks from economics and education, significant

## 48  *Creative democracy*

business leaders, education corporations, wealthy benefactors with various cultural affiliations, media barons and celebrity, public service bureaucrats, disparate members of parliament and individual party political operatives. Under these circumstances and global connections, it is possible for university academics and researchers to find a niche in policy formulation and sometimes in curriculum and assessment design, although it has become very difficult to successfully contest the economic ideology of neoliberalism as applied to education and schooling. This is particularly so in relation to so-called standards and assessment.

Since the release of the 'No Child Left Behind' Act in the United States (US, 2016), high stakes testing has become common around the world. While opinion varies on the impact of national and international testing of this type, there is no doubt that mass testing is a key ideological and accountability strategy of neoliberalism to support the marketisation and privatisation of education. Authors such as Hursh and Martina (2016) and Ravitch (2014) have clearly documented the impact of such tests. There is no philosophical basis for assessing the learning of humans, except in the most superficial manner. It is not possible, for example, to assess a person's understanding of the wheel (or any other thought object), as understanding discussed earlier depends on the experience and background of each person. It is possible to allocate grades of course in whatever way is decided, but such grades have little to do with learning. Alternatively, from a practice perspective and based on a broad view of teaching as 'intersubjective praxis,' we propose that *assessment of student learning occurs through a practice analysis of learning environments and the identification of new practices so created.* In a middle years' science class, for example, students may be investigating the states of matter and the differences between ice, water and steam. First, they undertake a description of 'practice situated' as they begin and their understanding of the composition of water, then the possible arrangements that occur or 'practice enacted' as water is cooled and heated and finally, their new understandings of the overall process they have created as 'practice emergent.' Artefacts and annotations may be included to focus, illustrate and concentrate discussions. Such a 'practice analysis' of learning undertaken by all participants discloses changes in thinking and understanding as experience evolves and new concepts and ideas are created and accessed as new practices. Pursuing this argument raises issues regarding the allocation of competitive grades for student assessment and whether external judgement is appropriate or not for collaborative participant 'practice analysis.'

Considering practice analysis as assessment constitutes a conceptual shift in thinking from 'assessment of students' to 'monitoring of practice.' This shift is significant in that it redirects attention away from the externally imposed products or assessment tasks of a teaching program, to the internally generated new practices that emerge from new thinking and new imaginings as experience proceeds. It is suggested that the 'monitoring of practice' (as discussion, ideas, concepts, proposals, redrafts, experimentation, projects) is co-ordinated through a portfolio process whereby groups of students compile artefacts of personal and community experience and culture, discuss the meaningful character of such artefacts and generate traces of importance for continuing investigation. For example, artefacts regarding family history (photographs, clothing, stories, immigration papers, interviews)

*Creative democracy* 49

could generate an investigation of the pathways taken by earlier groups or family members as they relocated and became more involved in local farming enterprises. This can be linked to broader issues of the time such as developments in science and technology that were impacting industrial and daily life and influenced previous family decisions. In making journal entries, notes, annotations, interpretations and reflections regarding portfolio discussions, students construct their own meanings that can then be considered in relation to official accounts from the literature, reports, media and the like. Exhibitions, roundtables and summaries of portfolio experience enable new practices to be identified as evidence of collaborative and authentic student learning.

Control of the school curriculum and student assessment remains the most difficult in education around the world. This is where ideology and political judgements collide and where economic systems expect adherence. Freire (1972, p. 65) comments on how transitions are possible under even the most difficult circumstances and describes as in earlier chapters, how societies or communities can move from more restricted and controlled to more accessible and fluid relationships:

> Although the qualitative difference between the semi-intransitive consciousness and the naïve transitive consciousness can be explained by the phenomenon of emergence due to structural transformations in society, there are no rigidly defined frontiers between the historical moments which produce qualitative changes in awareness. In many respects, the semi-intransitive consciousness remains present in the naïve transitive consciousness.

Freire goes on to describe how in more closed societies, the 'silenced' become more supportive of change as they experience new conditions and new opportunities. In terms of schooling and student assessment, it has taken the silenced some time to awaken, in spite of strong minority voices that have been raised with concern for many years, perhaps as long as schooling has existed. The education profession in all its aspects must accept much of the blame for this situation, allowing a detailed and critical philosophical analysis of education to be absent from political and professional debates in most countries. In terms of power and control of the curriculum and in particular schooling policy, there is an urgent need to pursue critique of the neoliberal economic and educational agenda in detail, from a democratic, comprehensive and progressive political and educational viewpoint. While education remains fragmented and disparate, this critique will not be possible.

## Generative themes for a cohesive education

Attempting to describe education in its broadest life, or birth-to-death sense as a philosophy of practice, will necessarily involve a thoughtful and prudent selection of principles and themes from all those available. From the previous four chapters, it should be clear that the basic paradigm from which this selection is being made is that of human action consisting of the social act, rather than the paradigm of existing expertness. The latter leaves aside the questions of where and how experts derive

## 50 *Creative democracy*

their knowledge in the first place. As a summary and starting point of considering specific principles and themes, we note that teaching and learning proceeds within significant economic and political institutions called school, college or university and the like. Formal education can be conceptualised as one aspect of a dominant economic system, existing within a complicated framework of bureaucratic regulation and procedure, aligned with and responding passively to changing political circumstances. Under these conditions, formal education will struggle to achieve some form of independence in its existence including implementation of policies and strategies to best meet the educational needs of all families and students. This will be the case under different variations of economic systems, such as welfare state, neoliberal, social democratic or socialist. Conversely, it is possible to conceive of formal education as one of a number of economic and political fields of human activity that exists in relation to all other fields in a constant process of interaction, tension and uncertainty. For example, it is possible to imagine a return to welfare state economics while under dominant neoliberalism, it is possible to envisage more democratic and more equitable distribution of resources while still enduring the constraints of capitalism. This imaginary delineates education as a semi-independent, usually somewhat weak field, still coming under the influence of all other fields and in particular, powerful economic imperatives, but it has an interrelational rather than subjugated position within the matrix of historical human experience. This is the significance of education as a coherent philosophy of practice in its own right, capable of shaping its own destiny regrading social and educational progress and indeed piece together different counter narratives against prevailing trends. A field analysis of this type indicates how a range of alternative policies, procedures and practices can appear and survive under very difficult conditions and provide evidence that progressive change is always possible. Attempting to theorise and structure education in neoliberal times as a field of human practice and based on discussion in previous chapters has evoked the thematic chart that follows (Table 4.1).

It can be difficult to think about education in this way, that is as an integrated field of philosophical practice, rather than being composed of splinters and fragments of knowledge fields and disciplines drawn from elsewhere. In discussing this issue, Biesta (2015d, p. 666) draws on the work of Dilthey (Makkreel and Rodi, 1989) who proposed education as *Geisteswissenschaften*, defined as study of 'culture and cultural phenomenon, or, to be more precise, those realities brought forward by the activity of the human mind (in German: *Geist*), both in their contemporary and their historical manifestation.' Biesta also makes the distinction between 'research that aims at generating (causal) *explanation* and research that seeks to generate (interpretative) *understanding*' (p. 667), such that the dualism between qualitative and quantitative processes (or between the sciences and humanities) under *Geisteswissenschaften* becomes at least blurred, if not vague and ill-defined. Connections with the theorising of Dewey are persuasive here, in his energies to bring components together in relationship, rather than in opposition. But what is the significance of thinking about education as a field of philosophical practice in this way, why not accept that formal education is merely a haphazard collection of data, information and knowledge from a range of different and detached areas of

*Creative democracy* 51

*Table 4.1* Generative themes for cohesive education

| Themes | Description |
| --- | --- |
| Philosophy of practice | Education as a cohesive, integrated, balanced and holistic field of practice with its own distinctive theories, practices and knowledge claims. |
| Pragmatism | Human understanding that is constructed from all the encounters of experience of the social and physical worlds. |
| Practice and praxis | Negotiated projects within agreed or contested parameters that ultimately support living well for the public good. |
| Democracy, equity, communication, interaction | Modes of respectful, associated living that sustain autonomous, communicative culture and experience. |
| Ethics and morality | Personal conduct and action regarding living well for the public good. |
| Creative action | Unorthodox solutions to encounters, problems and dilemmas to resolve further thinking and action. |
| Culture | Dimensions of the lifeworld that connect interest, history, language, community experience with current and new practices. |
| Transformational knowledge | New understandings that arise from practice that transform perceptions and conceptions. |
| Teaching/learning as intersubjective practice | Repertoires of formal, informal and transitional practices to engage and investigate ideas and problems such that new practices are created with and between participants. |
| Curriculum as emergent practice | Transforming discourses, practices and ideas that result from creative interaction between generative themes and negotiated tasks. |
| Assessment | Practice analysis of learning environments and the identification and monitoring of new practices so created. |
| Research | Engagement with reflective discursive practices that establish dialogue between participants to transform current practices into intersubjective praxis knowledge. |

mainly empirical study? This argument centres on what it means to be human. If, to be human, involves interacting with and learning about the different worlds of experience we encounter in contemplative, meaningful and satisfying ways, then this must proceed from the basis of all that we understand at a particular time. It is not possible, for example, to disconnect sections of our being when we come to engage a new object, problem or interest and attempt to comprehend, plan and enact our way forward. This occurs when making a sand castle at the beach, when discussing matters around the kitchen table or when designing a scientific experiment. It seems strange then to insist that a school student must be able to understand an explicit mathematical or language object at exactly the same time as everyone else, when the background experience of everyone else is different and at different stages of 'alignment.' Particular humans engage the world with holistic

## 52  Creative democracy

intellectual tactics and tentacles that are similar to but different from all other participants, regardless of the similarity with social and economic background.

A perusal of Table 4.1 indicates that practice exists in and arises from the general lifeworld of culture and experience, partnered with inquiries of interests and puzzles that are undertaken, the results of which become part of consciousness and awareness. This could be referred to as the 'three domains' of human existence and education, as shown in Figure 4.1. Habermas (1984) proposed a similar arrangement when outlining his views of lifeworld and also described the interconnections between experience, discourse and consciousness.

Finally, we come to the question of how we understand education itself, its purpose, direction and what could be called, its ontology or very being. For these questions to be pursued, a distinctive process of theorising education is required that may or may not include elements of other theories and frameworks. In defining education as a philosophy of practice, the means of theorising and researching 'philosophy of practice' need to be detailed such that key understandings, affordances or what Bellmann (2014, p. 77) calls 'normative categories' can be investigated. He goes on to suggest that 'The question as to what education ought to be, has overridden the question of how education is possible.' From this, it can be proposed inchoate that education becomes possible through the continuing, cyclical and integrated social acts of lifeworld, inquiry and consciousness such that humans become increasingly subjective and intersubjective. Particularities of this understanding will be discussed in following chapters. It does mean, however, that the theorising of lifeworld, inquiry and consciousness is possible, within the constraints of the time and that research paradigms and methodologies are available for investigations to proceed. At this point, a new form of theorising is required, one that conceives of the three domains of lifeworld, inquiry and consciousness as being in constant dialectical interaction and transformation, each impacting and being informed by the other. This is how we need to think about the process of sense making and how experience needs to be researched.

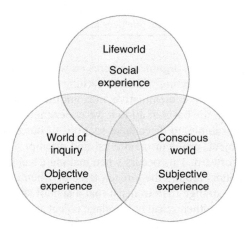

*Figure 4.1* Three domains of human existence and education

Creative democracy 53

The proposal that will be briefly introduced next and discussed more fully throughout Part II advances the concept of democratic and participatory narrative inquiry as the means by which executing and researching 'education as philosophy of practice' can be conceptualised. As initially discussed by Hooley (2009) but is extended here, Clandinin and Connelly's (2000) work on narrative inquiry drew upon Dewey's (1958) theories of experience when they proposed a narrative structure of three dimensions that looks backwards and forwards, inwards and outwards and considers the location in place of participants. When using narrative methodologies, researcher and participants alike are always in the position of crafting interpretations. This means working with the data for a long time, perhaps over many years, to be steeped in the data and experience, seeking facts, exploring confirmations, evaluating alternative viewpoints and developing different understandings. It is now suggested that a central feature of participatory narrative inquiry that enables the process of theorising to occur, is the notion of exemplar. The work of the philosopher Thomas Kuhn introduced exemplar as an important idea regarding progress in science and how theory develops. Kuhn saw 'knowledge embedded in shared exemplars' as a 'mode of knowing' and pointed out that such 'working knowledge' is acquired in the same way as other knowledge such as music or art (Mishler, 1990). For investigating communities of all types, the development and refinement of knowledge exemplars over times helps to clarify emerging and generalised ideas and helps guide ongoing pathways as experience and knowledge accumulates. A draft model of knowledge and practice discourse to guide exemplar production is shown in Figure 4.2 (see Hooley, 2009):

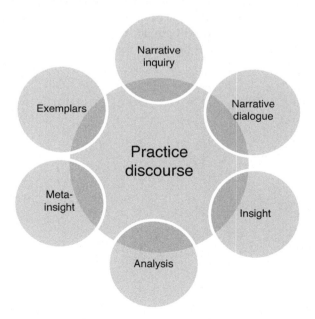

*Figure 4.2* Narrative exemplar process for philosophy of practice

54  *Creative democracy*

The notion of generative narrative exemplars described earlier is taken to be operating within the dialectical relationship of lifeworld, inquiry and human consciousness. It is how cognitive substance is made of sensorial experience and culture. For the purposes of participatory narrative inquiry and reflexive practice, the exemplars so proposed will need to begin with and be seen as credible by communities of practice if they are to contribute to and improve practice of those using the exemplars. The investigatory and research process described earlier has taken narrative inquiry as its mode of exploration and has proposed a series of practices to ensure that the inquiry is rigorous and systematic, links with the literature and can result in further practice that is informed by and can be critiqued by theoretical concerns. These practices are referred to as narrative dialogue, insight, analysis and meta-insight. A further step, that of sense making, involves the theorising of exemplars that capture the central features of the work being undertaken and which provides the basis for new forms of investigation and clarification of meaning for participants. There are thus two types of exemplar as the process continues, those that characterise a particular approach to practice and those that characterise a particular problem within a particular field of knowledge.

We now turn to Part II of this book that proposes an integrated, balanced and holistic concept or model of education as a comprehensive 'philosophy of practice' in its own right. This model will be detailed in relation to the 'generative themes' of Table 4.1 and be compared and contrasted to six other philosophies that will have similar and opposing characteristics. All philosophies are considered to be of equal importance, while recognising that the economic field continues to dominate and often distorts the others. It is to be hoped that discussion in Chapters 1–4 while brief and selective and perhaps at times a little disjointed in an attempt to ensure that main points are mentioned, will provide a sound basis for this construction and comparison. If so, there will be a more rigorous framework for debate that what currently exists.

# Part I reflections

A number of major theorists and some of their key ideas have been encountered throughout the first four chapters of this book. There has not been any attempt to provide an extensive discussion of their theorising, but rather to suggest some broad directions arising that demonstrate a clear line of demarcation with conservative and neoliberal educational thinking. From this broad overview, an emphasis on social practice and creative personal action are suggested as being central parameters that assist in establishing and maintaining an ethical, productive and communicative life. Such matters run counter to and do not figure in neoliberal education. These concepts are considered from an epistemological perspective with learning and knowledge arising from the comprehensive and discursive social act and seek to move beyond mere description that often dominates sociology. The significance of taking an epistemological perspective concerns the implications for action that relates to all participants, educators and students alike. At this point in our journey then, it is hoped that the educational map that has been sketched thus far indicates some of the foremost ideas and theories of philosophy and sociology that will impinge on and challenge our understanding of how to go about improving learning for all citizens around the world who wish to embrace knowledge and to live with dignity and satisfaction. Our journey of practice-theorising can be thought of as spiral rather than linear, whereby the ideas and practices we engage at one point, are brought to bear again at a later stage as our subsequent experiences and knowledges bring a fresh perspective to previous and continuing questions. Part II will provide some ways of thinking about this problem, especially in relation to a number of associated philosophies of practice

# Part II

# Thinking educationally

As an important feature of social and economic life, formal education is of great interest to neoliberal adherents. Its often fragmented character in many countries makes education an easy target for criticism and proposals for constant conservative reform, piece by piece. To provide a means of considering education in relation to a number of domains of criticism, Part II is not divided into separate chapters, but is structured around a series of scenarios that are intended to raise key philosophical questions. Following each scenario, there is some brief discussion and theorising of these questions, somewhat like an exegesis provides commentary on a creative activity. Such discussion and theorising draws upon the philosophical and sociological insights raised in Part I. It is not possible of course to discuss the six philosophies of religion, neoliberalism, conservatism, social democracy, science and Marxism in any depth via a series of short scenarios, but hopefully two or three central ideas from each will be illustrated. Part II is therefore intended to, in summary, outline a progressive and coherent view of education as a philosophy of practice that can then relate to other philosophies that impart both criticism and challenge. In becoming a more holistic, independent and stronger field of practice and action, education is better placed to act in the interests of all citizens, not totally at the behest of wealth and power. It is the case that under the dominance of the capitalist and neoliberal economic system, formal education will be dictated to by wealth and power, but this can be mediated by the systematic social action of citizens as they explore and implement ways of acting on the world to change the world for historical and social progress.

# 5 Education as philosophy of practice

Weeping willows show grief of war
strands of green cascading down
around the lake with bridge and boats
while lilies capture peace and calm
expressions of nature's essence
lie scattered across large panels,
liberated from tradition's staleness
revolution always ignores the cage
turning what we think inside out.

A philosophical view of humanity generally conceived, that is how humans conduct their lives and what they see as being important, suggests the following perspectives of the purposes and significance of education:

- to assist evolution of the species in harmony with the environment;
- to live well and virtuously in relation to the good;
- to learn actively, socially and communicatively;
- to respect and investigate all knowledge, ideas and practices;
- to support the interests and aspirations of democratic humanity; and
- to assist social and educational progress for all citizens.

Such terms are all available for definition and interpretation, but they stand in marked contrast to a view of education that has contracted economic outcomes for minority and privileged gain. A cohesive set of philosophical practices regarding the purposes of education can now be considered as constituting a consistent and interrelated discipline of education that usually does not exist at present. Current forms of education in many countries are often derived from a mix of disciplines and fields that has political and economic rather than educational intent. Therefore, it is now possible to consider and detail each of the main constructs of formal education – curriculum, pedagogy, assessment, research – from the perspective of these philosophical purposes and, once defined and elaborated, reconsider which philosophies that best support such constructs. In this reflexive way, both philosophy and education are in constant flux, change and formation to meet the needs of all participants, families, students and teachers alike (Roberts, 2015). The following integrated and combined discussion of Chapter 5 which aspects of curriculum design that encourage active learning and the 'social act' are supported most strongly philosophically? Which forms of assessment enable phronesis and praxis understandings of the objects and complexities of learning? Which paradigms of knowledge creation and evaluation support an ongoing understanding not constrained within rigidities and ideologies? Attempting to interrogate both philosophy and education as the basis of what it means to be human and of learning in formal programs will necessitate new concepts of investigation and organisation that move well beyond the neoliberal agenda. Specifically, the following:

1. A new knowledge discipline of education will emerge to be included with the current short-list of knowledge forms consisting of mathematics, physical sciences (physics, chemistry), human sciences (language, history), religion, literature and the fine arts (music), philosophy.

(Hirst, 1974)

2. A new concept of integrated 'educationist' will be created rather than those involved in education being seen as sociologists, philosophers, anthropologists, historians and the like, loosely drawn from other knowledge disciplines or forms.
3. A new concept of curriculum and pedagogy will be constructed that immerses all participants in understanding and interacting with the social and physical worlds as intersubjective and dialectical lifeworlds of experience, culture and practice for communities and for individuals.
4. A new concept of student assessment will be necessary that monitors changes in the practice environment of participants and does not attempt to measure the subjective learning and understanding of participants.
5. A new approach to researching the discipline of education will be required located within a new paradigm of integrated and holistic learning and understanding involving but different from other knowledge disciplines and fields.

To investigate this new realm of human existence, the following discussion or narrative will attempt to describe the relationships between education as a philosophy of practice and six other philosophies and provide examples and scenarios wherever possible. In structural terms, the discussion will be organised as in Figure 5.1:

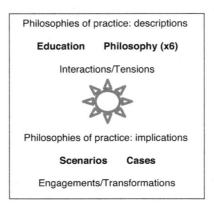

*Figure 5.1* Structure of Chapter 5

## Philosophy 1: education as a knowledge discipline

To conceptualise education as an independent knowledge discipline with its own authenticity based on a philosophy of practice, requires a close definition of each term. Bradatan (2015, pp. 5–6) comments that philosophy is an 'art of living,' a 'practice,' 'not something you store up in your books, but something you carry with you.' He then makes the telling observation,

> Indeed, to embrace the notion of philosophy as a self-transformative practice is to make yourself fundamentally vulnerable. If a philosophy is genuine only to the extent that it is embodied in the one who practices it, then the philosopher is not unlike the tightrope walker performing without a safety net.

It is unlikely that many teachers or academics will adopt this advice regarding how to live and work, that in the end, their only role is not to impose the 'truth,' but to investigate the 'real.' In relation to knowledge, the British philosopher of education Paul Hirst suggested that it can be thought of as becoming aware of experience regarding 'structure, organised and made meaningful in some quite specific way.' He went on to say that, 'To acquire knowledge is to learn to see, to experience the world in a way otherwise unknown and thereby to come to have a mind in a fuller sense' (Hirst, 1974). This conception sees knowledge as arising from and strongly linked with human action and involvement with the world. It lays the foundation for his later statement that, rather than formal education and the school curriculum, for example, being based on formal disciplinary knowledge, 'education is primarily initiation into social practices' (Hirst, Barrow and White, 1993). It can be taken that the notion of 'primarily' as used here means within an educational and social context that includes disciplinary knowledge that is not imposed as the endpoint of personal learning, but connects with and informs the ongoing findings of social practice. In noting that to qualify as a separate 'form' or discipline of knowledge a set of distinguishing features is required, Hirst (1974) broadly proposed

- specific concepts that are peculiar to and define the character or central appreciations of the knowledge involved;
- a relationship with experience such that experience can become understood;
- statements regarding knowledge that can be investigated and critiqued; and
- distinctive ways of exploring experience and understandings.

From this approach, the generative themes for education outlined in Chapter 4 must now be reconfigured to be consistent with the four distinguishing features as noted in Table 5.1. Some brief summary comments are provided in the table to indicate these connections. Comments have not been written in any particular order, or separated into separate cells in the table to emphasise the integrated nature of the discipline and the interrelated networking of all items with each other. It should also be noted that not all knowledge falls within the category of discipline, but that 'fields' of knowledge also exist. These include journalism, economics, biology, engineering, painting, computing, currently education and many others, that are not distinctive with their own features as outlined in Table 5.1, but consist of

*Table 5.1* Distinguishing features of education as knowledge discipline

| Theme | Specific Concepts | Relationship with Experience | Statements for Investigation | Exploring Experience |
| --- | --- | --- | --- | --- |
| Philosophy of practice<br>Pragmatism<br>Practice and praxis<br>Democracy, equity, communication, interaction<br>Ethics and morality<br>Creative action<br>Culture<br>Transformational knowledge<br>Teaching/learning as intersubjective practice<br>Curriculum as emergent practice<br>Assessment<br>Research | Processes of ethical, subjective living for public good<br>Understanding through experience<br>Negotiated social acts for equitable public good<br>Arrangements of associated living and communicated experience<br>Forms of conduct enacted for the personal and social good<br>New practices in response to new situations<br>Current and new practices connected with lifeworld experience<br>Designed to change current situations for improvement<br>New subjective awareness from experience<br>Generation of new practices through communicative and democratic practice<br>Monitoring of new practices arising from experience<br>Transformation of current practices into intersubjective praxis knowledge | Direct engagement with significant objects of experience<br>Modes of experience – e.g. art, history, language, physical, synthesised at level of knowledge<br>Experience located in lifeworld and particular aspects of lifeworld<br>Knowledge immersed in experience or abstracted from experience | Outcomes of practice available for monitoring and explanation<br>Provide integrity, ethos and culture of knowledge experience<br>Generalised for explanation and application within different situations<br>Verified and validated against experience | Theorising of practice to guide further practice<br>Integrated action and theorising to understand practice<br>Variety of methodologies as required to resolve dilemmas |

*Education as philosophy of practice*   63

a mix of knowledge and practices drawn from other disciplines and fields. Hirst's categorisation can of course be disputed, with disciplines being added or removed. The place of religion, for example, is particularly interesting and contested, as it can be considered as a grouping of disparate knowledges, behaviours, mythologies and rituals that have little connectivity, except being based on faith and hierarchy. Religion will be the next philosophy to be considered in this section.

We are now in a position to sketch an indicative outline of education as a philosophy of practice involving disciplinary knowledge in action. This will need to be done in systemic terms – that is, how a public system of education and schooling for the vast majority of the population will be constructed and operate. Themes and features as identified next will be construed in policy and practice terms and examples will be given to illustrate key markers for each. In some respect, this attempt will be idealistic and may be criticised as such, but some license needs to be given here to discuss and frame an education system that does not as yet exist. The level of resources needed to support the outline will not be excessive, but it is accepted that resources would be available in relation to the description given. This applies to not only buildings, equipment and grounds, but the number of teachers required and the extent and quality of teacher education (also covered in Chapter 8). It is taken that the principles, themes and practices will be appropriate for most countries regardless of economic and cultural disposition which raises serious questions of educational and cultural imperialism, not unlike that of neoliberalism we are attempting to combat. The debate here involves epistemological concerns around the nature of knowledge and learning, and how these are similar or dissimilar depending on cultural and political background. There is a philosophical standpoint that humans have great similarity about how they relate to and investigate their social and physical worlds and that this needs to strongly inform the public education systems of all countries. It does not constitute educational or epistemological dominance, but it does require very careful and detailed understanding of how humans learn and how this can be incorporated into different cultural systems and traditions. Chapter 10 regarding Indigenous education considers this problem in some depth.

## Scenario 1: education as philosophy of practice (from a teacher's perspective)

Jemma has been teaching a range of humanities subjects at a large secondary school for the past five years. She comes from a working class family where the common pattern is for children to try to complete secondary schooling, but to leave at the legal age of 16 or 17 if an appropriate job becomes available. Schooling is valued by families for its democratic and citizenship purposes, but the realities of economic imperatives at home often dominate. There is a lack of experience of university life in Jemma's family, but they were very pleased when she announced that she wanted to continue at school and go on to study history and literature, if possible. Although she spoke with her teachers at school about what to expect, Jemma was still surprised at how much choice she had in designing her own

## 64   *Education as philosophy of practice*

program at university and in attending lectures and tutorials to support her interests. Her lecturers encouraged her to read widely and to experience as much of university life as she could so that she had a broad base of information and know-how to bring to her studies. While Jemma was very interested in European history and culture, she found that wide reading and discussion helped her gain a deeper appreciation of past events and why actions and decisions were undertaken. As an active member of the film society, she found herself arguing with students from other faculties about the need to understand society and not to view the world as if from the bottom of a well. She began to take an interest in politics and the environment and realised that historical events did not merely happen on their own, but were interlinked in a maze of complicated social and community practices, all of which needed to be taken into account. This became clear at student meetings and rallies when speakers would rage against the inequalities and injustices they saw locally and around the world.

Teaching full time in a secondary school came as a shock. Like all new teachers, Jemma had trouble in making sure she was well prepared for all classes week after week, attended staff meetings and was able to contribute, followed up on student problems and absences with parents, adhered to what had been agreed on student assessment together with the responding to and recording of results and generally participated in the life of the school whenever she could. This activity was constant and exhausting, often frustrating and usually involved rushing from one class or meeting to the next with little time for thinking and planning. After a time, however, it occurred to Jemma that there was a common thread running through all this hectic activity – all teachers no matter what their subject area or personal interest were committed to the best possible learning experience for their students. She discovered that in spite of arguments at staff and subject meetings, teachers generally wanted to involve all students in their own learning and to encourage them to think broadly and creatively about what they thought and what they hoped. This reminded Jemma of her lecturers at university and their support for students to 'do their own thinking.' Discussions at the school curriculum committee also reflected this view, where teachers did defend their own subjects, but also recognised that constructing barriers between subject knowledge restricted markedly how understanding of complicated ideas proceeds. While primary schools had a strong tradition of play and exploration of integrated knowledge in an open-ended way, secondary schools often separated subjects one from the other and assumed that outcomes were known. Over a two-year period of discussions and investigation, the curriculum committee finally endorsed Jemma's proposal that the middle years of secondary school should combine subject knowledge as much as possible and organise classes around projects and experiments so that students could come to their own conclusions whenever possible. There were long debates around the committee table about this, about whether students had to always reach the same understanding about the water molecule, a significant novel or author, the nature of gravity or the nature of people and events. These were important questions that one teacher said had philosophical and historical importance for everyone and that needed to be confronted rather than denied.

*Education as philosophy of practice*  65

In the midst of Jemma's beginning years of teaching, there was much debate in the country about the introduction of a national curriculum for all schools. Where Jemma worked, the school curriculum was the responsibility of the elected school council (of teachers and parents) working with the advice of the principal and staff. The argument here was that the local school is best placed to understand the needs of its students and is more than capable of designing appropriate curriculum with the support and guidelines of state authorities. Most teachers also believed that it was their professional right to work with families and children in this way and not be directed from outside in the same way as lawyers, medical doctors and other professionals construct their work. National curriculum has been adopted by some countries for their own reasons, sometimes due to small populations and geographical areas, sometimes for political and ideological consequences. While they disagreed on a number of issues, Jemma and her colleagues were adamant that it was their right to design curriculum in the best interests of their students, but they had one major concern. To this point, the school curriculum did appear to be fragmented in organisation and intent and it was difficult to mount a consistent argument against the many comments, criticisms and questions that came forth from various sectors of the community. For example, mass testing was an important local and national debate, but there did not seem to be an overarching or philosophical view to put on where knowledge comes from and how it can be assessed accurately. For Jemma and her colleagues, the draft national curriculum was not the answer as it was mainly content driven and did not promote discussion of background issues to curriculum and knowledge. As a starting point, the teachers began to compile a set of principles that they considered infused all subjects and provided a framework for teaching and learning generally. As this work proceeded, they realised that what was central to their work with students and with each other was a combination of subject knowledge with thorough approaches to investigation of ideas such that new thinking for everyone became possible. The curriculum began to crystallise around these key ideas and practices where new thoughts were excitedly appreciated whether they fitted with accepted views or not, at the time. A closer alignment was always possible a little later.

Many of the research papers regarding teaching and schooling that Jemma read, did not appear to be of immediate use. There were plenty of studies that covered a wide range of educational issues, but not that many that hit the mark with the detail of what goes on in classrooms. Again, Jemma's mind went back to her history lecturers, who said that you have to be patient with research, in gathering the documents and making sense of what they are saying. It's like getting fit where, particularly after a period of inactivity, it may take a long time before any change is discerned. She did discover that journal papers may describe the general conditions that contextualise education, or take statistical measures of various types, but often did not do what she wanted, an integrated and comprehensive analysis of how teachers and students go about learning. Apart from the distinction of qualitative and quantitative research, she wanted to understand how those in their professional fields understood what they were doing and how this changed as situations changed, she wanted more detail of practitioner experience. Late one

## 66  *Education as philosophy of practice*

night, Jemma put the paper she was reading aside and sighed. She had been thinking a lot recently regarding her journey over the past few years, from a humble working family, to university student and now, to a responsible teacher, a person who was expected to do good work for many children from all backgrounds. She was satisfied with her progress so far, but at the same time, still felt lost in the education profession. What was lacking she thought was this consistent view that had been developed over many years by the profession, not to be imposed, but to be available for general guidance. It was difficult to speak with parents, teachers and students, let alone local politicians and the like, on difficult matters without strong, consistent, authorised and theorised backing. Professional knowledge in other words that was generally agreed and which was available for practitioners in their daily work and in their role as community practitioner-theorists. Underneath all her worries was the uncertainty of how practitioners thought about what they were experiencing and how they decide to do better.

Scenario 1 suggests that teachers work well under the conditions that they face, but that they are patently inhibited by the lack of a progressive, consistent and consensus educational framework. This involves not only the purpose and direction of formal education, but general schema to guide organisation and structure. In his famous early work, Lee Shulman went some of the way in outlining the various knowledges that he thought were required for teaching. It is worth repeating in full his opening remarks that are still relevant today (Shulman, 1987, p. 1):

> Richly developed portrayals of expertise in teaching are rare. While many characterisations of effective teachers exist, many of these dwell on the teacher's management of the classroom. We find few descriptions or analyses of teachers that give careful attention not only to the management of students in classrooms, but also to the management of *ideas* within classroom discourse. Both kinds of emphasis will be needed if our portrayals of good practice are to serve as sufficient guides to the design of better education.

Shulman went on to outline his seven categories of knowledge for every teacher and listed content knowledge, general pedagogical knowledge, curriculum knowledge, pedagogical content knowledge, knowledge of learners, knowledge of educational contexts and knowledge of educational ends, purposes and values and their philosophical and historical grounds. This is a comprehensive list that is still incorporated into many teacher education programs around the world. What is being attempted in this book is to bring such a list or similar list to Shulman's together, so that education and teaching is not fragmented into different items, but coheres into a robust knowledge discipline that is available for testing, researching, strengthening and critique. As mention previously, Shulman's later work involved an investigation of signature pedagogies that went across various professions such as law, medicine, engineering, clergy, teaching and nursing. He described 'signature pedagogy' as 'a mode of teaching that has become inextricably identified with preparing people for a particular profession' (Shulman, 2005). The three characteristics that were proposed for signature pedagogy were its distinctiveness to a profession, its pervasiveness within the curriculum and its inclusion across institutions and the profession. If we can combine the approach of Shulman into the knowledge discipline of education involving the knowledges of curriculum, pedagogy, assessment, research and policy, linked by a number of signature pedagogies distinctive to education, then a cohesive philosophy of practice begins to emerge.

## Tensions and similarities

It is difficult to conceptualise education as a knowledge discipline when it does not exist at present. It is easier to take another knowledge discipline such as language to consider how our understanding of knowledge connects with the world at large. Most people would say that they 'know' language in an intimate way. That is, they may accept that it is composed of a number of different parts, but it is understood holistically and used inclusively to express and communicate ideas and meaning. We 'know' language through its connectedness with us and how it is a part of daily life from birth to death. Other forms of disciplinary knowledge such as physics and chemistry are slightly more removed, although we draw upon specific aspects as the need arises. If these forms of knowledge including mathematics are reasonably accurate, then they will reflect the social and physical worlds as we engage them and help with explanation and realisation. Education, as a form of knowledge is not like this, but is generally broken up into various parts to be used as the occasion demands. Modern schooling, for example, can impose a formal view of knowledge discussed in earlier chapters, where the shift from concrete to abstract thinking is a confusing process to explain, formalised by school as requiring expert assistance and instruction. One way of considering how this process may occur, has been developed by Burridge, Hooley and Neal (2016), where they propose the concept of 'frames of practice' arising from their pre-service teacher education experience and research. They theorise the notion of 'frame' as 'a conceptual skeleton of understanding that arises from school and classroom practice and is formatted in practice' (p. 158). Drawing on the work of Giddens (1984) regarding 'practical' and 'discursive' consciousness, they distinguish between primary and secondary frames of practice as in Table 5.2 (p. 159):

*Table 5.2* Characteristics of frames of practice

| *Primary Frames of Practice* | *Secondary Frames of Practice* |
| --- | --- |
| Situated | Intersectoral |
| Connected | Entangled |
| Place-dependent | Place-independent |
| Closed | Fluid |
| Specific awareness, description | General awareness, explanation |
| Practical ideas of practice | Discursive ideas of practice |

## 68  *Education as philosophy of practice*

From an epistemological perspective, there is an ongoing transitional process between primary/naïve frames of practice and secondary/complex frames of practice as experience ensues and becomes more dense, generating new frames of understanding and learning. For the purpose of considering education as a knowledge discipline, there is a question as to whether there are frames of practice for specific topics, or whether frames bring together knowledge as integrated domains of understanding and perspective. It is interesting to think of the language example discussed earlier in this regard, compared with say physics. Perhaps it is appropriate to theorise a third category of frame, the tertiary, where the 'conceptual skeleton' of cognition has strengthened to the extent of enabling a broad overview of meaning and possibility (Table 5.3):

*Table 5.3* Characteristics of primary, secondary and tertiary frames

| *Primary Frames of Practice* | *Secondary Frames of Practice* | *Tertiary Frames of Practice* |
| --- | --- | --- |
| Situated | Intersectoral | Holistic |
| Connected | Entangled | Merged |
| Place-dependent | Place-independent | Place-autonomous |
| Closed | Fluid | Integrated |
| Specific awareness, description | General awareness, explanation | Abstracted awareness, aesthetic |
| Practical ideas of practice | Discursive ideas of practice | Creative ideas of practice |

This approach begins to flesh out what might be involved in education as a knowledge discipline and what is involved in its practice. It suggests a pragmatic relationship between initial forays into social action, how this transitions into the formation of tentative and evolving constructions of explanation and then, the growth of holistic subjectivities that enable creative and aesthetic views to appear and be shaped. The concept of 'frame' allows us to think about this process and to engage the world accordingly. If there are no rigid divisions between frames, with each interconnected with the other, then we can begin to envision education as we do language, an integrated practice, brought to bear on particular situations as they arise. When acting with and through disciplinary knowledge, an intimate dialectical relationship is established between the human actor and the object of experience, such that each is informing and is informed by the other. When observing the sunset, for example, the human participant brings their prior knowledge to bear on the experience so that understandings and impressions of light, colour, energy and universe are combined, while at the same time, every new sunset will change these understandings and thereby create a new object when observed the following day. Observing an eclipse of the sun will generate new meaning of the sun itself when it is observed at a later stage. Education as a form of holistic, integrated knowledge, that can then be applied to vastly different situations as the need to learn and gain meaning fills our mind, to resolve uncertainty and frustration, to pursue deep

*Education as philosophy of practice* 69

human interest, becomes the connection between consciousness and lifeworld, as we practise knowing. From the point of view of pragmatic philosophy, education is the practice and process of becoming human, the formation of intense subjective awareness that enables our continuing exploration of what it means to be human and the significance of our relationship with others.

## Exegesis: Jemma, education and pragmatism

In returning to discussion of Jemma's scenario earlier, it is a challenging task to expose a detailed explanation or understanding of her situation and corundum's without being able to consider her engagement with education as an academic discipline, a knowledge discipline or a philosophy of practice. Biesta, Allen and Edwards (2014, pp. 3–4) for instance pose the issue of

> whether educational research *necessarily* has to rely on theoretical input from (other) disciplines) or whether there are, or ought to be, distinctively *educational* forms of theory and theorising. This in turn raises the question whether education can and should claim to be an academic discipline in its own right or whether it should be understood as an applied field of study just like, for example, business studies or sport studies.

In this case, the notion of academic discipline needs to be differentiated from knowledge discipline in terms of areas of study undertaken at a university. An academic discipline may involve areas such as economics, psychology, engineering, technologies and such like that, with current studies of education, call upon expertise and judgements from elsewhere. There is also the concept of 'applied field of study' in the sense of areas of knowledge that do not involve theorising themselves for principles of deeper understanding and explanation. We therefore attempt to interrogate Jemma's experience not from the point of view of academic discipline, but from education as a discipline of holistic knowledge that enters into sustained dialogue with her lifeworld of culture, inquiry and consciousness. Coming from a working class family, Jemma saw knowledge as having both a use and exchange value, but this view broadened when she entered university and her lecturers encouraged her to explore and read as much as possible. Through her new experiences of student life including those of meetings, debates and rallies, she began to realise that her life intermingled with those of many others around the world and that she had an obligation to combat injustice and inequality wherever she could.

When Jemma started work as a beginning teacher, she could not avoid being immersed in curriculum change and development disputes brought about not only by external pressures, but by internal educational conflicts as well. She had to grapple with these problems from her past and recent experience as a history and literature graduate, while at the same time, extend her thinking into all other curriculum areas of the school. This was difficult, given that she found her mathematics and science colleagues in particular having what seemed to be a different view of what knowledge is all about and the role of the teacher. On the other hand, she

## 70 *Education as philosophy of practice*

thought that they had a very limited view of her work as well. Jemma surprised herself by taking the initiative and moving at the curriculum committee for a combination of subject knowledge during the middle years of secondary schooling and a greater emphasis on project work that would encourage student decision making. She was aware that her thinking was changing and that she was coming to accept that knowledge from all subject areas was connected in some way. Her reading and discussion with colleagues was important in this respect, but she realised that her experience of working with a range of students of different ages and backgrounds was pivotal in expanding her concept of learning. Jemma was coming to see that her main task involved taking a key idea and linking it to the student's experience in some way through a combination of discussion and experiment. This had to be done in an integrated process where the student could draw upon their own language, interest and culture to connect with the new idea being presented. In this sense, Jemma was supportive of the proposal by Gardner (1983) that we all used 'multiple intelligences' rather than only one to understand the world. When discussions of a national curriculum were raging at various staff meetings, Jemma was feeling more comfortable in participating and putting forward the view that teaching and learning was much more than merely accepting knowledge that was agreed by others and that teachers in all subjects needed to start with or at least incorporate and respect the initial thoughts of students. This raised a whole set of other problems of course, particularly those that involved exactly how to connect global and local concerns and how to ensure that all students did not miss what were considered important ideas in the time available. Jemma became steadfast in her view that 'learning had to be put first before subject content.'

Unfortunately, Jemma felt let down by the education profession and what she perceived was a lack of research support. She understood her growing frustration as the question of theory in education and perhaps, of education. What she was reading often did not connect with the problems she was facing at school, within classrooms and with colleagues. There was also the issue of how she should approach her own theorising of educational practice, what personal observations she should make and how to make sense of them. Jemma felt it was useful to consider the research and views of authors she was reading, but in the end, it was up to her to interpret and act with her own setting. Her mind drifted to a saying from her closest uncle, that she should never forget where she came from and no matter where she travelled and roamed, 'home and country will always call you back.' Jemma took this to mean that she had a set of values and ways of acting that had been generated from her family and community experience that will always constitute her and guide her knowing, of how to conduct herself ethically and with integrity. She had a 'feeling' that she understood this framework, but it was difficult to resolve the daily contradictions she faced with all the issues at school and the strain and anxiety of juggling the educational pressures that were constantly present. Jemma was coming to the view that she wanted to be a *practitioner-theorist*, where she could theorise her professional practice within an ethical structure that she could defend and one that also respected the social and cultural experience of the families and students she encountered. It seemed apparent that this could not

## Education as philosophy of practice   71

be done from a fragmented perspective, some psychology there, some sociology here, some mathematics somewhere else. Jemma concluded that she did not want to be an anthropologist, an economist or a biologist as such, even a historian, she wanted to be an *educationist*, investigating important issues that faced the world, families and students in a holistic and distinctive way.

In paraphrasing Raymond Williams, that 'culture is ordinary, a whole way of life' (Williams, 1989), it may be appropriate at this point to suggest that 'education is ordinary, a whole way of life.' By so doing, we are proposing that the manner by which we go about interacting with the world from birth to death, that is of being human, should be understood as the natural process of education, a holistic, deductive process that should be continued in formal schooling. It is accepted that schooling should also introduce students to new forms of knowledge and new experiences of understanding that connect with and build upon current comprehension. However, while akin to the 'zone of proximal development' (Moll, 2014), this process demands additional features that are more explicitly epistemological. For example, and for our guidance here, da Silva (2007, pp. 67–69) comments that the work of George Herbert Mead (Biesta, 1998) involves inter alia three main ideas:

- Conception of the self as emergent from social experience provides an alternative to Descartes's rationalism and atomism.
- Human beings are complex biological organisms whose selfhood is intimately related to linguistic communication and social experience.
- Theorising the dialogical social act locates individuals within the intersubjective social environment, so that the self is not opposed to the world, but is a part of it.

This view of what it means to be human will not be found in many schools around the world today. Jemma would certainly find it a new educational platform in her discussions of curriculum. What it is suggesting is that the human organism or self sets up a relationship with all the objects of experience such that dialogical social acts including communication enable intersubjective connection and response. It is through this intersubjective process between participants (objects of experience), that thinking as an 'inner conversation' takes account of others and of self in deciding how to proceed. From a broad understanding of the theory of pragmatism involving the inquiry of Dewey and the intersubjectivity of Mead, it would appear that Jemma needs to negotiate many projects with her students that bring their personal and community interests and culture to the fore, so that communication of ideas and opportunities flow freely and tentative conclusions can be arranged for continuing trial and error (Edwards-Groves and Kemmis, 2016). It is difficult to express the 'feeling of knowing' that emerges from such open-ended processes, but it must be similar to what we experience when eating chocolate, when reading poetry, when crying with sadness, when reading a bedtime story with grandma, when watching a spider spin its web. However, we 'know' the feeling and we 'know' what it means, for us. This is the essence of grasping the holistic integrated nature of education as a knowledge discipline. Many people would think

72  *Education as philosophy of practice*

that they have some understanding of an abstract idea such as atom, black hole, DNA, plastic, 'blues' in music, pathos in literature, where thunder comes from. With each of these ideas, there is some connection that has come from talk around the table when Cousin Billy visits, from the media, from school and from some type of direct or indirect experience. Language and communication are important in all of these. In many cases, we are content to let our overall understanding or perhaps social consciousness make sense of these inputs in a deductive manner, going from the general to the particular. We let that rest or sediment until such time as greater detail is required and we try to fill in the gaps. Similarly and as a generally abstract idea and practice at present, the concept of education as a knowledge discipline will be difficult to 'feel' and 'know' just yet, but it can be related to 'experience of the everyday, of the ordinary' as a personal means of investigating who and how we are. For this, we now turn to considering six philosophies that exist in harmony and conflict with education as a philosophy of practice and how each impact the other.

## Philosophy 2: religion, the sacred and profane

It may be an impossibility to write concisely about religion in general given its specific histories, characteristics and practices across the world. However, in following the work of Geertz (1993), it may be possible to ask questions about cultural phenomena not so much about what they do, but what they mean. Geertz commented that culture could be thought of as 'a system of meanings embodied in symbols' and that religion could be considered this way. In his essay on religion and Geertz, Chernus (2016) distinguished between religion as 'experience' and religion as 'guide to life.' Experience can be described as sacred, or holy, but also in relation to something infinite or beyond such as a wonderful landscape or night sky. A 'guide to life' generally means an agreed framework amongst a group of people that helps explain everyday occurrences without involving reference to supranatural force. In this context, three of the generally considered founders of sociology, Durkheim, Weber and Marx all placed importance on religion and its influence in societies around the world. Durkheim accepted religion as a cultural system of beliefs, texts and practices that are sacred to the group and which provide a unified means of understanding that can be generalised beyond evidence. As commented previously, this is his striking contrast between the everyday or profane knowledge and the generalised or sacred knowledge. In his work that linked religion with the rise of capitalism, Weber was particularly interested in why a divinity would create an imperfect world and the possibility of redemption. He posited that using the fruits of personal gain in appropriate ways could avoid predestination. Witnessing the cascading development and inequality of capitalism in Europe, Marx argued that human progress should be escorted by reason and the supportive evidence becoming available from the new science. He saw a connection between Christianity and capitalism whereby the poor will be favoured but within an ideology of private wealth. He of course supported a redistribution of wealth for all citizens. As a co-founder of modern sociology, Comte proposed

*Education as philosophy of practice* 73

the Law of Three Stages whereby society progressed from the theological, to the metaphysical and, finally, to the positive or scientific stage, when beliefs are justified by evidence, argument and causal effects. Comte theorised that sociology was the culminating science of knowledge and in particular, was based on a history of all other scientific knowledge so that a comprehensive overview and its connections was possible.

It is not intended here to provide descriptions and analysis of a number of the world's religions such as Christianity, Hinduism, Buddhism, Islam and Judaism but, like the European and American sociologists mentioned earlier, to suggest some general key features of religion that may then be contrasted with education as a knowledge discipline. In broad terms, these features are proposed as being

- an adherence to a system of symbols, texts, places, ceremonies and practices that assist and confirm continuing meaning and conduct, through conceptions of a 'general order of existence';
- an acceptance of beliefs and meaning either by faith, metaphysical conviction or experiential happenings;
- a presence of a deity for explanation, law, dogma or guidance; and
- participation in worship, ritual or ceremony as decided by appointed authorities.

There are obvious connections here between culture and religion, although these do not necessarily mean that they are the same. Political judgements need to be made on that question. For example, the notion of 'secularism' denotes a significant difference that may be irreconcilable. In a secular society there is a separation of church, state and judiciary, a separation between how citizens conduct themselves as individuals and how they are involved with community and state functions and a separation between the plurality of practices undertaken by the nation state and its citizens and with the distinct requirements of a particular religion. A secular state and its institutions do not deny religion, but respect a range of viewpoints and practices without imposing one. All citizens are equal under the law regardless of religious and economic background. For a democratic secular state, all political decisions that impact the citizenry are made democratically (at various levels of social organisation) and are not influenced by religious beliefs. While a pluralist society accepts a wide range of views, it is difficult to tolerate beliefs and practices that are strongly counter to dominant trends and may want to supplant them. Comte's three stages may come into play here, over long historical periods of time and change. Accordingly and perhaps for transitional reasons, religion, science and secularism need to come to grips with the notion of myth. Present in many cultures, myths are usually taken to mean stories or explanation of phenomena and events, often involving supernatural beings, that may not rely on empirical evidence. Fairy tales and fantasy in European culture are obvious examples. They usually relate to the 'difficult to explain' and may contain 'hidden' meaning that is passed on to each new generation. The French anthropologist, Claude Levi-Strauss studied the concept of myth with Indigenous South American peoples (Lévi-Strauss, 1978)

74  *Education as philosophy of practice*

and drew structural linkages between language, myth and meaning to the extent of noting similarities with how modern science is conducted. On this basis, some religions could argue that its purpose is not to answer complicated issues, but to enable consideration from a particular perspective.

Whether or not religion should be considered as a cultural practice, or as a distinct ideology will have an important impact on public systems of education. These matters will be discussed in more detail later. However, the particular political forms of government that operate within each country will determine how its institutions are created and behave. A church state that expressly undertakes decision making from a religious outlook will erect a society that has very different laws, procedures, practices, beliefs and schools in comparison to a secular state. This will depend on the religion in question of course and the historical moment. On the other hand, is it possible to claim that in a secular pluralist society, strongly ideological and dogmatic religion can co-exist harmoniously with a number of other viewpoints under the banner of 'cultural?' For instance, it can be argued that minority church schools that actively promote a religious view can exist adjacent to majority public schools that are secular. This is a different argument as to whether they should exist, that is whether it is ethical to enable religion to be promoted and imposed through schooling particularly when children are involved? Should religion be a family rather than state concern? Is the different religious purpose too great and contradictory to secular state purpose? In many countries, a political and practical compromise has been reached to accommodate this problem, rather than philosophical principle and integrity. To achieve the impossible description therefore, we can consider an ideological spectrum of understanding of religion (using highly contested words for discussion), from the mythological, dogma/faith-based life-strictures to the personal world-view/guidance-based life context and a mix of cultural symbols, texts, places, ceremonies and practices in the middle. This spectrum needs to be negotiated by states, communities, families, children, schools – and history.

## Scenario 2: religion (from the perspective of a secondary school student)

Getting up early to go to mass on a cold morning would not have been Emmet's first choice, but it only happened a couple of times a year, so he understood it as a personal obligation. He knew that his family had emigrated from Ireland during the potato famine of the 1850s and that they were Catholic. His parents were not strong churchgoers, but the local priest visited every so often particularly when mum was sick and his uncles were concerned that his father was not seen regularly at mass. As a 13-year-old, Emmet didn't quite understand what all the pomp and ceremony meant and he wasn't too keen on singing hymns either, given that the existence of God was still uncertain for him – although he found some of the stories about what might have happened a long time ago, interesting. He sometimes talked about this with his big sister Anita, but she was more interested in her school exams these days and seemed impatient with him. Emmet had been sent to a Catholic primary

*Education as philosophy of practice*   75

school where religion was not a dominant aspect of the curriculum but, at secondary school, he found it very difficult to settle down to a more traditional acceptance of religious views and rituals. While his father put up some resistance, his mother insisted that he go instead to the local public secondary school where his growing independence would be better suited. Emmet still found teachers a bit strict at this new school and his shyness prevented him from speaking with them very often, but he was interested in most subjects and his test results were generally good. He liked mathematics and science and the times when they were able to do projects and experiments and talk about how scientists had come up with their new ideas. Uncle Conor went to church on a regular basis and was worried that Emmet was drifting away from what he saw as essential teachings and understandings for living a devout and pious life. They would chat about this occasionally and while Emmet appreciated his uncle's concern, he would try to steer the conversation onto safer topics, such as what he had found in pond water under the microscope, or why plants won't grow in dark cupboards.

Sport was very important in a country town with football in the winter and cricket in the summer taking pride of place. Being on the coast, however, meant that Emmet was able to swim and run all the year round, which he enjoyed immensely. Perhaps the beach gave him the chance to express himself unhindered by teachers and adults and, being in the outdoors whether hot or cold, seemed to embrace him closely. There was the constant challenge of defying the excitement of big waves and of running until exhausted along the sand, knowing that each day or week or month you could run a little faster. Then, there was the time Emmet was sitting on the beach just after the sun had gone down. It had been a hot day and many locals, visitors and children were seeking relief in the shallows. Emmet felt pleased with himself after his exertions earlier and, for some reason, his eyes wandered skywards. He gasped. The sky was a brilliant darkness, but scattered about like specks of dazzling white paint on a canvass, where a multitude of stars blinking at him. Emmet could not remember seeing the sky like this before, perhaps he had not looked, or the time had not been right. As he gazed upwards, Emmet felt differently to what he had before, even a few moments ago. It was difficult to explain, but he felt more as one with the beach and sky, it was like they were speaking to him, as friends. Thoughts rushed through his mind about where the stars had come from, how big they were and how far away, what his science teacher had said about the 'big bang.' He had heard the priests mention this a couple of times as well, about how it had all started, but he couldn't remember his parents ever discussing the matter. The next day, the stars had disappeared and Emmet stood quietly looking at the ocean with new eyes. He felt a mixture of excitement and confusion, of wonder and perplexity, of many questions that he wanted to discuss about his experience the night before. These were new thoughts that the hymns and sermons would probably not satisfy and the knowledge of his science teacher might be inadequate as well. Emmet watched the waves curl and break on shore.

For the remainder of that year, Emmet continued to do well at school and most afternoons would find him running and swimming as usual. He continued to think about the night sky, although there were few direct observations to make during

## 76  *Education as philosophy of practice*

the rainy winter months. He often went into the reference room of the public library to read astronomy books that weren't available at school and marvel at pictures of the universe that were becoming available through more powerful telescopes. It was difficult for him to understand many of the articles that he came across, but it was giving him a chance to think more broadly about what it all meant. It was one thing to say that light took a certain amount of time to travel from a star to earth, but how did this actually work, what exactly was doing the travelling? He wasn't attending church and the priest hadn't visited for some time, but he was frustrated by not having his questions answered. He remembered in primary school that teachers had told him to just believe, but increasingly, this wasn't enough for him. It was not as if he was openly disbelieving, it was just that the answers weren't coming. He felt that if he couldn't understand for himself that it was not fair to ask him to simply believe. On one occasion, his science teacher had said in class that science was always changing as it did more experiments and scientists had to think very carefully about whether ideas would stand up to whatever experiments were conducted. Uncle Conor seemed to have a different view about all this. He had always told Emmet that the priests knew what was right and what to do and that we had to take notice of them. It was important to live as a moral Catholic person he said and the church would guide that in difficult and good times. Emmet could see what Uncle Conor was saying but, until now, the church had not explained the meaning of the stars and what he felt when seized by the ocean, its moods and beauty. He knew what he felt and wanted to know more, to find out for himself.

## Exegesis 2: Emmet, culture and knowledge

Children are inducted into family practices from an early age all over the world: what to eat and when to eat, to be wary and comfortable with various animals, how to speak to your parents, singing, playing sport, going to school, keeping secrets. Religion is similar. Emmet knew that there are ceremonies he is expected to attend even if unsure of their purpose. He is part of family, neighbourhood and school groupings that engage in these ceremonies together and which to some extent, binds them together. Cultural bonds also exist in communities and families, as noted by Matthew Arnold. Matthew Becoming Inspector of Schools in England in 1851, Arnold continued in that role until two years before his death in 1886. Being deeply religious, he saw human 'perfection' as doing God's will during a time of social upheaval and demands being made by the emerging industrial working class. He proposed the notion of 'culture' as a stabilising influence during this time such that 'The pursuit of perfection, then, is the pursuit of sweetness and light.' He detailed this inspiration in the following way (Arnold, 1932/1984):

> I have been trying to show that culture is, or ought to be, the study and pursuit of perfection and that of perfection, as pursued by culture, beauty and intelligence, or, in other words, sweetness and light, are the main characters. But hitherto, I have been insisting chiefly on beauty, or sweetness, as a character

*Education as philosophy of practice* 77

of perfection. To complete rightly my design, it evidently remains to speak also of intelligence, or light, as a character of perfection.

Arnold did not see culture being imposed on the working class, but rather the purpose of culture was 'to make the best that has been thought and known in the world current everywhere.' In a famous statement, he proposed that 'This is the *social idea* and the men of culture are the true apostles of equality.' In considering these ideas 150 years later, we need to be able to have our own concept of culture, how it intersects philosophically with modern education and how associated programs might be implemented. This is particularly important in terms of assumptions made about public and private schooling and the social and cultural background of families. Clearly, there is debate about 'the best that has been thought and known' and the values, practices and meaning on which such debate is conducted. There is debate about beauty, intelligence, truth and goodness and how these virtues are understood and defined. In grappling with these issues, Dewey attempts to explain 'religious' in terms of experience and the motivation that humans have of envisioning an ideal world of 'spiritual' goods to which we aspire. The title of his book *The Quest for Certainty* suggests that as humans we accept such goods existing in some type of ideal world accessible as we try to control the social lived environment. He comments (Dewey, 1906/2008, p. 9),

> Those who hold to the notion that there is a definite kind of experience which is itself religious, by that very fact make out of it something specific, as a kind of experience that is marked off from experience as aesthetic, science, moral, political; from experience as companionship and friendship. But 'religious' as a quality of experience signifies something that may belong to all these experiences.

These are significant distinctions for Emmet. His experience of the stars at night while sitting on the beach could be interpreted as either a part of his world of change and fallibility, the quest for the 'precarious' goods of knowing or his attachment to a world of 'stable' ideal being, the quest for 'religious' certainty. Either case does not necessarily involve a superior actuality of some type to be worshipped through ceremony and dogma, but both do connect our personal existence with something greater or beyond. What will cause Emmet to support or believe one prospect or the other is unclear, but will emerge from a combination of life experiences and what tends to dominate at any particular time. The notion of 'associative' learning as described by James (1899/2015), whereby we link or associate what we know with the new conundrum is a part-explanation from pragmatism. It is certainly an argument for formal education to include a broad range of practices and experiences that can then associate with the new and problematic. Whether or not Emmet will be strongly influenced by his uncle Conor or his parents and become more traditional or orthodox, compared with more progressive and creative in his own thinking cannot be predicted, although a detailed trace of his every encounter and experience with the social and physical worlds would probably provide substantial

## 78  *Education as philosophy of practice*

pointers and correlations. While family members may appear to have similar experiences, for example, a closer inspection will most likely reveal major differences at particular times that will encourage alternative pathways. Pragmatism does need to enable discussion of how different beliefs, values and emotions are generated through a range of practices at different stages of a person's life and for educators, how a different mix of democratic practices can support diverse and flexible thinking that is more unconstrained and imaginative.

## Philosophy 3: conservatism, what is or should be

Seeing the world and humanity epistemologically, from the point of view of American Pragmatism, is a difficult commission. Conservatism has been chosen as the next philosophy to consider, not only because of its extensive political and historical reach, but because it challenges pragmatism to explain its occurrence. The desire to keep things as they are – the quest for certainty – must compete with the tenacity to answer, change and create as new situations appear – the quest to know. As this process continues and contradictions come into play, the sum total of experience is constantly in flux while being brought to bear. It is this sum total that the pragmatists considered central to understanding, the broader the base the more likely that new situations could be encountered creatively. How these contradictions worked themselves out during the Industrial Revolution, for example, and the development of capitalism, can only be speculated, but as social classes developed unevenly across Europe in particular, different communities and individual members would have come to grips with the vast range of economic and personal problems they faced. Because of their experience, some would have felt compelled to accept while others to oppose the juggernaut, the enormous change happening around them. For those in power, it was in their interests to support their position and the status quo, that of compliance and subservience. Not all forms of political and cultural conservatism as it developed demands total obedience and some forms contain aspects of noblesse oblige. However, it seems entirely logical that pragmatism can generate both conservative and progressive viewpoints and practices as a result of the accumulation of experience, with all persons having their own uniqueness.

## Scenario 3: conservatism (from the perspective of a working class mother)

Saturday was generally basketball day and a hive of activity for the family. Sophia was just starting out with her primary school team, but Damian was already a veteran in the under 15 side. Her husband usually took care of transporting them to and from games, but it fell to Rydia to make sure that all the uniforms had been washed and were ready each week, that lunches had been packed and that all the forms regarding registration, injuries and the like were in order. She had not realised how costly sport for the children could be, or time consuming, but their enthusiasm and involvement with the local teams made it all worthwhile.

*Education as philosophy of practice* 79

Rydia was grateful that she had a job at the woollen mill working the night shift for most of the year because without this, the family income would be nowhere near enough. She found talking with other workers at the mill interesting and was gradually becoming more confident in asking questions about the quality of different types of wool, how the price of wool is decided and how the exchange rate of money can ultimately impact the number of jobs at the factory. She thought it was reasonable that she be paid what her friends thought was a proper wage, but was uneasy about the latest wage claim that was being strongly opposed by the mill owners. They were saying that the international price for wool was declining and that jobs had to go to pay for any wage rise. While many of Rydia's family were factory workers and union members, they were not strongly activist and she generally did not want to cause any trouble at work. She thought that it was best to accept the way things were and be appreciative that they had food on the table, the kids were healthy and there were no soldiers with guns in the streets. When they managed to find some time in the lunchroom, Rydia talked about these issues with her work mates, especially those who had come from other countries. They had similar views to herself, although some said that not everything was perfect and that they had a right to try and make things better.

In many respects, Sophia and Damian represented Rydia's hopes for the future. She had left school early, but was very conscious of the importance of education today and wanted her children to continue as long as possible and it could be afforded. Sophia was a quiet child and her reports from school were good, but Damian was showing signs of being dissatisfied and unsettled. With her lack of experience of the school's program, Rydia did her best in talking with Damian about the importance of school and how it provided a gateway to important knowledge that the family did not possess, knowledge about mathematics, important books, what science was all about and what scientists did, the history of many countries and events that she had not heard of before. She tried to talk with him about her limited understanding of the buying and selling of wool, but this did not interest him at all, apart from the cost of his latest footy jumper. While the family was not overly religious, Rydia thought that the church and school were similar in that they provided an ongoing set of ideas and traditions that were important to the country and to themselves. If Damian excused himself from these activities for too long, he would miss out on important knowledge that other people had and he would be excluded from many aspects that life had to offer. When listening to people speaking on television, for example, Rydia was often struck by their broad knowledge and how they could seemingly discuss and argue issues with a lot of background information that she knew nothing about. Some of her work mates had told her about dictatorships in other countries and she certainly did not want that. But it was important for the church and school to ensure that children understood their recent and ancient past and what was necessary to know to survive in today's world. Good literature, good music, good science were like the steering wheel of a car travelling any known or unknown road.

It was difficult for Rydia to balance her family and working lives and she was finding newer thoughts from the lunchroom at the mill conflicting with her own.

80    *Education as philosophy of practice*

She understood how the mill employers made a profit and established jobs, but she agreed with others that this had to be done without exploitation, for a fair day's pay. In other words, there were human values that had to be maintained like respect for the work that is done and the knowledge of workers, safe working conditions and participation in any changes proposed. Informal discussions like these prompted other thoughts regarding how things are done outside the factory and how decisions are made regarding other industries and institutions. Rydia thought it was important for everyone to have a say and to build upon his or her family, work and community experience, rather than being merely told what to do. She found herself thinking that some people might be in a position of making decisions for her, but she also had views of her own that deserved to be taken into account. Who knows best about what it takes to get a local basketball team onto the court, or how to ensure that the weaving machines keep turning, or what children really find interesting and want to know? It seemed appropriate that the local school board or town council should take notice of family opinion especially when it directly impacted adults and children alike and that participation in community affairs was a right. She realised that it is was more complicated at government level, but Rydia reasoned that those who are nominated to represent or serve – councillor, priest or teacher – should represent and serve with respect and humility. When she found a notice in the bottom of Damian's school bag that a parent meeting was coming up about changes to the mathematics program at school, it didn't take long to tick the required box about attending. The time had come to go along and put forward her views about mathematics, even if she wasn't too sure what they were just at that moment.

## Exegesis 3: Rydia, fractions and frictions

Where ideas come from remains a mysterious process, let alone how they transition and change into something else. As debated previously, how does the concrete/informal merge with and/or create the abstract/formal over time, or instantly? Rydia's lifeworld is strongly influenced if not determined by her economic composition, but she is coming to question some of its suppositions based on her direct experience. According to Habermas (1981/1987, p. 126), 'Communicative actors are always moving *within* the horizon of their lifeworld; they cannot step outside of it.' He goes on to explain,

> The lifeworld is, so to speak, the transcendental site where speaker and hearer meet, where they can reciprocally raise claims that their utterances fit the world (objective, social, or subjective) and where they can criticise and confirm their validity claims, settle their disagreements and arrive at agreements.

In this passage, Habermas seems to be suggesting that the lifeworld is somehow separate from the objective, subjective and social worlds that humans inhabit and it is within this separate world that we interact with language to consider validity claims and to make meaning. He adds, for example, that agents cannot establish

*Education as philosophy of practice* 81

the same relationship with their facts, norms and experiences as they can with language and culture and that 'speakers and hearers come to an understanding from out of their common lifeworld about something in the objective, social or objective worlds.' As is to be expected, this position enables Habermas to ensure that language has centre stage in human understanding and that action in all its forms is secondary. On the other hand, it is possible to conceive of the three worlds interacting in a continuing dialectical manner including when the young human does not have or has a restricted vocabulary. A young child may feel sad when her pet dog is injured, or feel excited when throwing and catching a ball or serene when looking at a picture book with grandma, but in each case does not have the words to express her experience, her social act. In each of these experiences, there could be a continuous dialectical process connecting her three worlds that result in a 'feeling of understanding' that cannot be expressed, there are no truth or validity claims at work, or agreements and disagreements to be negotiated. Understanding of the world comes about *in actu*, or through the act, that involves a combination of all that has gone before including language and culture, but necessarily arises from the act itself. What this suggests is that a combination of lifeworld and the objective and subjective worlds generates a notion of 'self' that is constantly in process as human communal experience and consciousness evolves. In writing about Mead, da Silva (2007, p. 34) puts it this way:

> For Mead, meaning was born when, at some point in evolution, the speaking primate learned how to respond to a vocal gesture in a similar way to its interlocutor. The consciousness of meaning emerged when primates learned how to take the role of the other; with reflective intelligence, primates began to perceive and manipulate the objects around them in a radically different way – they could now see the 'inside' of things ie their abstract properties.

These are important features of Rydia's life as she grapples with experience. She has her own language and culture from her childhood and family life that now sits alongside her working life at the mill. It is not possible to definitively distinguish between the locus of meaning, that of a separate language world or a dialectical action/self-world, but it does seem clear that Rydia's internal agreements, conflicts and thought patterns are emerging from her social experience of being, her daily role as an industrial mill worker and engaging in the many discourses that cannot be avoided. It seems clear it is the action component of this experience that provides the substrate of language and discussion and comes first before discussion of events becomes possible. Put another way, discussion without action proceeds in the abstract, remote from the objects under examination and their implications. As noted by da Silva earlier, it is through the manipulation of objects that we begin to see their internal or abstract properties so that more reflective thinking comes into focus. From the scenario evidence earlier, it is not possible to detail where Rydia's apparently conservative view of the world originated, but it is feasible to note that her new experiences offer a challenge. What might seem to be a minor action is extremely central to her place in society, when she decides to attend a school

## 82   *Education as philosophy of practice*

meeting about mathematics. For many parents, the formality of school mathematics represents all that is emblematic about the institution of schooling, its capacity to deal with what is considered to be abstract and immutable truth known by a few experts and communicated by their emissaries. Many parents may feel comfortable with the arithmetic and play of primary schools, but secondary school mathematics with its algebra, geometry, proofs and calculus can be difficult to grasp. Something must have happened to encourage Rydia to take this step, perhaps discussion of the latest wool markets, or the union's wage claim, but a combination of action, discourse and application (such as muted discussions with Damian) may have triggered new thoughts of quantity and relationship.

Pragmatism needs to enter the debate regarding how different experiences result in different understandings of the world. Why is it that similar experience of government, for example, or of sitting in a science class, produce acceptance or rejection from brother and sister of similar ages? In his criticism of Habermas, Joas (1993, p. 130) provides a clue when he comments,

> Habermas, on the one hand, insufficiently separates the question of overcoming the philosophy of consciousness from the reduction of the paradigm of purposive activity and the turn to communicative action; on the other hand, he incorrectly identifies a typology of action with a typology of the different kinds of *co-ordination* of action.

Joas offers an important judgement of the work of Habermas, but its sociological basis does not confront the epistemological issues noted earlier. Philosophy's attempt to deal with the question of consciousness remains work in progress, but American Pragmatism can explain the generation of human selfhood, values and morality through the paradigm of action. As noted earlier, the different outcomes for brother and sister may be explicable if all action and experience could be traced from birth. For Rydia, the turn to communicative or selfhood action rather than strategic or selfish action promoted by her changing social circumstances signals a shift from individual to public interest, from narrow to broader concerns and from the passive to active life. If Joas and Hooley are correct and Habermas has some issues that require further analysis, then this may lead to epistemological practice that strengthens our humanity and does not deny it. For educators, there are some obvious implications. In the first instance, it will be necessary to ensure that action or the social act take primacy in all programs of study. This does not diminish the role of language of course, but it means that all learning is taken to arise from personal, community and communicative action and is not entirely directed by the predetermined knowledge of experts and emissaries communicated through language alone or, in many cases, by assumption of silent acceptance. In the second instance, it is recognised that all action contributes to social understanding, even if the connection is not totally clear at any time. Energetic discussions that appear to harbour strong disagreement, for example, may in fact be responsible for uncovering deep personal realities at another time, hence supporting the view that broad experience of all types exists at the centre of new understandings. In

*Education as philosophy of practice*  83

this sense, the language requirements of Habermas regarding reaching consensus may need further detail and go through different stages of discourse that are both antagonistic and non-coercive at various times. In the third instance, the objects of communicative action need to be meaningful and real for participants, worthy of their attention, before the intensity of origin reaches an appropriate threshold. It there is little apparent point in solving an equation at Year 8, then why bother? This is the distinction between 'real' and 'truth' that must be made by the learner rather than the teacher. It is probable that Rydia's world is in transition as it wrestles with new factors that are presenting themselves, with how she and her family attempt to cope and with new thoughts being constructed that seemly help and hinder understanding at once and how to proceed. It may be of course that the social, political and educational context that Rydia experiences will dominate her thinking and make independent engagement and creation extremely difficult.

## Philosophy 4: neoliberalism, capitalism personified

It is not difficult to understand why the characteristics of neoliberalism have been extensively and enthusiastically embraced by the capitalist class of the world. They see the expansion of market ideology acting in their political and economic interests through concepts such as individual prosperity and private gain. What is difficult to understand is the extent to which such thinking and practice has been taken up by broad sections of the population throughout different countries of quite different economies, from strong to weak. During and after war, for example, the citizenry usually fight for a better world for all, one that is more democratic and equitable. Neoliberalism is therefore our next philosophy for reflection, as it tends to confound our understanding of what it means to be human and what most see as important for themselves and families. This does involve safety, food and shelter for all, but one would think that the pursuit of meaningfulness regardless of social background would be strongly supported. As neoliberalism separates, classifies and discriminates, prospects for equality diminish, but the price may be seen as being worth the cost. Neoliberalism therefore like all our philosophies has a moral dimension in that it trends away from the public, collective and the obligation that we have towards each other.

## Scenario 4: neoliberalism (from the perspective of a middle manager)

A fine mist rolled across the city as Emile placed some folders into his bag and prepared to leave the university for the night. It was unlikely that he would continue work on those projects after dinner as it had been a difficult day, but it was a ritual to be maintained. On the subway going home, Emile soon gave up trying to read the evening newspaper and instead gazed out of the train window, turning figures over in his mind. He had proposed a number of budget savings at the meeting that afternoon, but the committee felt they did not go far enough. His senior manager raised several major criticisms of the strategy and was insistent

## 84  *Education as philosophy of practice*

that costs had to be trimmed to the bone. This was a problem for Emile, as he recognised that the university had a finite budget based mainly on student fees, but that there was a limit to how much the budget could be reduced. He did not have extensive contact with academics across the university, but those he knew seemed reasonable to him and wanted to do the best they could for their students. As budgets shrunk and faculties were forced to do more with less, it became more and more difficult for staff to finely balance teaching and research responsibilities, to publish and to maintain a scholarly disposition. Still, it was Emile's job even at his level of middle management, to make ends meet and to ensure that the budget envelope was appropriate and sustainable. As the train negotiated suburb after suburb, Emile decided to go over the figures for each department again and to see what a further reduction of about 1.5 percent on key items would achieve. Academics had to be realistic he reasoned and pull their weight by doing more teaching if required. Taking another class or two each semester would require less casual staff where the biggest expenditure lay. It was a short walk from the station to his house, but Emile was glad that he always carried an umbrella when the weather was so changeable. He smiled to himself as he thought of his job as standing on the bridge, steering the university through stormy times as well, keeping the remaining staff and students safe.

In many respects, Emile considered budget planning at the university in a similar way to what happened at home. There was a certain amount of income that he and his wife Jill brought in each year and expenditure on major items was fairly consistent. Repayments on the house mortgage were the greatest drain and a new car was required every so often to keep the family functioning. Their son Darcel would be going to secondary school next year and he already needed a stock of computer equipment to keep him up to date. They juggled a number of credit cards for a wide range of incidental expenses including holidays and found the high interest required difficult to meet. Emile thought that the university budget should also be able to estimate big items quite accurately each year and deal with the unexpected and those at the margins with good planning and dexterity. He had grown up in a country town when no-one in his family or in most other families went to university and started work in local factories, shops and farms as early as they could. However, he studied hard and managed to get a scholarship that paid for his fees and some living expenses. Because of this hard work, he often found himself in disagreement with his father who would generally argue in favour of government entitlements or support benefits in the areas of health, housing and education when people were unemployed or required extra help. He had strong connections with his family, but Emile felt himself growing away from them, particularly through his study of economics and politics at university. He was not in favour of what were called 'hand-outs.' His lecturers explained that small government had the advantage of reducing public spending and of encouraging private enterprise to invest in productive economic activity. They argued that this is where the jobs for full employment were generated. This made sense to Emile then and certainly now as well, when he knew that he had to provide for his wife and son. There were some managers at the university and at the seminars he attended who

*Education as philosophy of practice* 85

thought that cost cutting can only go so far, but most were of the view that reducing budget outlays was always to be preferred.

As a budget manager at a university, Emile tried to read as much as he could regarding higher education, financial trends and economic arguments that circled the world, recognising that such influences were global. However, most of his views came from the social practice of his job and the expectations that were placed on him. He had a slightly and usually fleetingly uneasy feeling about this as it meant that he often had to proceed with the task at hand without being able to think too deeply about its social and ethical consequences. These matters were sometimes approached obliquely at meetings or over lunch with colleagues, but they never really were discussed in any depth. He had heard it said that others may have the moral luxury of sitting around and considering what it all means, but others like him had to get on with the job and make progress, to work in the interests of the organisation. Emile accepted this view of the world and was hopeful that if he conducted himself accordingly, that he could become a senior manager in due course. After that, who knows? He did find it difficult on some occasions to discuss these matters with Jill, as her family with a committed union background usually argued for what they called the 'public good.' Whenever this occurred, Emile quickly diverted the conversation fearing the inevitable quarrels that erupted around his ears. He understood the point and was somewhat trapped between these competing understandings of what life was all about, but he had to keep food on the table and, in his mind, it was his work not theirs that keep the wheels of industry and academia turning. It was difficult when jobs were lost to maintain the budget bottom line, and he felt for the families concerned, but at least the institution as a whole was kept on a stable footing. He had thought of enrolling in a humanities program himself, part time, to be more disciplined about his systematic reading of economics, history, philosophy and the like, although how he could find the time at this stage of his career was an insoluble problem. He did make up his mind to make sure that he read the financial sections of the newspapers every day.

It was going to be a difficult meeting. Emile had calculated that an additional 1.5 percent cut on major items of staffing in particular for each faculty would meet budget shortfalls for the year and would contribute to a small surplus recommended by the university board. He knew that there would be vigorous and outspoken opposition to this from academic members of the committee and that he would be strongly criticised. He reasoned that it was his responsibility to put forward the difficult decisions that had to be made in the interests of the institution overall. Previous meetings had stumbled at this hurdle and it was unclear whether his proposal would be supported in the end or not. The committee had to finalise its report to go to the next board meeting, so there was no alternative. Deep down, Emile was somewhat resentful that he was in the position of being seen as cutting the budget in a callous manner, without regard for the jobs of many university staff. This was unfair, he thought, as he was merely responding to the general settings of budget decided elsewhere in the university hierarchy and that was where responsibility really lay. He was just doing his job as a

## 86    *Education as philosophy of practice*

manager and providing realistic options based on the best data available. At some point, he wondered about whether following the rules is a good defence or if it is only outcomes that matter regardless of how you get there. Jill had mentioned that her father often talked about the 'virtue' of acting properly in the true interests of others, but he had remained a construction worker all his life and Emile was uncertain of the 'virtue' of that. As far as this meeting went, Emile decided the best plan was to outline his proposal as directly as possible, not stray too far from what the data were telling him and to confine himself to functional issues rather than their social and educational impacts. Emile knew his place around the table and within the structure of the university, he knew that colleagues generally followed the dictates of senior management and board and that they did not refer too often to the meaning of what they did every day. Yes, they talked of strengthening the institution, ensuring student numbers, of having the best possible cases to put to government for extra funding and, sometimes, of what quality higher education might actually consist. Generally, the ubiquitous spreadsheet dominated most committee meetings. Emile sat back, satisfied that he had argued the merits of his proposal well.

### Exegesis 4: Emile and the occasional dilemma of conscience

At present, Emile has made fairly definite decisions about his life, about what he thinks and where he stands. He works as a middle manager in a large organisation and implements budget policy as best he can. His family background, educational experience and social involvement have led him to accept his role within the overall scheme of the society he inhabits. Like all humans, however, he responds to changing circumstances based on his current thinking, circumstances that can emphasise existing frames of reference or that can suggest other ways of proceeding. In his work on the nature of decision making and therefore morality, Dewey was faced with a developing American republic and the need to consider how democracy across the land could be established (Feinberg, 2012). Within his general understanding, he saw democracy as arising from social inquiry as citizens grappled with changing conditions and hoped for outcomes. It was necessary for decisions to be made that reflected change, rather than some fixed ideal from another place and another time. Dewey spoke of the difference between 'ends and means' and of 'valuing and evaluation' when engaged in making decisions. He used key words such as 'prizing and appraising,' or 'esteeming and estimating' in make this distinction. Dewey (1939/1969, p. 35) as always related this process of approaching 'ends-in-view' to the actions that participants take and how ends and means are reciprocally related and change as action continues:

> Now, as has been so often repeated, things can be anticipated or foreseen as *ends* or outcomes only in terms of the conditions by which they are brought into existence. It is simply impossible to have an end-in-view or to anticipate the consequences of any proposed line of action save upon the

*Education as philosophy of practice* 87

basis of some, however slight, consideration of the means by which it can be brought into existence. Otherwise, there is no genuine desire but an idle fantasy, a futile wish.

It would seem then, that Emile is locked into a particular way of viewing the world that is difficult to refine without a clear analysis or understanding of the conditions that enable or inhibit a desired 'end-in-view.' This requires the capability of acting within those conditions to create a better and changed situation, to come to a deeper understanding of conditions, means and ends collectively. There are three aspects of what might be called Emile's moderate and personal 'conservatism' that need to be raised here, structured under neoliberal intent. That is, the desire to keep things as they are that lead to a shallowness of viewpoint and the inability to implement political procedures that when needed will enable groups of different opinion to work together. Conservatism can be thought of as a set of ideas and practices that support traditional convention, habit and relationship such that change is minimised and current social order is not disturbed. The Irish/English writer and parliamentarian Edmund Burke (Norman, 2013), is often considered as the father of European conservatism, due in part to his criticism of the French Revolution and its destruction of the monarchy, church, nobility and law, in favour of arbitrary power, liberty and freedom. In the broad sense, this must be a part of Emile's thinking as well. He must come to grips with the tension between maintaining structures and customs as they are and making progress with resolving the social pressures of the day. External tension will provoke internal conflict as well, the difficulty of denying or putting aside the social context in which one lives and which impacts others and personal aspiration that will need to be defended in some way, to yourself, but also with others.

Aristotle (2014, p. 39) considered happiness as being concerned with living well over a complete life and to be an end in itself. He recorded that 'Being happy, then and happiness consist in living well and living well is living in accordance with the virtues. This, then, is the end and happiness and the chief good.' It is unlikely that Emile connects his budget problems with the notion of being happy and, according to Aristotle, has not lived long enough to make an overall judgement. But, he may perhaps, use other words to think about his life, such as satisfaction, contentment and fulfilment. For some, the active pursuit of wealth, pleasure or authority may be central, while others may emphasise what Aristotle called the 'intellectual virtues' of knowledge, wisdom, intelligence and understanding. Associated with happiness, Greek philosophy of Aristotle's time also spoke of 'eudaimonia' or human well-being and a flourishing humanity. For Aristotle, eudaimonia consists of a life of practical reasoning in thinking intelligently about what we do and how we go about implementing that attitude and approach. According to Russell (2013, p. 13), 'the idea is that our capacity for practical reasoning shapes and interpenetrates every other aspect of our nature and makes our whole nature distinctively human.' These are difficult concepts for Emile to be conscious of and to live by every day, surrounded by the stresses and complexities of modern life. Yet they offer one philosophical framework by which personal meaning and a flourishing

## 88 *Education as philosophy of practice*

humanness can be respected and charted. There is a sense of course where moderate neoliberalism and conservatism overlaps with moderate progressivism, where both are concerned with the plight of the poor and speaking back to authority for improvement. This is where Emile's socio-cultural background comes to the fore, in accepting some level of economic equity and compassion for all citizens or in maintaining the hierarchical status quo. In becomes a question of establishing the conditions whereby at least a transition of thought and acts between possibilities can be realised or truncated.

From a sociological perspective, Emile's daily work enmeshes him in what Marx described as commodity fetishism. Here, the social relationships involved in production are conceived not as relationships among people, but as economic relationships among the markets of money and commodities. This tension between a denial of human value and the desire to live well compared with the inhumanity of value-free systems and bureaucracies, demands the formation of institutional arrangements that enable the capacity of people to conduct moral inquiry intelligently and knowledgeably. As a general guide, practical wisdom might suggest strategies of the following type:

- constructs of civil society and public spheres;
- democratic process, open communicative social sympathies and structures;
- habits of critical, experiential inquiry;
- communication that recognises the consequences of instituting norms; and
- social sympathies, to enable debate and critique of consequences of norms and the imagining of alternatives.

This understanding drove Habermas to propose his theory of communicative action, as a means of resolving the split between cognitive/instrumentalist and moral/aesthetic/practical rationality that he saw as horribly distorting human life and relationships. The pervasive capacity of neoliberalism makes the earlier strategies difficult to conceptualise let alone activate, but that is the circumstance of Emile and of many. For those wishing to live well, involving the vast majority of the world's people, ways must be found of acting around the notion of civil society and the establishment of public spheres (Kemmis and McTaggart, 2005). These ideas can be taken up with small-scale projects in the workplace, in a number of workplaces or more broadly across specific industries and occupations. Key principles need to be well understood before they can be applied. The right to open communication amongst participants must be ensured, recognising that this is often vigorously opposed by those in control. It can be difficult to predict the outcomes of communicate action, but consequences can be discussed and options planned. Above all, antagonism must not turn inwards, but always be directed outwards at the social conditions that exist and how these can be altered for improvement. Emile may not be aware that what has just been described is in his interest and in the historic interest of his colleagues and family. Whatever ideology is in play, lenient or sturdy variations of neoliberalism, conservatism or progressivism, there will be a strong hold on thinking and convention – or as James noted in

*Education as philosophy of practice* 89

*Table 5.4* Intersection of political-democratic tensions

| | *Religion* | *Conservatism* | *Neoliberalism* |
|---|---|---|---|
| Ideology | Higher authority, officer authority | Traditional texts and practices | Liberal, dominance of economics |
| Culture, aspiration | Faith, community, life meaning, ceremonies | Traditional, collective | Dispersed |
| Economic power | Institutional rather than social wealth, power | Elite, born to rule | Dispersed, new and old wealth |
| Decision making | Dictates, dogmatic to greater, lesser extent | Semi-regulated | Laissez-faire, enterprise operates under own laws |
| Public, private | Public or private, relates to group or humanity | Public or private | Private, individual |
| Individual role | Acceptance or choice of variation | Acceptance or choice of variation | Choice |

pursuing his 'flywheel of habit' metaphor, 'We are spinning our own fates, good or evil and never to be undone' (James, 1899/2015, p. 39) – and realistic proposals for change need to ring true to participants, as well as how they might be implemented. The ideological matrix will also most likely be complicated involving a number of socio-political trends and concerns that need to be untangled. If so, it may be necessary to concentrate on what are considered the major aspects of the matrix, leaving other more minor aspects to later clarification. At this point of the unfolding narrative then, Table 5.4 summarises some key features of the philosophies discussed earlier and how they might interrelate, or not. Would it be of some assistance to Emile?

## Philosophy 5: social democracy, in practice or in name

A choice has been made to consider social democracy as a political system as distinct from a broadly democratic society itself. This draws a distinction between the previous three philosophies (religion, conservatism, neoliberalism) and their similarities, with the three to come. The notion of social democracy attempts to improve the operation of democracy under capitalism and to succeed where the welfare state did not. This assumes of course that such improvements will be permitted by those in power and can be tolerated by the treasury. Again, it seems a logical step to argue for expanded services for the general population as the economy grows and the wealth for some accumulates. Education is a prime example of this, with expectations by ordinary people that education and schooling is a public good and should be available to all, at higher levels as the economy strengthens. It is not an accident that social democracy attracts greater traction in smaller countries with an appropriate budget trajectory, in contrast to much larger countries where the ruling class can vigorously argue budget deficiencies. However, the notion

## 90   *Education as philosophy of practice*

of greater support for public health, education, housing and infrastructure under capitalism, particularly the requirements of a global capitalism, is one where it would be expected to find public support.

### Scenario 5: social democracy (from the perspective of a trade union official)

It was a smallish country town, surrounded by green paddocks, dairy farms and the occasional sheep holding. The milk factory was the biggest employer and many families had generations of sons and daughters who had worked there. Andy was typical of this history, leaving school at the earliest legal age and getting a job as a storeman and packer in the distribution centre. He liked the physical nature of the work and how this added to his fitness as an enthusiastic tennis player. After a few years, he had been given more responsibility for ordering all manner of equipment for the factory and became the occupational health and safety officer as well. He enjoyed talking with his mates about what was going on in the factory and, when a friend was seriously injured on the job, had to negotiate the support that the employer was required to provide by law. Andy was about to be married and Heather's view that he should look for some type of office position posed a dilemma for him. He was quite proud of the fact that he was a manual worker and that at a young age, his workmates already looked to him for guidance on many issues. He knew that Heather would be generally supportive, but that she would worry about him being nominated for a union position at the factory and getting into disputes with management. From his experience so far, Andy was of the view that you could usually find ways of working with management, on safety, for example, but he understood that in matters regarding wages and conditions, they were often very stubborn and proved to be unreasonably obdurate, even to hold discussions to map out a process of bargaining was an effort. He finally agreed to be nominated for the position of membership officer and, to his surprise, was elected unopposed. Andy had voted in the previous two elections for the state government where he lived and he knew that in many countries around the world, people did not have the right to vote at all, or that voting was often manipulated in some way by those in power. He made up his mind to act in the most appropriate way in his new position, out of respect for his workmates.

If pressed, Andy would probably admit that he sometimes wished he had stayed at school a little longer. World events were often raised after matches at the tennis club and he felt that he lacked more detailed knowledge and understanding of why things happened. He did appreciate union meetings where more experienced members often talked about the history of disputes and famous win and losses of the past. It didn't take much for Jack to launch into his criticism of what he called the 'Westminster system' from England and how he thought voting was only one aspect, perhaps even a minor aspect, of democracy in a community or at work. Jack was able to cite chapter and verse of various government policies he had been involved with as a unionist and debates that were had in the upper and lower houses of parliament. He argued strongly for a separation between church and state

*Education as philosophy of practice*   91

and against interference from the public service and military; this was essential if the rule of law was to be applied equally to everyone. There wasn't much point to a so-called opposition in parliament if all major parties had similar policies, explained Jack. In general terms, Jack supported intervention by government to assist the population with employment, health, education and housing matters, but others thought that it was up to private enterprise to work things out for themselves and fail or succeed in the process. Under a welfare system, markets had to be regulated to ensure more democratic outcomes for the citizens and to ensure a fair distribution of resources. As he participated more in the life of the factory and was able to learn from more experienced union members, Andy felt more confident in what he thought and was able to put forward his viewpoint at various meetings. He tended to agree with Jack, that while voting was important, participation in all aspects of society was equally so, where ideas and proposals could be contested and outcomes should reflect the broad aspiration of those concerned. It didn't seem right that some should live in poverty and others in wealth, without government mediation and indeed from those who have wealth, trying to create a fairer society. Jack's view was that the Westminster system had failed the poor and those on low income, but Andy was thinking about how to make economic policy curb inequality and social division, how to make it work better. He understood that this would require major change.

One of the highlights of the year for Andy turned out to be the annual conference of his union. This was where elected delegates from all work places met for two days to thrash out union policy, both in the general sense for negotiation with governments and employers, but also to endorse strategies for a range of campaigns. Debate was often fast and furious on major questions as different political positions jostled for ascendancy. Andy was nominated as a counter and had to quickly count a show of hands on each decision. At one of his first conferences, there was an important debate on negotiations that had broken down with a government committee regarding health insurance for workers. Union negotiators reported that the committee was intransigent and progress impossible, probably because of a concern with the costs involved. A motion was unanimously carried that the union should bypass the committee and demand direct discussions with the relevant minister and that if this was not agreed, stop work action should be taken. Andy was excited but nervous about this debate and decision. He saw the logic of not being distracted by bureaucrats sitting on a committee, but he had not taken stop work action before and he knew that Heather and his family would be worried about not only the loss of pay but also the possibility of losing his job. At a conference lunch break, Jack had a quiet word and said that he had been through this before. He thought it was a good thing that the union was not deluded by so-called consultation with committees and it was about time that the minister was confronted face-to-face. Andy expected Jack to support action of course and for the first time, he began to understand the difference between consultation and participation. While the Westminster system was called 'representative,' it was not up to those elected to always represent viewpoints without having the participation of constituents as their reference and strength. Political theories were fine thought

## 92 *Education as philosophy of practice*

Andy, but in the end they emerged from what ordinary people like himself did and how this was reviewed, refined and redrafted as circumstances altered. You don't learn that in school.

In due course, the campaign that was hotly debated and planned at the conference Andy attended, was settled. Following a series of stop work days, the minister finally agreed to direct negotiations and a compromise proposal was developed. There was strong debate again when presented to a delegates meeting of the union, but it was finally approved. Back in the lunchroom, the process was dissected and critiqued, with Jack being critical of the outcome but understanding of the views of members to settle and to get on with work. For his part, Andy was coming to grips with what he thought about his new experience. He felt energised by standing together with his work mates and in reaching agreement with the government that had forced it to adopt a new policy. It wasn't all that the union had claimed, but there were important health benefits into the future. He thought that the process of decision making he had been involved with was good and most views were listened too respectfully, even if strongly disagreed by some delegates. He also now knew that he needed to see proposals in action before they appeared real to him. He wondered what it would be like to be a senior union official trying to deal with all of this, or a member of parliament, charged with representing the people in a very complicated political and economic environment. He thought that he would find it difficult to make the necessary compromises that seemed inevitable to settle policy and program disputes, but was this always necessary; perhaps there were occasions where principle rather than comprise should rule the day. Andy was convinced that government should support the population when needed and that it should be possible for major issues to be decided as a mutual responsibility of government, employers and the workforce. Exactly why this appeared to be not possible or unlikely remained a mystery to him, but according to the old unionists who had navigated this dispute, market and budget demands were a motive force. There needed to be a never-ending combination of consultation, representation and participation in every organisation to make sense of all this and to make progress.

### Exegesis 5: democratic thought and deed

If human history can be broadly seen as making progress towards social improvement, of a more just existence for a higher proportion of people, then versions of capitalism are an improvement on much of what has gone before, such as slavery and feudalism. Capitalism as a global movement can still involve such practices, but other aspects such as welfare, public services and representative voting can also be evident. Young Andy may not locate his experience of becoming a union delegate and being called upon to represent the views of members in this historical sweep, but he is part of a transition to a more egalitarian future. At some stage, he may join a political party that seeks to govern and he will learn more about how this difficult terrain must be navigated and ploughed. He will face moral and social dilemmas as his changing lifeworld interacts with him and he, in turn, interacts with it. In some countries, attempts have been made to ameliorate

Education as philosophy of practice   93

capitalism through a fairer distribution of wealth, resources and services so that the purposes of the state can be better met. Processes of representative democracy are generally seen to be a part of this and indeed, are key features of globalisation. Andy realised that the setting up of committee structures and the like did not ensure agreement and that (sometimes acrimonious) debate was an important part of coming to understand the way things were. He found a range of political views at work and in the union, from capitalist to socialist, where some workers argued that, according to Marx, a socialist society would need to be more productive than capitalism, so that public services could be more extensive and wealth distributed more evenly across the population. For his part, the British sociologist Anthony Giddens sought a 'third way' (Giddens, 1979) between capitalism and socialism so that appropriate human values continue to guide the lives of all while, at the same time, the drive for profit is situated within a more compassionate social framework. Giddens (1998, p. 66) identified 'third way' values as encompassing

- equality;
- protection of the vulnerable;
- freedom as autonomy;
- no rights without responsibilities;
- no authority without democracy;
- cosmopolitan pluralism; and
- philosophic conservatism.

These are very difficult values to establish under any political system, let alone a strong, increasingly globalised capitalism based on private property and individual gain. Exactly why they would emerge from a rearranged capitalism stretches the imagination. Giddens discusses each in a logical manner, commenting, for example, 'In a society where tradition and custom are losing their hold, the only route to the establishing of authority is via democracy' (p. 66). In this way, Andy is at the forefront of significant social change, when he sets about his role of representing a diverse union workforce. Giddens here may be talking about state authority, but the argument applies to the authority of citizens in their daily encounters as well. His view of 'philosophic conservatism' is interesting, meaning that as society breaks down through the pressures of late modernity, it is necessary in Giddens's terms to use the tools at hand, those that exist, to cope. This is a conservatizing force and neglects the possibility of radical change generating new approaches to social problems as they emerge, a more creative imaginary to challenge the status quo. While it secured its strongest foothold in the United Kingdom during Tony Blair's time as prime minister, 'third-way' social democratic politics never established itself as distinctive policy or gained strong support from the British people. One could suggest that capitalism under any other name is still capitalism, with, in particular, all major economic settings remaining in place.

Political parties that exist under modest and restricted representative parliamentary rule, such as the Westminster system, may take many configurations, but can usually be categorised into those that have a base and purpose arising from

## 94 *Education as philosophy of practice*

working people and those that are more connected with wealth and individual interest. The former are often called 'labour' parties and the latter, 'conservative' parties. Both arose from the Industrial Revolution and the process of modernisation that has formed social classes and both now can take various and similar programs quite different to their precursors. Andy's workmates and those in other unions will most likely be attracted to a 'labour' party that purports to govern for the benefit of all citizens including working people, although some will align themselves with a more conservative approach, perhaps for individual gain. In an earlier time, this division may have been clear-cut, where social division between the rich and poor, between the powerful and disenfranchised was clearly visible every day. Under these conditions, the quest for equality, at least in relation to the basic necessities of life such as food, housing and health care, was a quest to unite large numbers of people. The growing dominance of neoliberalism since the1980s has weakened this understanding to the extent that parliamentary parties tend to occupy the middle to right of the political spectrum and concern themselves with managing budgets and debt, ensuring that resources are still unevenly distributed towards the privileged minority. This has been a major success of neoliberalism and of capitalism reinventing itself despite ideological and practical challenges. For young workers like Andy, who may be on a reasonable wage, the contradiction between rich and poor may be somewhat masked and difficult to engage. In the weaker economies of the world, social division can be more clearly evident and still involve violent confrontation between social classes.

What Andy is facing here is the construction of personal meaning from his own and collective experience. He must work this out for himself within the context of local and general conditions that exist and his evolving sense of ethical conduct. At one point, Dewey (2012, p. 257) commented,

> Plato defined a slave as a person who carried out the orders of another person. The evident alternative is an active share in forming the orders, the ends and regulations to be executed. In idea, the freedom for which democracy stands is freedom of the mind, that is, of examination, criticism, involved in discussion, taking an active part in conference, communication and decisions that determine general social policies and the ways and means of their execution.

Creating the conditions where 'freedom of the mind' can flourish is just a little difficult all over the world and requires constant action and vigilance. In this regard, we recall the insight of Habermas describing the legitimation crisis of modernity, where many citizens have lost confidence in the capability of social institutions to deliver their intended support and benefit for society in general. As mentioned earlier, systems of money, law, regulation and power seep into and take over or colonise the lifeworlds of people, such that human values, relationships and ethical bearing are subsumed and neutralised if not distorted and become ineffectual, not able to guide benevolent social demeanour. Andy will be conflicted by his thoughts on giving orders to others or finding alternative avenues in forming the orders. This is a key aspect of the relationship between system and lifeworld, between external and internal authority. Resolution of this dilemma will occur through a delicate combination of agreements and disagreements, tensions and contradictions, quickly or over longer periods of time. Whether resolution will align more closely with the status quo or with innovative understandings depends on the complex mix of experiences that is brought to bear on each and every event. It may be that the certainty and security of what is known, such as a representative form of vertical decision making, will be favoured over a more radical reshuffling of horizontal processes and that new compilations or readjustments of thought will remain acceptable until novel and challenging experiences come into being. How Andy will decide between an approach to living that supports the latter over the former, not only in relation to his union work but towards all other vicissitudes of social and cultural existence will be a never-ending process of trial, experimentation, discourse and reflection. To do otherwise is to argue for life contained within a sealed container disconnected from all that surrounds, remaining stagnant and inert. Evolutionary life on earth, however, is not like that, instead enacting, absorbing, transforming as the years advance. The inevitability of change is what must be confronted for life to continue.

## Philosophy 6: science, explanation or understanding

An obvious contender for inclusion in our list of philosophies of practice is that of modern science. Arising from the Industrial Revolution and the Enlightenment period, science became separated from religion as a means of explanation including that of origin and became known as natural philosophy. Its defining features were that of experiment and a determination to investigate rather than merely accept tradition and dogma. For some, modern science has taken on a dogma of its own, when it is claimed that the laws and precepts of its various fields must be accepted. This criticism is usually wielded by those who have little experience of the practice of science and its determination to do the exact opposite. Science is also criticised on the grounds that its view of knowledge and how knowledge is produced, is limited, not taking account of human culture, dispute and emotion that is highly significant for humans in other fields. The counter argument asserts that these are features of modern science and again, shows a restricted understanding of how science proceeds. The place of science in schooling has a reasonably recent history as well, but this has mirrored the development of curriculum since World War II, the continuing expansion of secondary schooling and the need for appropriate equipment in schools. Science itself is a historic and contested field of practice that sets up a problematic relationship with formal education and with society in general.

## Scenario 6: science (from the perspective of an industrial chemist)

It was a simple enough experiment. Luis was able to connect a series of paper clips together, in a vertical line end-to-end, while leaving a small gap next to a magnet at the top. They appeared to be suspended in mid-air. Most students were fascinated

96    *Education as philosophy of practice*

by this and had many theories about what was happening. Exactly how magnetic force or attraction was transferred or travelled from one paper clip to another along the chain always caused some excitement whatever the age of his students. Luis had come into teaching for precisely this reason, to encourage children to be curious about the universe they inhabited and to conduct small experiments for observation and explanation whenever they could. Learning by doing was always best, he thought. Luis had studied chemistry at university and had then worked for a few years as an industrial chemist for a multinational pharmaceutical company. He enjoyed chemistry and science in general because it enabled him to appreciate what he saw around him every day and, in his work, he could interact with the physical world and see how it could be acted upon and changed for social benefit. He remembered sitting in science classes himself as a secondary school student, while the teacher sometimes demonstrated a science principle or idea at the front bench. This did not happen all the time, but he found himself interested in what he saw – small pulleys lifting weights, colourless solutions producing coloured solids when mixed, extracting chemicals from plants using methylated spirits, dissecting animals or animal organs and describing what was inside – although he usually had to strain to see when sitting at the back of the class. It seemed to Luis that a study of science at school could open up new understandings for children that they would not experience elsewhere. This could be done through books, photographs and videos, but there was nothing quite like conducting an experiment yourself, even if you were not quite sure what you were doing. He tried to impress upon his students that science depended on the thirst that people have to know and of moving into unfamiliar areas of investigation, wherever knowledge and interest took them. There would be possible reasons to explain why things did not work out as expected, providing new studies that had not been thought of before.

There was little attention given to the philosophy of science during the university course that Luis undertook. He did remember one unit that mentioned major scientists, but this was in the context of their work, not so much where their approach fitted within a philosophical view of science itself. He was aware of Galileo and his observations of the night sky, Isaac Newton and the notion of classical mechanics and Albert Einstein of course regarding relativity and atomic energy: where there any science students who at some stage had not travelled on a light beam along with him? There were surprising few female names, but he heard about Marie Curie who gave her life when working on radioactivity and Rosalind Franklin of DNA fame. There was debate about why she did not receive the Nobel Prise it appeared. Luis struggled with the ideas of Karl Popper regarding the falsification of science conjecture, but he thought what he understood of Thomas Kuhn and the theory of scientific revolutions, was reasonable. Some of his colleagues when working for the pharmaceutical company were interested in the background of science, but when he began teaching, he found that very few could distinguish between what Kuhn had called 'paradigms.' They were more concerned with getting through the specified curriculum and ensuring that all content had been covered before examination time. It occurred to Luis that

*Education as philosophy of practice* 97

all students should be inducted into what might be called 'scientific method,' but there were many views as to what this was, even a view that 'method' itself did not exist. After he had gained some experience with his teaching, this problematic nature of 'method' caused Luis some problems, as he struggled to involve students in reflecting on their experiments, rather than merely the excitement of using equipment and 'doing' in the science room. In discussions with other teachers, he began to devise a framework of science teaching that not only involved students in conducting their own investigations but also encouraged small-group discussion of results and looking at a variety of possible outcomes. This seemed to him to create a sense of what science was all about and enabled children to use their imaginations and inventiveness.

Perhaps the most difficult issue that Luis faced as a teacher was arranging science content in some sort of order so that what was covered was not too confusing for students and could build in difficulty. There was a problem here, however, as different children had different interests in science and they often seemed to think in haphazard rather than linear ways. The best that Luis could do was to arrange his class in small groups and to assist each group in working out what they wanted to study and the most appropriate and manageable ways of proceeding. Without really understanding the process, Luis reasoned that opening up the possibility of learning was more likely to engross young learners rather than imposing what should be done, by him. For this to work, he spent countless hours compiling lists of projects and experiments that could be undertaking by students at any time. He also had to have all the necessary equipment and chemicals readily available and, if possible, a senior student as lab assistant to help him prepare each day. In this way, Luis was able to participate with all the groups in planning, conducting and reflecting on their projects, as distinct from being too concerned with traditional classroom supervision. Over time and especially as his classroom became full of detailed science projects, students were able to organise themselves with little teacher intervention. They became more observant of what was happening at each stage of an experiment and even, to notice the unexpected. They were encouraged to keep a lab book where they jotted down these incidents or events and to make some rough notes whenever they had a thought. Diagrams and sketches helped with this process of reflexivity or the constant thinking backwards and forwards of science practice. Most students were capable of this approach once they had a storehouse of experience to draw upon and they began to see connections between their observations with a certain experiment one day and those of the next. This was a case of trial and error for Luis, as the mainly young science teachers at his school were conservative in outlook which, for Luis, was unfortunate in the field of science and research; surely flexible and innovative would be more likely to encourage creative open-mindedness in the pursuit of knowledge and understanding.

It was relentless and tiring, but searching through countless textbooks, Internet sites and apps and other materials for the better experiment, the more interesting project, the latest kit of equipment, was the lot of the science teacher. In putting the pile of books aside one evening, Luis thought about the differences between

# 98    *Education as philosophy of practice*

his time as an industrial chemist and as a secondary science teacher. It was strange to realise that his own lab work was not that creative and that he had been mainly concerned with technique, the testing of chemical product along the chain of production to ensure that each stage of the process was proceeding as anticipated. Of course, if his testing showed results outside of a particular range, he would alert the factory workers to what changes needed to be made. He thought that science therefore involved a mix of regular practice and interpretation and sometimes for irregular action arising. The creative act of science may not be possible at all times, but occurs when unexpected consequences are apparent and some type of problem solving is called into being. This gave him a clue about how to conduct his science classes at school. It may be necessary to involve students in fairly standard science technique for some of the time, but to try and encourage more unorthodox thinking along the way, that is when personal experience has been accumulated and allows such thinking to occur. After all, they have to have something to think and reflect about, rather than nothing. He wondered why no-one had told him about this, either at university or now at school, but he supposed it was about the pressure that all teachers seemed to be under these days, especially with high stakes testing being so prevalent. Luis began to reconstruct his own understanding of science and how he might more systematically create the conditions in his classes for all students so that they might shift from concrete to abstract thinking and science practitioners. This would be a far cry from sitting at the back of the class, straining his neck to see what those pulleys were doing in the hands of an expert teacher or what was holding those mysterious paper clips together. Was it possible for all students to begin to think and act like a scientist, in doing science, or to be meagre and inadequate replicas?

## Exegesis 6: principles of the everyday and everyplace

In some of the most famous writing about the philosophy of science, Kuhn (1962/2012, p. 10) described a science paradigm as being able to transfer the attention of scientists to a new mode of thinking and practice and being open-ended to the extent that a new range of problems were created. He commented that paradigms 'provide models from which spring particular coherent traditions of scientific research.' In an amazing statement, he goes on to say (p. 24),

> Few people who are not actually practitioners of a mature science realise how much mop-up work of this sort a paradigm leaves to be done, or quite how fascinating such work can prove in the execution. And these point s need to be understood. Mopping-up operations are what engage most scientists throughout their careers. They constitute what I am here calling 'normal science.'

Luis finds himself in the middle of this conundrum. Working as an industrial chemist, he was mainly involved in testing materials using standard techniques and looking for results that indicated processes in the chemical plant were as expected. When he became a science teacher, he was suddenly involved in

*Education as philosophy of practice* 99

setting up situations in the lab where young students could not only experience the thrill of discovery, but were encouraged to think for themselves about meaning and options. That is, while the idea of surface tension may be accepted, he wanted his students to think about all sorts of creative reasons as to why certain insects could walk of water. Luis found himself wanting to challenge accepted explanations and to leap into the unknown. He recalled comments from Einstein about the importance of imagination in learning and how humans had become what they had become. He felt that he had a larger calling as a teacher than merely 'mopping up' what was already known. Was it possible for him to craft learning situations in the classroom that would transport students into new and unknown worlds that would grip their imagination and curiosity like never before. In this way, Luis felt himself drawn to the likes of Kuhn and other philosophers who were creative thinkers and were courageous enough to confront and reconstruct knowledge regardless of its pedigree. In particular, he had to grapple with what was called 'scope and sequence' in education, where clumps of subject content were arranged in order across the year levels of schooling. This didn't seem right to him. Surely, humans embraced knowledge when they needed to understand an event, whether they be 5 years old or 80 years old. This caused many arguments with his teacher colleagues, who were concerned that a more open approach to knowledge would make regular testing of content very difficult. Luis was not convinced that knowledge existed in vertical columns and horizontal layers, but rather as networks of understandings that were accessed when necessary. He needed to draw upon other viewpoints than the paradigm in which he found himself.

One way of thinking about the constrictions of a current paradigm was encountered earlier in regards pragmatism and the approach of Dewey and Mead. In placing emphasis on human action, the social act and inquiry learning, pragmatism theorises that learning arises from the resolution of dilemmas when current experience must deal with new situations. Bourdieu had similar interests and, in work published after his death (Bourdieu, 2004), undertakes a wide-ranging discussion of the nature of science. He expresses concern for the economic and political pressure under which science is now placed and the need for historical and sociological analysis. This should 'enable those who do science to better understand the social mechanisms which orient scientific practice' (p. viii). Bourdieu is not attacking science in its contemporary forms nor indeed the project of modern science itself, but is pointing to the dangers of socio-economic corruption. In a most significant passage that draws attention to his view of science and the difficulties of coping with the biological and the logical, Bourdieu comments,

> It is however in a Kantian perspective – but one totally excluded by Kant, in the name of the break between the transcendental and the empirical – that I have placed myself, by taking as my object the search for the *socio-transcendental conditions of knowledge*, that is to say, for the social or socio-cognitive (and not only cognitive) structure, empirically observable (the field etc), which

## 100   *Education as philosophy of practice*

makes possible phenomena as apprehended by the various sciences or, more precisely, the construction of the scientific object and the scientific fact.

(p. 79, italics in original text)

In seeking the most appropriate means for his students to engage the richness of science, Luis, too, may be trying to establish the *socio-transcendental conditions of knowledge*, in his classroom. Following Bourdieu and indeed pragmatism in general, it may be appropriate for him to take the socio-transcendental as the essential characteristic of practice and that the pursuit of understanding through practice in classrooms is achieved as learners bring together the social and transcendental as they construct, investigate and critique their own knowledge and that of community. This is what Bourdieu may be recommending by his notion of 'construction of the scientific object and the scientific fact.' In positing that the scientific object and fact are human constructions of science, Bourdieu encourages learners from all backgrounds to build their own understandings and by so doing, to link across the borders of knowledge. His notion of '(and not only cognitive) structure' suggests that learning is located in the cultural and personal field and that the relationship between the social and cognitive provides all learners the scope for creative and expansive science knowledge. The ongoing development of new practice and a new understanding of practice by social actors arises not in isolation from doing or thinking about doing, but from dialectical practice itself as the relationship between the social and the cognitive is impacted by experience, experiment and reflection.

Under the influence of high stakes testing, it does seem apparent that Luis will be expected to have a 'mopping up' science role at his school, merely inducting students into what is, rather than what could lie beyond. This is an important task no doubt and there are many enthralling experiments and activities that he can employ along the way. A line of magnetised paper clips opens up many questions about the universe. But Luis has grander aspirations for all of his students, remembering that Marx pointed out the difference between the architect and bee was that the architect raises structure in imagination before erecting it in reality. This was his task, to ensure that in his contact with staff and students and indeed members of the local community, that he was not only able to discuss and provide possible explanation for what was observed, but to go further and articulate what could be possible with clarity and lucidity, to make such phenomena and ideas accessible and intelligible. Luis was coming to the position that science was philosophy of practice and knowledge and that he should not be bound by the orthodox and the taken for granted. Under what circumstances would rainbows be square rather than circular, does gravity always pull down when in space there is no up or down, how does human conscious evolve from matter and energy? It was not his role to impart 'truth,' but to investigate the 'real' as experienced by his students, their families and himself. He would have to be careful in raising these issues with his colleagues and the school principal, who would immediately question his capability of ensuring that all subject content was covered, in sequence, for the next round of examinations. Luis figured, however, that he had a moral

Education as philosophy of practice   101

obligation as an educator and scientist to make other paradigms of knowledge available to all so that what lay beyond could be imagined and accessed. He was not a scientist otherwise.

## Philosophy 7: Marxism, social class and social division

According to Karl Marx and Friedrich Engels, 'the history of all hitherto existing society is the history of class struggles' (Marx and Engels, 2015). This statement was presented in the middle of the nineteenth century as the development of capitalism proceeded quickly. If accurate, it means that the dominant feature of political, economic and cultural life is that of social class, with other aspects taking a secondary or at least a related position. A class analysis of society generates enormous implications and ultimately postulates war and aggression. For these reasons, Marxism is our final philosophy of practice, contrasting dramatically with all others. Also, for these reasons, the contradictions of a Marxist understanding of education cannot be reconciled with a capitalist understanding of education, as each have diametrically opposed purposes, principles and outcomes. Except, both support a rigorous approach to knowledge as generally understood by society and how that knowledge can be utilised for the benefit of society. Which particular groupings in society are privileged and exactly the nature of that benefit, differs. A Marxist or socialist approach to schooling would move well beyond any of the other philosophies discussed earlier and indeed, could only be possible in its fullest extent, if it were based on a totally different economic system.

## Scenario 7: Marxism (from the perspective of an artist)

It is not always easy to capture the soft, morning light, especially in winter. As the feeble dawn tries to spread itself across the landscape, the mist and fog struggle to retain their hold on the grass and trees, let alone the imagination. Ella loved this time of day as she witnessed transformation before her very eyes, moisture disappearing, the wind gently finding its place alongside the songs of birds, spiders inspecting their constructions of the night and farmers staring at the skies for some indication of what the day might bring. She had not been painting for very long and was still experimenting with oils and colour to interpret what lay outside her experience. Of course, she saw and felt the sun and wind and rain every day, but she was trying to express their essence, what they really meant in the cosmos and for her. For some reason, she had always remembered a comment from her science teacher some years ago now at secondary school, when he said that the universe and everything in it was really just different arrangements of matter and energy that would stay that way for a while and then reform into something else. If that was true thought Ella, how could she depict a flower or atom or elephant or person and the relationships between them? She was attracted to the idea of Indigenous peoples that everything is connected to everything else, meaning that the universe is composed of infinite respect and ethical affiliations. And, the very real possibility of constant change as the flower, atom, elephant and person

## 102  *Education as philosophy of practice*

interact and learn from each other. In her discussions with other artists, Ella was impressed that many grappled with this question and seemed to have an open, philosophical view of the world and their role. They saw the artist as engaging with the social and physical environments, making what sense they could of them and returning interpretations for further consideration and discussion. Why Ella felt like this was unclear, but she knew deep down that her creative role of expression and interpretation was one that had existed throughout history and that she could encourage an open-minded view on many matters, rather than one that was stale and moribund.

Despite her expanding experience, Ella was still uncertain as to where the creative act came from and whether it could be analysed and documented in some way. She admired the work of Picasso and thought she understood his political intent, but the surrealism of Dali was still confusing. As an Australian, she felt connected to the work of the early painters who set out to portray the virgin bush landscape, unknown to the world at that time. They had to readjust their European eyes to the blinding light, striking blue skies and flora and fauna that were revealed, a continuing lesson for Ella as she also struggled to grasp what she saw. As well as the distinctive bush of Australia, she was fascinated by the ocean and long golden beaches that circled the continent. While the land mass was so vast, most Australians lived within 100 kilometres or so of the coast and frolicked with its hospitality as often as they could, a democratic and engaging playground. Here was another puzzling contradiction for the artist to confront, to display the formation of character and aspiration within such contrasting settings and to try to decipher the impact of history and struggle. Her artist friends had told her over many cups of coffee that creativity was unfathomable, it came from within and that it was important to become immersed in events so that it could emerge, unfettered. This was fine and had to go hand in hand with the experience of painting itself in various styles and with different implements, let it unfold, without explanation. But Ella was uneasy with this, she was curious about the world and indeed the universe itself and wanted to at least have an overview of why things existed the way they did, including humans, so that she could try to resonate with a deeper meaning. When she had her first and very nervous exhibition of sketches of the local countryside where she grew up, a combination of farming land and calm and wild coastal excursions, Ella found herself being asked many difficult questions by residents as to why she had taken liberties with how they understood where they lived. It was at that point that she realised she was trying not to merely reproduce a beach or tree or river, but to expose the essence or meaning or what constituted physical and social life. This was not exactly Picasso commenting on fascism or Michelangelo setting free the beauty within, but it was the same hope, to interpret, to challenge and to express a higher good.

As rain clouds started to amass and the west wind strengthened, a sure sign of a change in the weather, Ella hastened to pack up her paints and not be caught in the open, as had happened a number of times before. She smiled to herself in thinking that her painting may not be greatly improving, but she was becoming

*Education as philosophy of practice*   103

an expert weather forecaster. Sitting in her cluttered van as the rain swept in, Ella suddenly felt enveloped by the natural world and realised again, that she felt at home whatever the weather. There was some connection she sensed, that spoke to her, with the natural surroundings, of which she was an element. She pondered the idea that she was trying to express matter and energy in all its wondrous forms and its transformations on a moment-by-moment basis. Was this truly what the universe was about? She knew of course that art was often talked about in terms of beauty and aesthetics, but this could be said of mathematics and other knowledge as well (she had heard). She kept coming back to the essential difference that art is ineffable, indescribable, whereas other knowledge such as mathematical and science principles were explicable and logical. Was this the major finding of history: that human experience falls into two broad categories that may have some overlap, but are generally discrete? There are domains of knowledge that rely on evidence, but others that rely on belief and conviction, they do not have to be explained and justified. Perhaps art was the mechanism through which we sought understanding between these two categories, a process that is nowhere near complete at present. A small clap of thunder reverberated around the van as Ella wiped paint off her hands with an old cloth dipped in turpentine. Well, this may be it, she thought, why am I using turpentine and not water in my artistic endeavour, do I need explanation or merely accept that's the way these materials relate? Where does smelly turpentine come from anyway and why does it dissolve paint, unlike water? She wondered if Picasso and Dali knew the answer and how Michelangelo coped with cleaning his brushes.

Back in her converted garage that Ella somewhat graciously called her studio, there was the usual process of getting out her sketches and rough experiments with colour and attempting to recreate in her mind the experience of before. This was not easy to do and resulted in what she described as 'approximation of the unknown': how exactly did those purple clouds look, how to depict flowers and leaves 'wafting in the breeze,' what do we 'feel' when standing by the river? She worried about this stage of the process, where decisions of some type had to be made, really, on the sum total of her experience, not just the immediate. She had grown up here and knew the stories of the land and people, the ships and lives that had been lost at sea, the droughts and floods that took their turns, the good times and the bad as sickness, war and love circulated through society. In many respects, Ella saw the artist as a storyteller and, like all stories, having some freedom to adapt and emphasise as she saw fit. This was the creative act she thought and her responsibility. Perhaps science and mathematics could cover the links between this and that, the patterns that exist in matter and energy, this was surely at the centre of meaning for us. But there needed to be deep human connections with something else that may be difficult to explain, something else gets to the heart of what it means to be human, warm, compassionate and ethical, dedicated to the social and emotional public good of all humans, regardless of background and status. Ella hesitated at the word 'emotional' as it occurred, but she couldn't think of a better description, perhaps sensitive, expressive were similar but not quite the same. In any case, she was pleased to see herself as part of history and trying to continue

104   *Education as philosophy of practice*

as artists had for centuries, interpreting the world and challenging the understandings of other citizens. In some strange way, this made her a part of everything, transforming itself beneath her very feet and mind.

## Exegesis 7: aesthetics of matter and energy

It is difficult to understand why Leonardo da Vinci's Mona Lisa is considered most famous painting in the world. There are many others from different eras. As Bourdieu might say, however, it probably has extremely high cultural capital formed over the years since the early 1500s, compounded as the celebrity, tourism and media of capitalism have extended during this time. It may be that da Vinci has embodied the smile, eyes and mystery of inherent beauty recognisable through the centuries. Ella is coming to grips with painting the characteristics of her subjects as well, the splendour of clouds, the dignity of a child's activity, the structure of an autumn leaf. There are vital connections here with what Dewey has outlined as the five conditions of aesthetic form, those of continuity, cumulation, conservation, tension and anticipation (Jackson, 1998, p. 45). According to Jackson, the notion of continuity indicates what is stable and ongoing in experience, such as the physical properties of materials that artists use and the cultural and historical ideas that they bring to the work. Dewey thinks of cumulation as the build-up of experience and values as the creative work unfolds and of conservation as the energies and meanings that inhabit art as the artefact changes in form and detail. He sees movement in this process, as one energy or impulse for a certain direction is opposed by another impulse direction. What should be emphasised in the next chapter of a novel, for example, should a painting show the depression of winter or the remarkable structure of snowflakes? In regards the property of aesthetic tension, Dewey considers all art to involve the resolution of difficulties along the way as ideas and opportunities jostle for prominence. Rather than being seen as unfortunate obstacles, difficulties enable different pathways to be considered and, in so doing, provide deeper understandings of the issues at hand. Anticipation of an artistic experience is not something that can be described in advance, but depends on the experience itself. Going to the theatre to see a play depends on previous plays that have been witnessed, but it is known that the outcome may be quite different. In summary, Jackson (p. 51) contends,

> The true appreciation of an art object, for Dewey, is not the causal listener or viewer. Rather it is someone who has spent time with a work, has found it engaging, stimulating, puzzling, perhaps even troubling and, as a result of this sustained exploration of it, has undergone a significant change of some kind.

In this way, a combination of the five properties of aesthetic experience noted earlier, combine and integrate the new and old understanding, 'They form a new pattern, a new way of perceiving.'

As an artist, Ella has this type of experience every day. Dewey's thoughts on aesthetic *experience* in effect, guide her actions as she makes decisions, interprets

*Education as philosophy of practice* 105

the world, selects colour and form and unites them into a cohesive whole. Her life is *experiential* in that it is framed by action and experience that then informs her thinking and reason. In a similar manner, Marx saw the key influences of the social and physical worlds as *materialist*, whereby human knowledge, understanding and values arise from evolutionary social acts that occur collectively throughout the centuries. As mentioned earlier, he saw consciousness as an outcome of the interactions of matter and energy, rather than being present in some unclear way that then impacts the social and physical worlds. Central to the philosophy of a materialist existence is that of *dialectics* (Engels, 1954), involving constant transformation and change between all aspects of the universe, including humans. As well as dialectical materialism, Marxism also advocates historical materialism, where the previous arbitrariness of history and politics gave way to a consistent and harmonious view of human progress as the norm. Here, as a consequence of the growth of productive forces, out of one system of social life another and higher system develops. Marxism contends that just as human knowledge reflects nature, so social knowledge including philosophical, religious, political and cultural, reflects the dominant economic systems of society. Finally, as a key determinant of knowledge and contrary to conservative economists, Marx proposed that the relations between people must be held uppermost. This raises the most important unresolved issue of knowledge discussed earlier in this book, the inability of the schooling system all over the world to cohesively integrate practice and theorising for all students. Obvious inability of this type signifies that the capitalist economy has little interest in resolving this dilemma for the vast majority of children, indeed citizens, the contradiction between school mathematics, science and the humanities, between concrete and abstract knowledge, between creative artistic projects and predetermined instrumentalism, between autonomous play and experiment and preformed outcomes established a long time ago in places far away. It seems apparent that Ella's life of the artist, can be seen as one of dialectical materialism, moving from practice, to consciousness and back to practice, as her ideas develop and transform.

As noted earlier, Dewey's colleague, George Herbert Mead, in his discussion of the 'social act,' raised the issue of what he called 'gesture.' By this he meant the movement or attitude that serves as the impulse for interaction between social agents. The notion of 'a conversation of gestures' understood in this way, opens up a deeper analysis of how and indeed why interaction between humans and other primates occurs. Within relations, a situation occurs that requires resolution of some type, resolution that must take place socially. This refers to Mead's concept, discussed earlier, of 'intersubjectivity,' where new and current experience come together between humans to bring forth the new. Human consciousness is therefore social rather than being attained at higher levels by some individuals and not others. Gesture or attitude as part of the social act can be thought of in a variety of ways involving, for example, the interaction between Martin Luther King and a huge peace rally, a painter recreating what they see and interpret on canvas, a photograph of the Beatles on the cover of an album or a singer communicating with thousands of concert goers via a big screen and physical actions and movements on

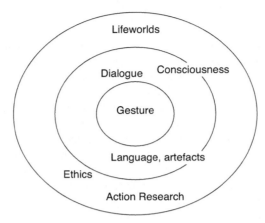

*Figure 5.2* Evolutionary development of gesture, lifeworld, dialogue

stage. The gesture indicates an intention or attitude towards a particular situation, that can be seen as hollow, false, or being in deadly earnest. That is, it can be bold, weak or foolish depending on the judgements made. It is located deep within the lifeworlds of participants and must be interpreted by each. It connects with others via diverse cultural experience including dialogue and social practice (Figure 5.2).

Seen in this way, social act and gesture are immersed in the cavernous cultural experience of the ordinary of all humans and link with lifeworld via language, ethical conduct and social practice, guided by consciousness and awareness. Understanding the world and experience is not the preserve of some, of a privileged elite, but is available to all, a democratic process that constitutes social being: it is social being that determines consciousness of the species, not a predetermined consciousness that determines social being. For Mead, consciousness emerged when humans began to take or see the role of others and began to relate to others with a new or heightened understanding. In this regard, the concepts of social act and gesture can relate closely to the work of Einstein who considered physics to have great cultural significance and in developing an overall philosophy of a comprehensive world. The German words of 'weltbild' and 'weltanschauung' having this meaning were central to the development of science and physics in Germany at the time and, according to Sonnert (2005, p. 287),

> What is perhaps most astonishing about Einstein's work as a physicist is his courage to place his confidence, often against much of the available evidence, on a few fundamental guiding ideas, which he called categories in a non-Kantian sense i.e. freely choosable.

These categories or *themata* included for Einstein, ideas such as simplicity, symmetry, unity, synthesis and wholeness, ideas that connect with those of the German poet and writer Goethe and with central precepts of German culture (Kultur) generally. Associating with the central thesis of this book, it is worth quoting Cassidy (1995, p. 14) in full on this point (cited by Sonnert, p. 291):

> Einstein's concern with a unifying worldview and adherence to a research program derived from it were not unique to him nor to physics. The 'unifying spirit' as it was called, pervaded much of European thought at the turn of the century. German idealism, neo-Romanticism and historicism, stretching from Immanuel Kant and G. F. Hegel to Benedetto Croce and Wilhelm Dilthey each pointed to some sort of transcendent higher unity, the existence of permanent ideas or forces that supersede or underlie the transient, ephemeral world of natural phenomena, practical applications and the daily struggle of human existence. The scholar, the artist, the poet, the theoretical physicist all strove to grasp that higher reality, a reality that because of its permanence and transcendence must reveal ultimate 'truth' and hence, serve as a unifying basis for comprehending, for reacting to, the broader world of existence in its many manifestations.

## Confirmations and conflicts across philosophies of practice

Our creative quest for education as a cohesive knowledge discipline that can be theorised as a philosophy of practice having similarities and tensions with other philosophies of practice, relates strongly to the views of many philosophers such as Einstein and Dewey. We too are investigating the dualisms and antagonisms of opposing states in the interests of resolving contradictions so that a higher state of harmony and understanding is reached. At least for a time. To summarise, the extended discussions of scenario and exegesis noted earlier have attempted to outline some key features of a unified education and six other philosophies of practice, to the extent that possible major and determining interrelations between them can be identified and analysed. In this way, the independence of each can be established, as well as the approximate nature of the influences between them. In attempting to work with possible, major and determining features, Table 5.5 summarises some political-democratic features of the philosophies encountered. A consideration of this table indicates differences and similarities that can then be compared with the suggestion earlier for a more cohesive view of education. These tensions and correlations are shown in Tables 5.5 and 5.6.

The significance of Tables 5.5 and 5.6 can best be appreciated by consideration of two specific examples. Over recent years, the dominant influence of neoliberal economics globally and applied to education specifically, has generated a large industry of high stakes testing. Many countries now see their test results as a marker of economic progress and an appropriate means of comparing economic health across countries. It is, however, very difficult to engage a serious and accurate debate regarding international test results because of the manner by which formal education and schooling are arranged. As mentioned earlier in this book, in the middle and stronger economies, formal schooling is usually organised around a strange mix of political imperatives rather than educational philosophy. This

Table 5.5 Intersection of political-democratic features of philosophies

| | Religion | Conservatism | Neoliberalism | Social Democracy | Science | Marxism |
|---|---|---|---|---|---|---|
| Ideology | Higher authority, officer authority | Traditional texts and practices | Liberal, dominance of economics | Representative government, welfare support | Knowledge through experiment, constant change | Social class, materialism, dialectics, practice and theory |
| Culture, aspiration | Faith, community, life meantime, ceremonies | Traditional, collective | Dispersed | General community | General community | Working class, general community |
| Economic power | Institutional rather than social wealth, power | Elite, born to rule | Dispersed, new and old wealth | Greater equity, wealth dominates | Equality of knowledge, little impact on power | Working class not bourgeoisie power |
| Decision making | Dictates, dogmatic to greater, lesser extent | Semi-regulated | Laissez-faire, enterprise operates under own laws | Representative within context of economic relations | Broader knowledge impacts appropriate decision making | Representative, with decisions at each level made by those directly concerned |
| Public, private | Public or private, relates to group or humanity | Public or private | Private, individual | Mix of individual, private within more equitable systems | Processes independent within political context | Public, collective only |
| Individual role | Acceptance or choice of variation | Acceptance or choice of variation | Choice | Choice as much as possible | Communities of practice | Member of collective with individual interest |

*Education as philosophy of practice* 109

*Table 5.6* Tensions and correlations between education and philosophies

| | *Tensions with Education* | *Correlations with Education* |
| --- | --- | --- |
| Religion | Acceptance of higher authority of various types<br>Faith-based not evidence-based<br>Dogmatic to greater, lesser extent regarding beliefs, practices, ceremonies, texts | Consideration of a greater good<br>Shared cultural, community experiences<br>Community cohesion |
| Conservatism | Acceptance of higher authority of various types<br>Elite, born to rule<br>Acquiescence regarding current arrangements of society, schooling, knowledge | Shared cultural, community experiences<br>Informative texts, practices |
| Neoliberalism | Dominance of economic views, systems, markets<br>Dominance of economic views over knowledge<br>Performativity, privatisation<br>Increasing economic difference between social groups | Encouragement of individual achievement |
| Social Democracy | Economic difference between social groups<br>Private, individual achievement<br>Traditional views of schooling, knowledge | Increased support for participation<br>Social rather than private context |
| Science | Uncertain, ambiguous mix of technical and communicative rationalities<br>Production of new knowledge | Cohesive, unified view of universe, society<br>Emphasis on explanation, understanding, innovation<br>Processes for change, improvement, creativity |
| Marxism | Adapting complicated social class perspective in contradiction with traditional, conservative views of society, schooling, knowledge | Social class perspective supporting democratic, cohesive, unified view of universe, society, schooling, knowledge |

means a collection of subjects derived from psychology, sociology, politics, economics, sciences, mathematics and the like, chosen more for their political importance in each country and not the integrity of their philosophical basis. Because of this philosophical weakness, mass tests are also impossible to define, also being a mix of psychometric and political requirements. Whether or not literacy and numeracy, for example, are defined accurately, are organised appropriately in schools, are taught with pedagogical consistency and whether students receive appropriate support and monitoring, is irrelevant; mass tests are administered in flagrant disregard to the actual social and educational context of schooling for the entire population. This means that criticism of testing generally adopts a 'taken for

## 110   *Education as philosophy of practice*

granted' approach, not one of serious educational critique. Students are seen to be put under pressure to perform on exams, they may lack experience of exam technique, or they may not have covered the necessary subject content at their school. More substantial comments include the lack of resources and qualified teachers in particular subject areas and a disconnection between the school curriculum and the cultural background of families. All of these are important issues, but they do not cohere in any meaningful way towards a general critique of schooling, knowledge, teaching and learning. The model of schooling and knowledge that still dominates around the world is essentially sociological rather than epistemological. Table 5.7 changes this dynamic markedly. It is now possible to critique mass testing using the key correlations identified as coming from the six philosophies discussed and compare those with the philosophical and indeed political basis of high stakes testing. Based on these correlations, the questions that can now be raised are of the following form (Table 5.7):

*Table 5.7* Questions for education as philosophy of practice

| *General Paradigmatic Question* | *Specific Characteristics of Action* |
| --- | --- |
| How does the organisation of schooling, arrangements for teaching and therefore the nature of testing correlate with the philosophy of education as a social practice involving for all students:<br><br>• Investigation of a greater good for humanity?<br>• Shared cultural and community experiences?<br>• Development of community cohesion?<br>• Immersion with informative texts and practices?<br>• Engagement of individual and collective achievement?<br>• Support for social and educational participation?<br>• Connecting with social rather than private context?<br>• Seeking of explanation and understanding?<br>• Experimenting with processes for change and improvement?<br>• Incorporating social class perspectives that support democratic, cohesive, unified views of the universe, society, schooling and knowledge? | • Working class orientation<br>• All cultural knowledge respected<br>• Democratic forms of organisation<br>• All formal knowledge respected<br>• All learning progress valued and respected<br>• Democratic participation of all<br>• Support for public good<br>• Participatory inquiry available for all<br>• All knowledge subject to critique<br>• Incorporating social class perspectives that support democratic, cohesive, unified views of the universe, society, schooling and knowledge? |

These ten questions can be asked of any system of education and schooling around the world at present. Obviously, each can be interpreted differently and has the legitimate possibility of conservative or radical comments. What exactly is a greater good for humanity, how is a student immersed in an informative text,

*Education as philosophy of practice* 111

where does explanation come from, can we have a unified view of the universe? There are two important responses to this possibility. First, any proposal for the realignment of highly significant aspects of society will be argued from a radical or conservative position. A set of ten points will not change the dominant class, wealth and status determinant that exist. What is different about these points is that they have arisen from a detailed consideration of six crucial philosophies that exist around the world and therefore exhibit tensions and correlations with education as it is known. This means that logically, all adherents must consider their own viewpoints and be able to defend them in sensible ways. The ten points are also essentially epistemological, they all involve taking action of some sort, without being diverted into passive cul-de-sacs where the 'taken for granted' is what currently exists. These points are therefore radical in character, designed to get to the heart of education through serious debate and to change education and therefore society in fundamental ways. Second, these points do not constitute the basis of high stakes testing around the world and therefore challenge its validity and integrity. International and national testing of this type is simplistic and unreal, not connecting with the culture of ordinary lives and the experience of communities. The points show that mass testing does not have a substantial philosophical base and its results are therefore dubious. Claims that relate test results and family background cannot be accepted for either the wealthy or the poor and disenfranchised. Our list of ten questions and the characteristics of action that arise therefore sets up a radical program for democratic schooling.

## Investigating how, why and what we know

An additional issue (or set of issues) does arise from this discussion regarding the process of transitioning from a derived, disorganised and disconnected system of schooling, to a coherent and systematic co-production of knowledge and understanding by all participants, families, students, teachers. That is, what to retain and what to discard in terms of knowledge and process. As mentioned earlier, Giddens suggested 'philosophical conservatism' as one of his 'third way' values. By this, he meant that respect for the past and history should be maintained as major change took place around us at dizzying speed. In somewhat of a similar way, Leiviska (2015, p. 581) comments that Gadamer's concept of tradition while often misunderstood also has an important place in the philosophy of education. Leiviska refers to the debate between Gadamer and Habermas on the question of tradition where conservatism is often taken to mean in education the preservation and insistence of established ideas, practices and institutions. She continues (p. 582),

I argue that although Gadamer challenges the ideal of preconditionless understanding, he does not suggest that questioning or challenging existing traditions is impossible. On the contrary, Gadamer perceives tradition as an inherently reflective ontological structure that is in a continuous state or revision and self-transgression through processes of understanding where historically inherited presuppositions are relentlessly questioned and challenged.

## 112 *Education as philosophy of practice*

This viewpoint goes to Gadamer's notion of the 'fusion of horizons,' where the interpretation of a text, experience or another person relies on a fusion of current understandings, prejudice and bias, with a different perspective. Whether or not such a fusion will lead to a serious review or critique of different viewpoints is not precluded, but will depend on the range of experiences that have been encountered and how problems and situations have been resolved to create new possibilities. This process can be called learning. The issue occurring here is that of educational research in the broad sense, that is how the practice of education as a cohesive field goes about investigating how, why and what we know. The following section will provide some examples of issues arising from education as a philosophy of practice, including research. However, as neoliberalism strengthens its hold, the issue of educational research comes under increasing pressure to be reified and objectified in terms of metrics, productivity and performativity. Such an approach denies human communities, practices and values and from where they spring, experience and participation. Educational research needs to ensure therefore that investigations of the social and physical worlds are intimately based on democratic participation with them, over time, in concert with all those who have an interest in understanding and improving. It requires recognition of background culture and history, including prejudice and bias, so that appreciation of others is respected, thereby strengthening appreciation of ourselves. The market must not inhabit the social under any circumstances. This is the key lesson for educational research that emerges from the discussion thus far of education as a philosophy of practice, with its own knowledges, claims and imperatives. We demand acceptance of a basic human right to public education that involves all participants in confrontation with the real, a basic human right to investigate the real and, through association with others, to come to our own understanding of what it means to be human.

# Part II reflections

It is very difficult to discuss the principles, benefits and criticisms of education when it is fragmented and inconsistent. Part II therefore has attempted to sketch or map education as a progressive and cohesive field of human action and then to compare this integrated corpus of knowledge and practice with six other philosophies of practice. This has been done through a narrative process, where brief scenarios have been drafted to indicate some key ideas from each philosophy. For example, in terms of religion, the thoughts of a young boy are described as he considers his personal experiences and feelings when observing the beauty of the stars at night and what he is taught from the church regarding origins of the universe. In the scenario regarding Marxism, a young female artist seeks to depict the natural world accurately and creatively and is therefore intimately involved in understanding her deepest experiences and feelings from a materialist rather than idealist perspective where matter, energy, ideas and practices are constantly being transformed. The scenarios in general attempt to highlight the crucial place of experience and inquiry in human learning and by so doing, show the importance of culture, experience and community. Neoliberal education pays scant attention to these aspects of the lives of ordinary people worldwide. The relationship between education and these six other philosophies of practice is of course extremely complicated and involves the exercise of power for sectional interest. Economic gain for the wealthy and influential will dominate, but a more rigorous and comprehensive analysis rather than what the fragmented and inconsistent can provide, will enable a stronger principled, systematic and nuanced contest between philosophies. Part II also suggests a summary series of principles on which this contest can be based. A number of these principles have been acted upon in various countries and by many progressive educators at all levels of education over previous decades but, in general, they have been very difficult to maintain let alone extend across systems during the neoliberal era of the past 30 years. Part III will outline some specific examples of application, each of which will need to be adapted depending on the local conditions that exist.

# Part III

# Thinking democratically

Taking the ideas and practices outlined in Parts I and II, it now becomes necessary to discuss how they might be applied in specific circumstances. In summarising and returning to some of the key ideas encountered earlier, Part III attempts to offer some advice in this regard, bearing in mind that practitioners around the world will need to act in accord with their own economic, political and cultural settings. The following chapters therefore review and comment on the nature of class ideology and society, education that takes place within an Indigenous context, teacher education that must grapple with the complexities of democratic and inclusive education and finally, an overview of our approach that supports a genuinely radical and pragmatic philosophical understanding of existence and knowledge that combats the pervasiveness of neoliberal dogma. Social class is taken to be the dominant aspect of this philosophy, but this is difficult to define in relation to a paradigm shift from the bourgeois to the proletarian, under a capitalist system. Indigenous questions are raised because they offer a clearly alternative viewpoint to much capitalist thinking that enable discussions of ethical conduct and knowledge from a base of experience and community culture. Restructuring teacher education to support discursive and democratic education and schooling will require a courageous and determined approach to reform, again taking place within a neoliberal and capitalist context. Finally, we encourage all peace-loving and democratic peoples around the world to consider the true meaning of radical and democratic knowing, of how all people regardless of background can embrace the local, infinite and universal in their historic quest to contribute to their own humanity and to that of their communities. This is the significance of our journey described in these pages, dedicated to becoming human through our personal narratives, thinking and practices, to recreate the world in the real and still-emerging interests of humankind.

# 6 Social class, equity and socio-economic positions

Extant in dark recesses
surviving on putrid fruit
and composting debris
of affluence, the senses
honed by generations
of squalid existence;
undaunted, strains of cockroach
endure for thousands of years.

What is important about humans conducting themselves ethically or in constructing a framework of living for themselves that consist of values and principles that
enhance their humanity? That does not necessarily have to be the case. Pragmatism
would suggest that there is a human disposition to change situations for the better
and that the direction of such betterment is understood and agreed through action
taken over very long periods of time. The difficulty of progressive change as a
historic process is frustrating and debilitating, especially when war, aggression and
acquisitiveness at every level of human existence continue to dominate social life.
But we now pursue deeper understanding of these questions through application
of Table 5.7 (see Chapter 5) within the context of social class, equity and socio-
economic positioning. Later, particular consideration of feminism will be given in
relation to social class and education.

Dewey will be helpful to this discussion in his deliberation on the concept of
habit and, in particular, how habits that are strong and ingrained, can be changed.
He argued that through human interaction, communication can increase the number of habits and link them together, thereby opening up the possibility of new
modes of endeavour. Dewey (1958, p. 281) writes,

> Now an animal given to forming habits is one with an increasing number of
> needs and of new relationships with the world about it. Each habit demands
> appropriate conditions for its exercise and when habits are numerous and com-
> plex, as with the human organism, to find these conditions involves search and
> experimentation; the organism is compelled to make variations and exposed to
> error and disappointment. By a seeming paradox, increased power of forming
> habits means increased susceptibility, sensitiveness, responsiveness.

## 118 Class, equity and socio-economic positions

*Table 5.7* Questions for education as philosophy of practice

| General Paradigmatic Question | Specific Characteristics of Action |
|---|---|
| How does the organisation of schooling, arrangements for teaching and therefore the nature of testing correlate with the philosophy of education as a social practice involving for all students:<br><br>• Investigation of a greater good for humanity?<br>• Shared cultural and community experiences?<br>• Development of community cohesion?<br>• Immersion with informative texts and practices?<br>• Engagement of individual and collective achievement?<br>• Support for social and educational participation?<br>• Connecting with social rather than private context?<br>• Seeking of explanation and understanding?<br>• Experimenting with processes for change and improvement?<br>• Incorporating social class perspectives that support democratic, cohesive, unified views of the universe, society, schooling and knowledge? | • Working class orientation<br>• All cultural knowledge respected<br>• Democratic forms of organisation<br>• All formal knowledge respected<br>• All learning progress valued and respected<br>• Democratic participation of all<br>• Support for public good<br>• Participatory inquiry available for all<br>• All knowledge subject to critique<br>• Incorporating social class perspectives that support democratic, cohesive, unified views of the universe, society, schooling and knowledge? |

In the way that groves on a plastic recording can combine and interact to produce wonderful sound and music, Dewey goes on to describe habits as being both durable and unstable, predictable and novel, separate and associating, harmonising and contradicting. Habits in action therefore are a significant aspect of Dewey's view of the social world and how humans construct their social spheres. This causes a reconsideration of the notion that humans reason their way through situations in a deliberative way in selecting how to act from a set of preformed beliefs to meet a certain end. Rather, humans work or act their way through situations where habits are conflicted and where responses are required, not predetermined, to resolve the conflict and move forward. As well as the personal, we can see how historically and economically this general process ensues between the bourgeoisie and the proletariat, as the members of each, united by world view and aspiration, attempt to decide problems and issues in their own interests. There may not be a telos or ultimate aim at play here for each, but current habits – grooves in the social fabric of the affairs of kinfolk – can be deliberative and innovative at once. Consequently and as a general means of considering how social class influences or dominates formal education, Table 6.1 attempts to summarise key characteristics

*Class, equity and socio-economic positions*   119

of bourgeois and proletarian characteristics of living. This summary is necessarily broad, an overview of two competing world views, but will hopefully provide signposts for the educational discussion that follows.

There is a close similarity between the characteristics shown in Table 5.7 and the proletarian world view described briefly in Table 6.1. Conversely, it is clear that the bourgeois emphasis on the ownership of production, the importance of private wealth and power for personal authority and its apprehensiveness towards any form of social action that may challenge position and status, is contradictory with the philosophy and practice indicated by a cohesive, integrated and participatory education. Education in the broad sense of the birth-to-death process of exploring the relationships between humans and nature and those that exist within human societies, the process of becoming more subjectively human discussed in earlier chapters, has a dialectical materialist character with materialist and social change and transformation at its heart. Under capitalism and neoliberalism, social life is reified to the production and exchange of commodities where money transactions avoid considering what commodities represent in social terms. In this way, exploitative systems of wage labour are ignored and the human goods of ideas, values and philosophies inherent in productive outputs are dismissed. This bourgeois economic world view cannot acknowledge where ideas, values and philosophies come from and therefore must distort and frustrate the learning process in formal education systems. Under the pernicious influence of neoliberalism, personal learning is corrupted and in effect, is reduced to pre-specified garbled and deformed commodities (equations, grammars, rules,

*Table 6.1* Characteristics of bourgeois and proletarian viewpoints

|  | *Bourgeois Characteristics* | *Proletarian Characteristics* |
|---|---|---|
| Relation to Production | Ownership, disconnected to various extents; linked by management dictates and procedures; dismissive of human value and understanding so created | No ownership, direct, connected by manual and intellectual work to various extents; respectful of human value and understanding so created |
| Wealth and Power | Ownership, private, central to human existence | Limited ownership, significant, but not essential for human satisfaction and progress |
| Culture | Elitist, supportive of private, individual aspiration and achievement | Inclusive, supportive of community, collective, individual aspiration and achievement |
| Life Opportunities | Individual effort, win or lose | Collective responsibility, support for all regardless of background |
| Social Action | Fearful, apprehensive of change that challenges status, wealth | Accepting, essential for social progress, equity, democracy |
| Ideology | Conservative, maintain status quo for benefit of minorities with power, authority | Progressive, radical, to change status quo to benefit majority of ordinary people |

## 120   *Class, equity and socio-economic positions*

conventions, symbols, abstractions) that cannot be grasped and manoeuvred (Collyer, 2015; Naidoo and Williams, 2015). Formal education thus becomes indecipherable and alienating for most.

## Social class in education

It is difficult to understand why the distinction between theory and practice still governs formal education with an iron grip around the world. A dictatorship in fact. There are cracks within the façade, but they are difficult to expand. From the discussion outlined in this book, the theory-practice gap would seem to act against the interests of working class families and children as it makes the application of real-world or socio-cultural knowledge to more abstract problems, difficult to navigate and evaluate. Case 1, for example, shows the necessity of building on previous abstracted knowledge at ever-increasing levels in school mathematics to make sense of generalised appreciations that may emerge.

### *Case 1. Contemplating the cosine rule*

Wednesday afternoon dragged on. As I sat at the back of the class, I observed 18 or so students quietly copying down what the teacher was revealing on the white board. It took my mind back when I did much the same, trying to engage 16-year-old in the mysteries of school mathematics. The young pre-service teacher had drawn a non-right-angled triangle, labelled the apexes A, B and C and had dropped a vertical line from the top apex to its opposite side, point D, thereby forming two right-angled triangles within the original. In using what had already been taught about trigonometry and sine, cosine and tan – such as the mnemonic SOHCAHTOA and the rule of Pythagoras $A^2 + B^2 = C^2$ – the pre-service teacher in a few lines of logic, derived the famous cosine rule – i.e. $C^2 = A^2 + B^2 - 2AB\cos\theta$. I was ecstatic at what I had witnessed, as I recalled the beauty of mathematics and how it opened up our thinking about the nature of universe, let alone how humans had evolved to the point of thinking and abstracting in this way. As he walked around the room, the pre-service teacher also made a further generalisation about triangles, almost to himself, that if angle C were a right angle, the cosine of angle C would be zero and the theory of Pythagoras would result! This stirred me even further, an amazing insight about the universe and triangles, surely a thing of splendour and puzzlement for the students so assembled. Outwardly, the ambience of the room did not change as the students finished copying down the equation and turned to the chapter in their textbook for the inevitable examples to calculate. I could not complain, as my memory of doing exactly the same came flooding back over the years. No-one had ever suggested that I should investigate where the equations came from and what prompted mathematicians of the day to investigate the physical world in such a way. Another weakness of the profession and practitioners in schools. As I got up to speak with students about question 1 from the book, it occurred to me that they had just been involved in an unmasking of philosophical thinking and investigation about the very nature of being, an event

*Class, equity and socio-economic positions* 121

that might excite and perplex them for many years to come. I assumed that when I reported to my good friend Chris, he would make his usual comment that families on low income are not interested in such things.

This case is epistemological in character. It describes students from ordinary families being exposed to the logical mathematical thinking of experienced adults that is seen as having inherent human interest, yet is removed from the daily cultural practice of children. It links with a sociological view that income determines intellectual engagement in a manner yet to be determined. What is also at stake here of course is that it is the school curriculum that decides which slices of knowledge should to raised with students of particular ages and what the outcomes of that engagement should be, at particular dates and times. The case indicates how knowledge is turned into symbols that are then manipulated to create new arrangements of symbolic complexity. This approach is not beyond the capability of working class children, but it does require procedures and thinking about the world that are not steeped in practice and culture. Vygotsky (van der Veer and Valsiner, 1994), for example, spoke of how the 'emotional lived experience' or '*perezhivanie*' contributed to the child's understanding of the world:

> The emotional experience (*perezhivanie*) arising from any situation or from any aspect of his environment, determines what kind of influence this situation or this environment will have on the child. Therefore, it is not any of the factors in themselves (if taken without reference to the child) which determines how they will influence the future course of his development, but the same factors refracted through the prism of the child's emotional experience (*perezhivanie*).

In this statement, Vygotsky is bringing together the effects of the child's experience with the situational conditions within which the current experience is taking place, described as the 'emotional lived experience.' In a similar way, Dewey (1958, p. 21) comments that 'For things are objects to be treated, used, acted upon and with, enjoyed and endured, even more than things to be known. They are things *had* before they are things cognised.' This is a further remarkable assertion by Dewey, in that he distinguishes the act from the thought, impossible as it is to verify and perhaps with an imperceptible gap between them, seemingly all acts and thoughts occurring simultaneously as life proceeds. But Vygotsky and Dewey appear to be getting at the same issue here, as they grapple with the notion of where thought comes from and how new and different thoughts arise from similar experience. Such active engagement with life and nature through daily experience is central to all humans and is the way by which working people come to validate their culture and knowledge. To deny such experience in a school curriculum or a school subject denies learning, indeed life itself.

In discussing the decline of social class as a major sociological determinant, Reay (1998, p. 259) observes that 'regardless of whether we see ourselves in class terms, class just as much as race, gender, age and sexuality shape and goes on shaping, the individuals we are and the individuals we become.' She does concede,

## 122 *Class, equity and socio-economic positions*

however, that a rethinking of social class is necessary, particularly as many commentators accept a major shift in society from production to consumption. That is, many economies have transferred large areas of their productive and manufacturing capacity to 'off shore' nations, particularly those where more oppressive labour conditions prevail. Where employment and wage levels are 'reasonable,' workers can still manage a modest living supplemented by new technologies that bring concerts, sporting, entertainment and celebrity events into their homes. In educational terms, however, working people continue to experience lives that require constant problem solving, investigation of social regulations and procedures, management of family finances, schooling for their children, engagement with materials and processes of production and construction, and a resulting paradigm of common community, culture and experience. Indeed, there is a thread of personal consumption across this activity and direct involvement with the production of commodities is not as apparent as in previous times. Yet people around the world of different nationalities, ethnicities and genders that encourage particular patterns of consumption of goods and services are still united by their relationship to the economic system, globalised and neoliberal. Whether or not such an understanding as 'class consciousness' exists today across and between different countries, can be debated, its form and content needs to be elaborated, but connections exist between those who work for a living and have very limited resources are real and enduring.

Mead's discussion of this question in the broad sense centred on the relationship between mind, self and society. How does society influence the creation of mind and, in turn, how does mind influence society. This can be restated as the connections between social class and the human mind, each influencing the other, emphasising pragmatism and action as the major originating influences. In some respects, Savage, Divine and Cunningham (2013) paint a similar picture to Reay earlier, when he suggests a reworking of the notion of class in the United Kingdom to include not three but seven class categories: elite, established middle class, technical middle class, new affluent workers, traditional working class, emergent service workers and precariat. It seems that this analysis focuses on work occupations and the reproduction of wealth and positions, rather than the formation of class stratification in the first place, via exploitation and manipulation. Fragmenting class structure also has the consequence of overly dividing the interests of groups of people, rather than seeing their class concerns as being similar if not identical. Mead would comment that connections between the 'I' of self-awareness and the 'me' of social interaction with the 'generalised other,' would collapse many of these strata around a common experience of exploitation, corruption and maltreatment, forming links of solidarity and empathy. As mentioned previously, communication between social actors is the key feature of this process, as each responds to gestures of the others. In this way, all social institutions and communities need access to open, honest and continuing practices of communication that establish shared understanding and ultimately, ethical conduct. Social class as a concept, practice and process therefore exists in the formation of mind and as a result, is redrafted by mind as experience is gathered. Like all other experience, social class emerges from human pragmatism (economic, political, cultural) throughout the centuries.

*Class, equity and socio-economic positions* 123

## Feminism, pragmatism and equity in education

It may have been apparent to readers of this book that feminism has not been mentioned before this point. As a powerful social movement around the world, this may have been a political mistake. However, the stance taken has been in the first instance epistemological, within a sociological context no doubt, but epistemological in that this is where the action of learning must be understood, designed and implemented, if progress is to occur. As has been mentioned in earlier chapters and will be noted next, other sociological trends are often listed if not in opposition to social class, then certainly as a means of weakening its influence, trends such as racism, ethnicity, gender, disability, geography and sexuality. These are referred to as 'identity' politics as distinct from 'class' politics.' In this book, such features are recognised as being significant and strong including for personal identity, but it is considered that social class remains the dominant and unifying aspect of national and international life. The discussion that follows, therefore, attempts to consider feminism from a class perspective and, more particularly, from the perspective of pragmatism (Seigfried, 1993; Livingston, 2001). Dewey and Mead continue to be the main referents as it is argued that concepts of feminism arise from the lifeworld of total experience in the same way as other concepts. From this perspective, the implications of feminism for schooling and curriculum will fall within the same framework of inquiry and social act as has been described earlier. The main purpose of this small section therefore is to open up discussion of the connections between feminism, epistemology and pragmatism without making claim to any definite answers.

There seems to be little reason why boys and girls should learn differently, except their different cultural and life experiences of course. According to the British eighteenth-century author and feminist, Mary Wollstonecraft (1792/2016),

> My observations on national education are obviously hints; but I principally wish to enforce the necessity of educating the sexes together to perfect both, and of making children sleep at home that they may learn to love home; yet to make private support, instead of smothering, public affections, they should be sent to school to mix with a number of equals, for only by the jostlings of equality can we form a just opinion of ourselves.

From this point of view, in effect the viewpoint of inquiry and pragmatism, boys and girls will both engage their worlds through a collection of experiences and will construct meaningful, ethical and knowledgeable humanities through reflexive considerations of what occurs. There is no evidence to suggest that epistemological structures are different, or that cognitive processes are of a primarily different nature between male and female reckonings. On the other hand, social class and cultural influences are strong, varying as they do across different communities and countries. For example, family wealth or poverty will impact sons and daughters in different ways, as too will connections with war, aggression, democracy, fascism, religion and ideology. These impacts may be intertwined and be strengthened at

## 124 *Class, equity and socio-economic positions*

particular historical times. Arrangements for and purposes of schooling can support, influence or moderate external factors depending on the aspirations of local communities (Lingard and Sellar, 2014).

### *Case 2. Learning with the senses*

A number of small glass bottles were arranged along the front bench of the science room. As Year 8 filed in after lunch, chattering, they made various comments about the activities to be considered that day. If nothing else, I was determined that all students would be encouraged to interact with the world around them and think about their own thoughts arising. After our few weeks together, they knew what to expect. Some sheets of guidelines would be available, briefly outlining some questions and some suggested investigation. They had been using equipment and were well aware of safety requirements. As each small group settled, they gradually got organised and agreed on what needed to be done. They took a selection of six unlabelled bottles from the front and returning to their place began to identify the contents. As the caps were unscrewed, perfumes were quickly recognised by boys and girls alike, with various comments and jokes about what is used at home. Kerosene, methylated spirits and other household solvents were familiar to some, while lemon juice was quickly noted. Soapy solutions were easy, but mothballs were not known to many. After 20 minutes or so of animated discussion, one or two groups were asked to report to the entire class on what they had found and on what basis they had identified each unknown material. When asked about what caused a particular solid, liquid or gas to smell in a certain way, there was a general consensus that the smell 'spread out' from the surface of the material and was able to fill the surrounding area. Different flowers were mentioned. When one student used the word 'particle,' it generated a number of comments about how all materials are made up of tiny grains or specks that move all the time and could therefore move about the room. Exactly how or why this happened was unclear. It was agreed, however, that perfume was a very good example of this. Some students had come across this idea on the Internet or had heard such words in passing from teachers, parents and big brothers or sisters. Mary reported that she dare not interfere with Cara's make-up kits in her bedroom. Tom wondered about how his torch worked and how batteries produced light that got from the globe to the pages of his book, read under covers each night. I suggested that each group could try to draw some rough diagrams of a number of their materials to illustrate how they thought smell occurred and if they wanted, to include other events such as light and the effect of batteries. Nicole glanced up at me with a grin as she tried to sketch Beyoncé on stage, whom I gathered was involved with all of these features.

As a close friend of Dewey's, Jane Addams and colleagues established Hull House in Chicago, in 1889. Hull House was founded by university women to support immigrant, poor and working class people through a process of social reform that involved education and research. Dewey was inspired by the work at Hull House and wrote many letters to his wife and children in Europe 'regaling

*Class, equity and socio-economic positions* 125

them with tales of his encounters with Jane Addams's (Durst, 2010, p. 19). Addams expressed some criticism of philanthropy in being concerned with helping rather than with interpretation and noted that 'The only way they could take their learning to anyone was by turning it into action so that it could be seen – people were already talked to death and written to death.' Additionally, any consideration of feminism and pragmatism should include the work of the French theorist, writer and activist, Simone de Beauvoir. In one of her famous statements, Beauvoir (1973) proclaimed, 'One is not born, but rather becomes, a woman.' To achieve this, women must have the freedom to transcend their own existence and to engage in whatever projects they decide regardless of the risk and dangers involved. Speaking pragmatically, Beauvoir 'prides herself on thinking, taking action, working, creating, on the same terms as men; instead of seeking to disparage them, she declares herself their equal.' This pragmatic theme is continued by the feminist writer Judith Butler (1986, p. 36) when she comments,

> In other words, to be a woman is to become a woman; it is not a matter of acquiescing to a fixed ontological status, in which case one could be born a woman, but, rather, an active process of appropriating, interpreting ad reinterpreting received cultural possibilities. For Simone de Beauvoir, it seems, the verb 'become' contains a consequential ambiguity.

Beauvoir's relationship and collaboration with Jean-Paul Sartre is subject to ongoing critique and scholarship and must have influenced her thinking as a major component of her life. She may have seen significance in an open relationship in deepening her understanding of the 'ambiguity of existence' in the pursuit of freedom. As a third reference point for feminism and pragmatism, the Australian writer and academic Germaine Greer is cited. Greer became famous through the publication of her book, *The Female Eunuch* in 1970, establishing herself as a feminist who did not want women to be the same as men, but enabled to determine their own lives as they saw fit. Once again, the emphasis here is on action and personal authority, in powerful learning from action individually and in concert with others. Jane Addams, Simone de Beauvoir and Germaine Greer are examples of feminists who engage the world from the perspective of pragmatism and who want to transform passivity into activity for all people in all fields of endeavour. While there are various anthologies and interpretations of feminism, this is a common feature that formal education can incorporate.

From an epistemological standpoint, social acts immersed in the human lifeworld involve inquiry of objects (thoughts, artefacts, practices) and how we make sense of those objects, expressed as a never-ending dialectical relationship between lifeworld, objectification and subjectification. Male and female humans will both proceed to change and be changed by their social and physical worlds in this way. Table 6.1 would seem to be inherently feminist on this count. All students are inspired to investigate, interpret, criticise and develop their own views through ongoing discourse and reflexive activity. Their education emerges from personal

## 126   *Class, equity and socio-economic positions*

and community lifeworlds, respecting and responding to others. Defined as such, education is ethical and democratic not as a result of programs of study, but as the basis of programs of study and personal understanding. As ethical beings (Levinas, 1969/1991; Strhan, 2016), humans work their way into the world as they encounter the objects of existence, rather than are formed this way initially. This responding and responsibility to others as the 'generalised other,' is the process whereby new thoughts, artefacts and practices as object are created, influenced by of course, culture and gender, but as Dewey said, being 'had' by the practitioner before being cognised. According to Butler (2016),

> The distinction between sex and gender has been crucial to the long-standing feminist effort to debunk the claim that anatomy is destiny; sex is understood to be the invariant, anatomically distinct, and factic aspects of the female body, whereas gender is the cultural meaning and form that that body acquires, the variable modes of that body's acculturation. With the distinction intact, it is no longer possible to attribute the values or social functions of women to biological necessity, and neither can we refer meaningfully to natural or unnatural gendered behaviour: all gender is, by definition, unnatural.

This definition also fits nicely with the central concepts of pragmatism and provides strong support for application of Table 6.1 as combatting discriminatory sexism in schools. In this regard, Mead is also generally attributed to being the key founder of what is called 'symbolic interactionism' where, according to Blumer (1969), the following perspectives are applied:

- Humans act toward things on the basis of the meanings they ascribe to those things.
- The meaning of such things is derived from, or arises out of, the social interaction that one has with others and the society.
- These meanings are handled in, and modified through, an interpretative process used by the person in dealing with the things he/she encounters.

Thus, in tracking these core tenets of Blumer, the symbolic interactionist approach reveals that reality as we recognise it is an active social construct produced through constant social interaction and only exists within a given social context. (For a critique of symbolic interactionism, see Puddlephatt, 2009). These epistemological concepts of, for example, pragmatism, inquiry, social act, symbolic interactionism, the ambiguity of existence provide a strategy for incorporating feminist understandings in classrooms around questions of knowledge co-production, rather than merely observing classrooms from the sociological outside. They encourage all teachers and students to work together on the big and historic issues of the day, to combine the personal with the general through lifeworld experience and, rather than assuage difference between boys and girls, to build upon their common human interest for peace, justice and satisfaction.

## Socio-economic position and culture

Social stratification under capitalism is the norm, with differences rather than equity between wealth, position and status being the natural order of things. For schools, this raises moral and democratic as well as educational dilemmas. Bourdieu and Passeron (1977, p. 54) theorised this situation and process as 'cultural reproduction' in terms that became famous within the sociology of education:

> Every institutionalised educational system owes the specific characteristics of its structure and functioning to the fact that, by the means proper to the institution, it has to produce and reproduce the institutional conditions whose existence and persistence (self-reproduction of the system) are necessary both to the exercise of its essential function of inculcation and to the fulfilment of its function of reproducing a cultural arbitrary which it does not produce (cultural reproduction), the reproduction of which contributes to the reproduction of the relations between the groups or classes (social reproduction).

In discussing what they label as 'a cultural arbitrary,' Bourdieu and Passeron show that the cultural stance of schools (in generally democratic countries) is open to choice, a decision by the school and its teachers and not imposed from elsewhere. They are of course, subject to social, economic and political context that can be difficult to resist or mitigate. Nevertheless, independent decisions can always be made by participants at specific levels of educational systems.

### Case 3. Uniforms of convention

Shelly was not her usual bubbly self that evening. She seemed a little distracted, even when her mother asked about how basketball training had gone that day, her favourite sport. As a typical 14-year-old, Shelly was finding it a little difficult to juggle all the activities she was pursuing at school and at home. Her father had a good job as a construction worker, but was often working different shifts and did not see a lot of the family when deadlines had to be met. Her mother worked part time as a carer at an elderly person's home that enabled her to spend time with Shelly after school and on weekends. For her part, Shelly wanted to do well at school and was trying to fit in sport and music with a fairly heavy exam schedule. The school had introduced unit tests every few weeks in all subjects which meant students had to be up to date all the time. She was also interested in the Internet and felt left out of things if she was not constantly in contact with friends and with popular sites on social media. But she was worried about a couple of developments at school. She had to select her subjects for next year and in addition, there was a choice that senior students could make between the regular program conducted by similar schools and the International Baccalaureate (IB), just being introduced. Last week, the principal addressed the senior students and said that the IB was recognised around the world and may have advantages when applying for university or for a job. He said it was hard to compete these days. Shelly thought this was a

## 128  *Class, equity and socio-economic positions*

bit strange because it meant that the school's current program was not thought to be as good. She didn't quite understand the connection, but the school was also talking with parents about a much stricter school uniform policy that may include hats and gloves for girls. Up until now, the school uniform was flexible with some basic items and colours being enforced, such as tee shirts and shorts in summer and long trousers in winter and this was seen as being sensible by students and parents alike. Shelly and her friends were unsure why major changes were in the wind and what it would mean in relation to their wider circle of friends from other schools. Up until now and as far as she knew, the local neighbourhood schools were much alike, although there were some different specialist programs in the senior years that influenced decisions about which subjects to take. Shelly was thinking about the biology and ecology program at her school, but couldn't work out whether the IB would be better when she came to apply for uni. If she did of course; after all, neither mum or dad had. And hats and gloves, ugh! She hoped that her parents would not check their email for a while yet, announcing whether the IB was going ahead.

Shelly of course is confronting the influence of 'cultural capital' as a key determinant of capitalism, head-on. In many respects, it cannot be escaped. A useful distinction here is the *Gemeinschaft – Gesellschaft* contrast proposed by Tönnies (Deflem, 2016) to suggest the difference between community and society authorities. This indicates the personal values and practices established through local interactions compared with social rules, roles and values that occur because of broader connotations. Shelly is struggling to come to grips between her local experience at school and home every day and the pressures being exerted by the economic system to conform. The status of her school within her community and beyond has become a major factor for the principal, teachers and governing board as they seek to strengthen its reputation to attract families and students. For many schools, it seems that the appearance of formal student uniforms disseminates a sense of stability and continuity throughout the community, while the inclusion of an international rather than local or national program of study proves high quality education. Both approaches are essentially superficial in regards the learning of all students and focus on façade rather than substance. Issues such as these may be somewhat easy to identify and expose for critique, but they represent much deeper economic, political and cultural concerns as discussed earlier. It has been argued that the factors contained in Tables 5.7 and 6.1 provide a theorising framework that emphasise key factors of epistemology as an action agenda for educational change. A point of criticism of this approach may come from Connell (2007, p. 1), when she argues that a concentration of European theory from the dominant 'northern metropole' can overlook different views of the world from the 'southern periphery':

> Open any introductory sociology textbook and you will probably find, in the first few pages, a discussion of founding fathers focused on Marx, Durkheim and Weber. The first chapter may also cite Comte, Spencer, Tönnies and Simmel, and perhaps a few others. In the view normally presented to students,

*Class, equity and socio-economic positions* 129

these men created sociology in response to dramatic changes in European society: the Industrial Revolution, class conflict, secularisation, alienation and the modern state.

It is correct that European thinking has strongly influenced the thinking about education, teaching and knowledge raised in the pages of this book. This is my heritage. Freire is a major exception to this trend. Feminist thought has not figured greatly. Indigenous Australian culture and knowledge is acknowledged and discussed later as a significant epistemological dynamic. What has been consistent throughout has been an emphasis on action and inquiry as the means of engaging and understanding the world, based on philosophical pragmatism. I argue that this is common across countries and culture, across history and experience and across social classes. To argue that large groups of humans interact with their social and physical worlds in fundamentally different ways sets up paradigms of division and elitism and the concepts of deficit and inability. As mentioned earlier, cultural backgrounds of language, history and community strongly influence how dominant issues of social class are managed, but these factors are situated within social class nevertheless. In pursuing this journey, Shelly may attend a session with or watch a video of the British physicist Professor Brian Cox (Cox and Cohen, 2016), or the environmentalist David Attenborough (2002) or the feminist Germaine Greer (2008). All of these communicators along with many others articulate the difficult ideas and practices of the social and physical worlds so as to make them accessible to general publics in all countries. There is no difference here between male and female, city and country, rich and poor, older and younger, local and visitor. All bring their life experience to bear on the wonders of the natural and built universe and attempt to construct meaningful understanding as they navigate problems and imperatives.

In attempting to distinguish between bourgeois and proletarian characteristics earlier, the question of action looms large, perhaps most importantly. Table 6.1 notes the bourgeois as being fearful and apprehensive of change, particularly that which challenges wealth and status, while the proletarian accepts change as being essential for social progress, to bring about more equitable conditions for everyone. In this regard, the former supports an ideology of maintaining the status quo, while the latter determines a radical philosophy of getting to the kernel of issues for comprehensive change and progress. Capitalism is therefore caught in the jaws of necessity, to maintain a conservative political ideology, yet at the same time to develop innovative procedures and practices that enable new markets and profits for some, but not the many. Since the Industrial Revolution and European Enlightenment, progressive schooling has responded to this dilemma of capitalism by attempting to find strategies of incorporating radical epistemological approaches into curriculum and pedagogy that can be defended and yet challenge conservative capitalism ideology at the same time, for the many rather than the few. Philosophical pragmatism has been available for progressive educators around the world for over 100 years in this regard. For example, in discussing the notion of 'associated learning,' William James (1899/1962, p. 42) writes,

## 130  *Class, equity and socio-economic positions*

Meanwhile it is a matter of the commonest experience that our minds may pass from one object to another by various intermediary fields of consciousness. The indeterminateness of our paths of association *in concreto* is thus almost as striking a feature of them as the uniformity of their abstract form. Start from any idea whatever and the entire range of your ideas is potentially at your disposal.

This insight opens up the notion of historical pragmatism and dialectical materialism for all citizens at any time. From Einstein's thinking about the nature of space and time and the relationship between mass and energy, to the nature of consciousness and Chalmer's hard question of philosophy, James is suggesting that our experience and thinking of any idea takes us to all ideas. From this it follows that the more extensive our ideas and practices, the more they can become associated with any idea when confronted. Einstein's thinking about photons and their momentum, for example, might be associated with what he understands of a box floating in space, an encounter with the amazing from experience of the ordinary and banal. Pragmatism then is at the service of the proletarian, of all peoples from all countries and cultures, to work themselves into the objects of experience, to reflect and critique and to push forward into new, unexplored terrains. This is not only the role of imagination and curiosity, but the basis of imagination and curiosity, what makes us human. Such a change process is available to all regardless of background, skin colour or gender, regardless of barriers that have been placed in our way until now. Social class and other sociological categories do influence us mightily, but they provide for our emancipation hourly, daily as we live and transform, determined to make our experience and existence meaningful and satisfying, knowledge within us reawakened. We are trapped, our destinies made, whether voluntary or not.

# 7 Connecting with Indigenous education

Contemplating the view from Robben Island
for many long years of enforced slavery
demanding strategies to unite the entire people
against injustice and violence of superiority
chiselled formations appear in the stone quarry
refined at night behind wire and locked doors
with segregation of truth a hopeless cause
destined to be transformed into its opposite
when thought and action inevitably converts
intransitive consciousness for coming generations
and the gates of freedom swing open wide
(historical irony is not lost on the old fighter
when honoured by the privileged world
his London statue is placed near that of Smuts).

The continued refusal of modern education systems within major world economies to recognise and respect the knowledge and culture of marginalised families and students diminishes the quality of teaching and learning for all. There is something most profound and equitable about appreciating knowledge and ways of knowing and applying new and challenging perspectives across all subjects of a school curriculum. Accordingly, this chapter reports on the nature of a 'discursive' and 'bricolage' approach to schooling that has arisen from researching the educational needs of UK Gypsy/Roma/Traveller and Indigenous Australian children. We have identified a series of curriculum principles and features that are located broadly in the culture and experience of families and children concerned and which can realistically be incorporated into the policy and practice of regular schooling. Rather than assuming that some minor adjustment to the regular curriculum can accommodate the learning needs of all children, the chapter argues that a fundamental reconstruction of curriculum is required. It is proposed that all children including UK Gypsy/Roma/Traveller and Indigenous Australian will benefit from a 'discursive' approach to teaching, learning and curriculum that encourages community knowledge, history, language and storytelling across the curriculum for understanding to be explored and strengthened. Recognising the context of schooling as 'bricolage' where participants draw upon a wide range of cultures, knowledges and

## 132  *Connecting with Indigenous education*

practices at hand to pursue their learning acknowledges the social and educational authority of all marginalised children. Drawing on these considerations, a new model of Discursive Cultural Knowledge Formation has been theorised.

## Marginalised knowledge

After decades of work in separate research contexts (Indigenous Australian[1] peoples and UK Gypsy/Roma/Traveller[2]) we have each reached the conclusion that the educational experiences of children from those communities are enhanced by the inclusion of the world views of Indigenous and marginalised groups within the mainstream education system. Indeed, we would argue that such inclusion is to the benefit of other youngsters, too, challenging and enriching their perceptions of the world. As marginalised groups living within two of the world's major economies, Indigenous Australian (IA) and Gypsy Roma Traveller (GRT) children continue to experience the discrimination and indignities of racism and colonialism. The fact that such conditions still exist within national consciousness and procedure shows that inequality is still a key factor of economic relationship.

Elsewhere a background to the make-up of these groups has been provided (see Hooley and Levinson, 2014; Levinson and Hooley, 2014). For the purposes of this chapter, it is important to bear in mind that both groups have suffered a history of oppression, that their traditional lifestyles have become difficult to pursue and that their distinct cultural identities have been undermined (in general) by engagement with mainstream education. The knowledge and skills that form the basis of the cultural capital of each group may have acquired a certain 'mystique,' but in each situation, constitutes a weak currency in the context of technological economies. In each context, youngsters have been confronted by contradictions between both the nature of knowledge and modes of transmission at home and school. In the case of both IA and GRT communities, there is a central role for families and community members in supporting cultural formation. Youngsters from each group have found themselves caught between home and school learning environments in which there are discontinuities and tensions; they have been further disadvantaged by educational systems that do not have the flexibility to incorporate elements from the home-place (Levinson, 2009).

Within this context, consolidating community and personal identity is a crucial historic task of survival for all social groups, but especially so for those who are excluded and disenfranchised (Ma Rhea, 2012). This takes place within the power and economic structures of the dominant society and raises questions of difference, essentialism and authenticity. Conceptualising marginalised groups as being defined by a list of unchanging essential characteristics that sets them apart from the privileged ensures notions of deficit and insufficiency. For citizens of whatever socio-economic background who want to participate in all aspects of social life as a human right, creative ways must be found of maintaining the values and practices of culture while at the same time being able to exist within the systems and customs of alienating if not oppressive conventions. Writing on this dilemma from the perspective of an Indigenous academic, Martin Nakata suggests the notion of

*Connecting with Indigenous education*   133

the 'cultural interface' where 'Western and Indigenous domains intersect'(Nakata, 2002, p. 285). Nakata explains,

> At the interface, traditional forms and ways of knowing, or the residue of those, that we bring from the pre-contact historical trajectory inform how we think and act and do. Western ways and for so many of us a blend of both has become our lifeworld. It is the most complex of intersections and the source of confusion for many.

Living at the cultural interface requires a strong commitment to a particular way of life while at the same time interacting with new and challenging ideas that may suggest a different direction and understanding. This is a demanding task where the pressures exerted through social interaction can either be resisted in total or in part, or be adapted in some way to personal understanding. As this process continues, the knowledge of participants changes so that new standpoints come into play (see Dakich, Watt and Hooley, 2016). For some issues of course, interaction at the cultural interface has little impact in the short term and requires substantial commitment over a long period of time. As people interact at the work place, shopping centres, sporting clubs, political parties, educational programs and with neighbours, new ideas need to be confronted and accepted or rejected in some way, depending on values and beliefs. Some concepts are indelible in experience and boundaries are difficult to modify or cross. The historic persecution of IA and GRT populations results in in-group scepticism about the value of contact with mainstream populations. Hancock (2002, p. 58) notes that this lack of contact can lead to assumptions that Gypsy/Roma/Traveller people are 'secretive and must be hiding something.' He goes on to comment,

> The need to keep the non-Romani population at arms length has also prevented investigators from gaining too intimate an acquaintance with the Romani world, which has led to highly embellished and stereotyped published accounts. These in turn have kept alive the 'otherness' and distance of Romani communities, both of which factors have helped sustain a literary or fantasy image and which have worked very effectively against Romani issues being taken seriously.

Keeping at 'arm's length' may be historic reality, but given the difficulty of different cultures really understanding and respecting each other for 'togetherness' rather than 'otherness,' key strategies must be enacted to bring the 'cultural interface' into effect. Through the experience of diverse cultural issues that are usually not encountered and grappling with practical and mutual problems that are important to all, participants can reflect upon their own standpoints and open up the possibility of changing their own knowledge, practices and beliefs, indeed their own identities. This may be seen as dangerous territory for those who distinguish a challenge to custom and association. For most cultural groups, the question of who we are, who my family are, where we have come

## 134 *Connecting with Indigenous education*

from and where we are going, is confronting and eternal. A classroom that is teacher-dominated could be altered so that there is much greater opportunity for personal discussion between students and between students and teachers. The classroom could be transformed into a learning environment in which the intention is not to teach fixed knowledge and understandings into something more democratic, inclusive, and open to alternative skills, knowledge and values that emanate from the home environment. In strengthening one particular cultural aspect of learning, such as the role of language, the teaching becomes more understanding of different cultural views to teaching and learning. Country, community and language are key components of culture and therefore need to be incorporated into schooling. If a cultural context for schooling is not established then learning becomes meaningless or distorted and children will become alienated from mainstream classrooms very quickly. Taking advice from Williams (1989, p. 4) indicates why the practice of the 'cultural interface' can be a threatening strategy:

> A culture has two aspects: the known meanings and directions, which its members are trained to; the new observations and meanings, which are offered and tested. These are the ordinary processes of human societies and human minds and we see through them the nature of a culture: that it is always both traditional and creative; that it is both the most ordinary common meanings and the finest individual meanings.

Williams appears to view 'culture' here as a way of significant life and meaning that is ordinary, or one that is encountered every day, but one that involves human meaning that is individual and collective, traditional and creative, fixed yet at the same time dynamic. A culture of this type is relational with other key ideas such as social practice, learning, art, democracy and transformation impacting original standpoints. The strong connection between culture and meaning raises questions of epistemology regarding how meaning is actually approached and apprehended in the human realm.

### Discursive learning

The slow progress by educational establishments in responding to the particular issues of children from marginal and marginalised groups is due not only to lack of leeway within curricular frameworks but also to the fact that groups tend to be considered on a very individual basis. This can mean that there is no persuasive case made in relation to particular groups, but rather issues are reduced to matters of 'inclusion' within specific programs and institutions. As Kincheloe and Steinberg (1998, p. 7) have powerfully noted, 'Traditional colonialism was grounded on the deviation of those colonialised from the norm of rationality.' Educational systems need to evolve to deal with the many dilemmas confronting children from marginal groups especially those that emanate from disjuncture between home and

## Connecting with Indigenous education   135

school learning environments. Otherwise, problems of engagement will persist among those from such communities. We have previously written about these issues, but in this chapter, we seek to go a little further by proposing a model for a cultural interface that enables youngsters to engage with the contrasting learning environments constituted by home and school. We therefore bear a heavy responsibility in working within formal education systems for the benefit of all families and their children. We do not presume to speak on behalf of different groups of citizens who have different perspectives of education and expectations of that which they consider regular schooling to provide. However, our commitment to social justice and equity in schooling impel us to challenge existing structures and procedures, and to propose others that are supportive of human interest and more equitable and democratic.

With regard to another Indigenous group, the Native American academic, Sandy Grande (2004, p. 107), has pointed out that

> American Indians are not like other subjugated groups struggling to define their place within the larger democratic project. Specifically, they do not seek greater 'inclusion'; rather they are engaged in a perpetual struggle to have their legal and moral claims to sovereignty recognised. The duration and severity of this struggle for American Indians removes the question of identity from the superficial realm of cultural politics to the more profound area of cultural survival.

The questions raised by Grande create serious problems for socially just teachers and academics who work within the mainstream. In the first instance, Grande assumes that all American Indians are not concerned with colonial democratic life in association with all other national citizens and that the notion of 'inclusion' means inclusion in structures of this type that are essentially 'assimilationist' and are not supported. Progressive educators do work within current understandings of parliamentary representative democracy and while attempting to move beyond strive to make learning and curriculum more inclusive of these features. In the second instance, Grande insists that understandings of identity and culture must be non-trivial and communal and be strongly located in the main historical and anti-colonial project of survival. Progressive educators recognise this imperative and work within schools to ensure that knowledge and learning provide support for community aspiration and activism. Such questions will no doubt continue to be a source of tension between different groups as they endeavour to create a fairer world for their children and strategies for their resolution will need to be found. We propose that concepts of learning discursiveness, critical pedagogy, bricolage, funds of knowledge (FoK) and participatory practitioner research as discussed next will assist this difficult process.

In previous research and taking the earlier issues of Gypsy/Roma/Traveller and Indigenous identity and culture into account, we theorised the notion of 'discursive learning' as appropriate for disenfranchised groups (Hooley and Levinson,

## 136 *Connecting with Indigenous education*

2014). In particular, we outlined a set of principles and curriculum features for implementation in Table 7.1:

*Table 7.1* Principles of discursive learning

| Principle | Curriculum Features |
| --- | --- |
| Learning requires respect for and recognition of different worldviews of knowledge and learning | Philosophical investigation of knowledge, values, beliefs, viewpoints |
| Learning connects with the local and general physical and social environment | Country, geography, sacred sites, philosophy, customs |
| Learning integrates local and general knowledge | Community and family events, oral and written history, stories, artefacts |
| Learning arises primarily from holistic knowledge, inquiry processes and language practices | Projects, themes, learning circles, celebrations, communication |
| Learning respects community interest, knowledge and experience | Community and family curriculum decision making, history, events, stories, ideas, interpretations |
| Learning involves community members and Elders | Narratives and accounts, community visits, guest speakers, revered knowledge and wisdom |
| Learning occurs within community structures and protocols | Ways of knowing, community codes, ceremonies, conventions, extended time |
| Learning intensifies when 'community friends' assist knowledge production | Background and cross-cultural knowledge, advice, formal experience |
| Learning requires appropriate support structures | Community tutors, discussion sessions, meeting places, parent rooms, outreach scaffolding |
| Learning involves local and general protocols of monitoring, appraisal and consensus | Oral and written descriptions of learning in relation to local and general knowledge over extended time with community involvement |

In broad terms, discursive learning was described as open and discursive arrangements that encourage student action, experimentation and intellectual risk. The notion of a discursive environment for teaching and learning invokes an atmosphere of respect, recognition and reciprocity where participants communicate, question and encourage each other on significant issues. This means that the principles and features in Table 7.1 must be implemented across the curriculum at all levels and encourage the broad framework of country, community and communication/language for all students. Four examples of integrated projects follow:

- **Ecology/Environment**: In small groups or learning circles, students discuss their interest in the environment and list their main questions, sketching connections on a concept map that may be rough and incomplete at this stage. Arrangements are made to chat with parents and Elders about events that have occurred such as local floods, droughts, heatwaves and stories about local rivers, lakes, plants and animals. Various references are obtained via newspapers, books and Internet. At an agreed time, each group reports progress of their investigation and issues they will pursue next.

- **Creativity/Theatre**: In organising their annual production, a class group undertakes to arrange the music score involving both well-known and original tunes. Adopting the general theme of 'imagination' for the play, the group uses a computer synthesiser to compose appropriate music around their poems and lyrics. Some of the group are learning a musical instrument, but in general, they have little practical experience. They arrange to discuss their draft material with one of the parents, who is an accomplished violinist who advises on how to create the ambience of wind and trees.

- **Community/History**: After listening to a talk by a group of parents about how their town was settled about 200 years ago, students decided to construct a timeline as a long mural on the school walls. Old photographs and newspaper items were collected as a first step to understanding where the first residents came from and why they decided to live in the local area. A workshop was arranged where parents and Elders came together to make a first rough draft of the timeline and to suggest where further information could be obtained. Students worked through a number of possible designs with their art teachers.

- **Flora/Fauna**: During an excursion to the local botanic gardens, students collected samples of various flowers and plants together with many photographs taken on their tablet devices. They were able to discuss the characteristics of many species with the gardeners present. Back in class, they drew outlines of the main features of each sample and compared these with other shapes they were able to compile from books and Internet. A series of large colourful wall posters were drawn and displayed in the local shopping centre.

These four projects are significant for a number of reasons. While they encompass some of the key learning areas of the regular curriculum such as science, art, history and mathematics, they also embrace many of the features of discursive learning. Specifically, the overall aspects of country, community and language are clearly present with knowledge being seen as integrated and holistic across domains. Local community members and Elders are included as much as possible, with appropriate protocols being developed to ensure that offence and misunderstandings do not occur. The notion of discursive knowledge is enhanced through the consistent use of language in negotiating, implementing and communicating projects across the curriculum. Learning is taken as work in progress with usually tentative outcomes available for ongoing discussion and connections being made with recognised knowledge and viewpoints to bring local and general perspectives together. Such holistic projects enable opportunities for interaction and learning at the 'cultural interface' as participants engage ideas and practices in democratic, non-coercive ways.

## Funds of knowledge

Schools located in working class and lower economic communities have an extremely complicated task in connecting the valued knowledge of the mainstream curriculum with the life experience of children and families. Teachers in such schools attempt to utilise different pedagogies that relate specifically to students from various cultural groupings and in doing so can be considered as 'cultural brokers.' Delpit describes cultural brokerage as something that doesn't happen automatically but needs to be learned: 'Teachers really are cultural brokers who have the opportunity to connect the familiar to the unknown. We teachers have to work at learning to do that' (Delpit, 2006, p. 226). Such a role presupposes that teachers need detailed understanding of local communities and can then build cognitive bridges between the areas of interest of school, home and child. This proposition raises the question as to whether the major influences on learning exist outside of a particular school or inside particular schools and classrooms. Studies of 'school effect' (Marks, 2010) attempt to isolate such factors and determine which are more influential. In many respects, however, this is a false division, as very few teachers work in an intellectual vacuum where connections with what the child is assumed to know are not made with what the school wants the child to know. In her discussion on the meaning of culture, Gonzalez notes the various approaches and definitions that have emerged over the years and expanding on Williams (noted earlier) describes culture 'as a holistic configuration of traits and values that shaped members into viewing the world in a particular way' (Gonzalez et al 2009, p. 34). She comments on the notion of 'cultural hybridity' where all citizens draw upon an 'intercultural and hybrid knowledge base' (p. 38) as the all-embracing processes of globalisation continue. If this viewpoint offers a useful frame of analysis, then the role of the teacher in navigating and brokering cultural values and practices is exceedingly complex.

In an effort to take account of these issues and to respect and recognise the culture and experience of local communities, the notion of 'FoK' has been introduced:

> Although the term 'funds of knowledge' is not meant to replace the anthropological concept of culture, it is more precise for our purposes because of its emphasis on strategic knowledge and related activities essential to households' functioning, development and well-being. It is specific funds of knowledge pertaining to the social, economic and productive activities of people in a local region, not 'culture' in its broadest anthropological sense, that we seek to incorporate strategically into classrooms.
>
> (Moll, Amanti, Neff and Gonzalez, 2009, p. 85)

The sorts of insights into human experience offered, for example, by Shakespeare, Einstein, Hawking and the like should be accessible to all, regardless of social class or parental income. Grappling with the complexities of our common culture is one of the main aspects of schooling. The role of the school is to deal with issues that are central to our culture. Various attempts have been made throughout the

*Connecting with Indigenous education* 139

twentieth century to resolve the issue of how schools can comprehensively and inclusively interact with culture. In connecting culture and education for working class and lower economic families and communities, the 'FoK' approach investigated by Gonzalez, Moll and Amanti (2009) attempts to honour the economic, productive and social capacities of local communities and to connect with a broad and accurate view of culture rather than rely on stereotypes and assumptions. For example, if we consider the extensive problem-solving capacities of citizens in their working and daily lives, then we might expect to note a similar approach to teaching in all classrooms. If we consider a direct approach to practical situations and explanations in terms of interactions, language and communication, we might expect to see a similar approach to teaching in all classrooms. The issue here is how to take the privileged knowledge that schools and society value – and which all working class families should expect to encounter in public schools and connect meaning and understanding with the 'FoK' that communities embody? In this way, working class and lower economic culture and knowledge is not seen as a deficit or a barrier to school learning, but the broad, dynamic experiential base on which reflection takes place and from which new and transforming ideas are composed.

In researching the different approaches to 'FoK', Rodriguez (2013, p. 95) has identified three main themes:

* engaging students in the co-construction of knowledge to deepen or extend academic knowledge;
* utilising home/family and youth/popular culture and knowledge; and
* moving beyond the connections between student/family/community understandings and school content to classroom transformation and students and teachers being active agents of learning.

Some guidance about how FoK might be implemented as a pedagogy for GRT and IA youngsters (as well as for other students form Indigenous or marginalised backgrounds) has been provided earlier through Table 7.1 and also through the notion of discursiveness. This is not under-estimated as a difficult process for all schools and teachers. As an initial step, teachers will need to compile what could be called an inventory of 'cultural wealth' (Rodriguez, 2013, p. 111) involving a range of specific capitals that reflect the child's cultural, economic and community background so that local ideas and practices can be connected with school knowledge. For example, family members who discuss engines and motor mechanics around the kitchen table provide a close link with school mathematics and general science. Similarly, farriers and blacksmiths have an intimate knowledge of metallurgy, nurses of biology and health, construction workers of materials, clothing machinists and design, journalists and reporters of writing and expression, grandmothers of local and national events. The second step, however, for teachers involves taking major aspects of personal family knowledge and connecting those with key aspects of school knowledge. A discussion of perspective and angles can be related to the experience of the crane driver, or consideration of structures can draw on the work of the bricklayer and plumber. Compiling the inventory of

## 140 *Connecting with Indigenous education*

cultural wealth can be undertaken through continuing discussion with community members so that their stories, knowledge and wisdom can be expressed and documented. Over time, the collection of such knowledge around themes of interest can be compiled as community 'exemplars of knowledge' and form the basis of the school curriculum. It needs to be emphasised that 'FoK' pedagogies requires teachers to be able to draw upon the corpus of information available to bridge local and family knowledge with school knowledge and to encourage children to participate with the construction.

### Researching the bricolage

For the purposes of this study, research can be considered as developing new universal or personal knowledge, or new perspectives and arrangements of knowledge. This is a major philosophical issue at any time given the different stances towards knowledge that are possible, but becomes even more problematic when non-mainstream knowledge and experience are involved. For example, Denzin and Lincoln (2008, p. ix) lay down a powerful challenge when they declare that it is time for non-Indigenous scholars 'to dismantle, deconstruct and decolonise Western epistemologies from within, to learn that research does not have to be a dirty word, to learn that research is always already moral and political.' The Native American author Margaret Kovach (2009, p. 44) outlines a research methodology based on the traditions of Plains Cree people that include 'holistic epistemology, story, purpose, the experiential, tribal ethics, tribal ways of gaining knowledge and an overall consideration of the colonial relationship.' There is a broad distinction being drawn here between knowledge that is theorised from quantitative methods and numerical measurement compared with knowledge and ideas that are based on qualitative, descriptive and interpretive methods. For Gypsy/Roma/Traveller and IA peoples, as well as external academic researchers, these are critical questions, perhaps involving a combination of different methods of data gathering to ensure a range of evidence. The issue becomes one of developing a practical understanding of experience by inquiry, reflection and theorising that builds on community values and wisdom, not by separating practice and theorising, not by cleaving a 'low culture' disregarded form of knowledge from a 'high culture' privileged form of knowledge. For community and external researchers working together on projects of various types, this is a most complicated process and requires the generation of an agreed protocol for research guidance. Such a protocol is suggested in Table 7.2 (Hooley, 2009, p. 146).

A protocol such as this for non-mainstream research is fundamentally different to that of regular scientific research and extends past the usual ideology of consent that seems to dominate ethics procedures of formal programs. It recognises the significance of key political issues such as community identity and consciousness that cannot be ignored. It highlights the notion of practitioner research, not only in terms of participants but outcomes of research must be available for community change and improvement. The protocol suggests that any problems associated with power, bias and influence can be overcome through having longer timelines

*Connecting with Indigenous education* 141

*Table 7.2* Practitioner and community research protocol

| 1. | Community | That a program of community research will be conducted by the community in the interests of the community. |
|---|---|---|
| 2. | Ownership | That the design, implementation and evaluation for research must be undertaken by the community through informed consent with the material and intellectual outcomes remaining the property of the community. |
| 3. | Consciousness | That community research will enable questions, issues and knowledge to be pursued and at the same time, enable each participant to reflect upon their own values, practices, history, identity and land and kin relationships. |
| 4. | Culture | That knowledge is located in the culture of researchers demanding that research methodologies are non-hegemonic, explicit and culturally inclusive. |
| 5. | Readiness | That research and knowledge production should be unhurried, humble and patient and be respectful of the manner in which knowledge is socially transferred and constructed within communities. |
| 6. | Ethics | That an ethical framework for research should outline the rights and responsibilities of all participants, the nature of the interactions between them and the manner by which research principles will be met. |
| 7. | Participation | That when conducting community research, all participants will be considered as equal and will be encouraged to participate fully in all aspects of the agreed work. |
| 8. | Narrative | That the research program should become a part of the narrative of the local community providing data and experience to enhance cultural life. |
| 9. | Critical Friend | That community research will enable critical friends to participate fully in the program to assist with background knowledge, experience and advice regarding the issues under investigation and the nature of the research process itself. |
| 10. | Validation | That data, explanation, general findings and theoretical ideas emerging from community research will be validated by reference to other groups, community learning circles and communities in ongoing cycles of democratic investigation and reflection. |

that enable the discourses, ideas and generalisations that accrue being investigated through many cycles, indeed, unending cycles. A communicative rather than instrumental reason is supported, such that emerging knowledge and understanding is considered by consensus and is not imposed by outside experts. Research of this type is not separated from life, but becomes a part of life for all participants.

All research including practitioner research is theoretically grounded in some way but also takes place within a local context. This includes the social background, experience and prejudice of researchers, the capacity of the research team in resolving problems and economic and professional pressures that impact the research program. Gaining ethics approval for non-traditional research programs

142 *Connecting with Indigenous education*

can be an involved process. The interpretation of data can also be difficult, relying on different understandings being accommodated so that findings can be agreed. The type of discursive, qualitative, practitioner research outlined earlier will draw upon the diverse resources available to the program and team and the facility of the community in bringing such resources together. The US theorist and writer Joe Kincheloe was well known for his support of 'critical pedagogy,' a comprehensive approach to teaching and research that saw learning and knowledge located within the political and power structures of society and which therefore considers the wide range of factors mentioned here. Kincheloe (2009, pp. 2–3) notes, 'Critical teachers must understand not only a wide body of subject matter but also the political structure of the school.' He then states that critical pedagogy necessitates 'alternative bodies of knowledge produced by marginalised or low-status groups, the way power operates to construct identities and oppress particular groups, the modus operandi of the way social regulation operates, the complex processes of racism . . .' Kincheloe had worked with Native Americans and had written on Indigenous epistemologies and saw critical pedagogy as a broad framework within which the struggle for educational liberation is built. The exact manner in which this proceeds needs to be worked through by all colleagues concerned.

Kincheloe also identified the French concept of 'bricolage' as a philosophical approach to learning, knowledge and research and a means by which the various features of human life and scholarship impact on knowing, the features of history, economics and the like noted earlier. Drawing on the work of Levi-Strauss (1966) and Denzin and Lincoln (2000), Kincheloe argued for the conception of teacher and researcher as 'bricoleur' such that diverse methodologies and understandings are brought together in the act of inquiry and research. He recognised that the complexity of the bricolage required knowing well a range of knowledge disciplines and that

> any social, cultural, psychological, or pedagogical object of inquiry is inseparable from its context, the language used to describe it, its historical situatedness in a larger ongoing process and the socially and culturally constructed interpretations of its meaning(s) as an entity in the world.
>
> (Kincheloe, 2011, p. 180)

This is no easy task and will probably require teams of practitioners bringing to bear their combined disciplinary know-how, philosophies and experience on difficult problems and ideas. One lifetime is not enough. A critique of both quantitative and qualitative methods in the social sciences and humanities would reveal issues of bias, accuracy, consistency and authentication as well as the lack of relationship between the objective and subjective that raise many troubling issues regarding the stability and trustworthiness of educational research. Kincheloe's commitment to establishing a new comprehensive, cultural, respectful, inclusive approach of knowing, of rigorous interpretation of experience and of theorising through the bricolage opened up a new vision of learning and schooling for teachers and students alike.

Advocating the practice of research bricolage has the advantage that it is highly respectful of community culture and values. However, it has the disadvantage of not yet having gained acceptance as a recognised research methodology and the validity of its outcomes. There is extensive debate in qualitative research generally regarding new methodologies and like all innovation, new approaches go through a process of trial, documentation, discussion and refinement over a period of time before being accepted into the pantheon. Given that the proposal for discursive knowledge and research bricolage is being advanced for those communities that work within mainstream environments such as regular schooling, then ways must be found of data gathering and theorising of findings that relate directly to systemic operation and enhancement. For example, consider a group of community members who are concerned about improving the literacy and numeracy achievement of their children together with their engagement with schooling. They develop a practitioner research protocol with a team of academic researchers and utilising their inventory of cultural wealth set about detailing the literacy and numeracy experience of their children at home. This involves discussion with parents and Elders, talking with friends and family, attending local events and ceremonies, interacting at sport and hobby clubs, visiting work sites, browsing newspapers and magazines, utilising computer applications, journeys through cities and countryside, writing letters, notes and e-communications and visiting libraries, museums and galleries. From this catalogue, key features of social life and knowledge can be connected with a broad understanding of literacy and numeracy and how they connect – or do not connect – to main factors of school life and knowledge. Community experience can be documented in various written, visual or oral form. Academics or others working as critical friends analyse community-school experience and can suggest explanations and other data to collect in a next cycle. A number of these steps are commonplace in recognised research, but the range of data collected and the relationship between participants are much more personal and non-traditional. For GRT and IA groups who are concerned with impacting systemic practices, establishing trust with a recognised academic team who are keen to confront the bricolage and change the world is an ongoing task.

## Conclusion: cultural change for recognition and respect

We have been concerned with designing a pathway into privileged knowledge encountered in mainstream schools for Gypsy/Roma/Traveller and IA peoples – and indeed, for disenfranchised peoples generally (Levinson and Hooley, 2014). In democratic countries, access to such knowledge is an indispensable human right regardless of socio-economic background. Throughout the discussion earlier, we have identified a number of issues that impinge on this process, issues such as cultural interface, identity and culture, community and school knowledge, discursive teaching and learning, bricolage and bricoleur, FoK, critical pedagogy and participatory practitioner research. Combining and interrelating these factors generates a model of Discursive Cultural Knowledge Formation which we now propose as shown in Figure 7.1:

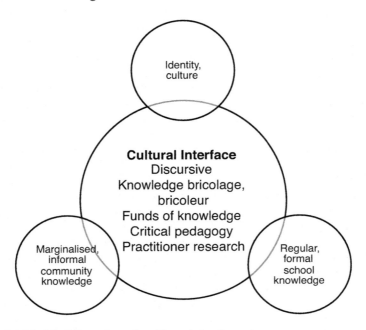

*Figure 7.1* Model of discursive cultural knowledge formation

Proposing a generalised model of Discursive Cultural Knowledge Formation should make available to schools everywhere an approach that engages not only marginalised and alienated students but students from a variety of backgrounds. It follows that the factors so identified in the model are not usually characteristic of curriculum and teaching either because more traditional approaches dominate or procedures and resources make them unfeasible. Interestingly, there is a view that rather than concentrating on traditional mathematics and science at the heart of European Enlightenment, and as a basis for educating more scientists and engineers, there is a need for pedagogical approaches that result in students who can 'think broadly' (Brooks, 2013, p. 38). In recognising this task as a difficult one, Brooks comments on 'abandoning the culture of grades and exams and moving to assessments centred on a student's portfolio of projects.' This will be to the advantage of marginalised (if not all) students and suits the discursive cultural basis of our approach as the emphasis on predetermined slices of knowledge is reduced. The model is essentially epistemological in that all factors are considered a part of the learning process and the construction and reconstruction of knowledge and meaning by participants. As a model, it does not solve all the pedagogical issues faced by teachers in different subject areas; these issues must be solved by the teachers themselves in relation to particular groups of students they encounter at any given time. However, the model does seem to favour rich-language, negotiated project, student-centred/teacher guided relationships and deep human interest in wanting to know.

There is a further significant aspect of the model of discursive cultural knowledge. A major difference between conservative quantitative approaches to knowledge production and progressive qualitative (and/or mixed methods) approaches is the impact that conducting the research has on participants themselves. Progressive researchers do not adopt a remote, unemotional 'fly on the wall' position. That is, regardless of research findings, a racist researcher can remain a racist, a violent researcher can remain violent and an elitist researcher can remain elitist. On the other hand, when researchers open themselves up to the research process as a participant and experiences, the reality of problems, contradictions and challenges to their own views, their appreciation and understanding begin to change. This is the consequence of working at the cultural interface rather than in a separate isolated domain. There is a major lesson here for understanding how curriculum and pedagogy can change to meet the learning needs of all groups in the classroom. Teachers who pursue projects at the cultural interface and a mix of factors so outlined in the model are committing themselves, courageously, to respecting the role of community identity and culture in learning and schooling. They will construct and reconstruct their own knowledge, practices and bias in light of new discursive evidence and experience. Ultimately, racism and colonialism, ignorance and cant will not withstand the strength of truthfulness and reason shaped by the citizens themselves.

## Acknowledgement

This chapter draws upon the research of Dr Neil Hooley, College of Education, Victoria University, Australia and Professor Martin Levinson, School of Education, Bath Spa University, United Kingdom. Both authors are committed to social justice and educational equity. They work and learn with IA peoples and Gypsy/Roma/Traveller peoples respectively to document and better understand community culture, values and practices so that regular schooling can become more informed and respectful of all families.

## Notes

1 The term 'Indigenous' used in this paper refers to Aboriginal peoples on the mainland of Australia and the island state of Tasmania and to the Torres Strait Islander people of the Torres Strait between the state of Queensland and Papua New Guinea. The terms 'Aboriginal,' or 'Aboriginal and Torres Strait Islander' are preferred in some areas. There is discussion across Australia regarding the crucial differences between the words Aboriginal and Indigenous and how they are interpreted by different groups of people. When being introduced, most Indigenous people note their country of origin within Australia such as Yorta Yorta, Gundijtmara etc. A capital letter is used for Indigenous in the same way that capital letters are used for English, French or New Zealand peoples. A capital letter is also used for the word 'Elder' as a mark of respect for experienced,

146 *Connecting with Indigenous education*

responsible and wise community members. The titles 'aunty' and 'uncle' are used to designate community Elders.

2 The term Gypsy/Roma/Traveller is used in this chapter although there is fluidity in the use of terms to describe this group. This is an outcome both of shifts in policy usage and also to changing preferences with regard to self-ascription. For many years in the United Kingdom, there was a preference in policy documents and amongst practitioners to use the term 'Travellers.' The word 'Gypsy' had been used pejoratively in the media, and this seemed neutral. However, the term 'Travellers' fails to acknowledge any rights as a separate ethnic group, and is based purely on lifestyle. Moreover, there was resentment within the group of New Age or New Travellers who were often linked to the traditional Travellers and were perceived by many as having brought about repressive legislation, restricting movement. Within schools, younger members of the group have often opted for the term 'Traveller,' as it is neutral, but this varies. In recent years, the term 'Roma' has begun to be used more widely. This provides a means of differentiating between the communities who are long established in the UK and those who have arrived in recent years from Central and Eastern Europe. At the same time, it should be noted that many of British born Gypsies would also describe themselves as Roma. And once again, within the group many who perceive themselves as 'true Roma' do not include other Travellers, such as those from Irish or Scottish Traveller backgrounds, within that category.

# 8 Appraising the practice turn in teacher education

> Reaching down into the hidden depths
> reveals intensities and uncertainties
> that challenge our very subjectivity
> contradictions that need to be confronted
> if clarities of our being are embraced
> unconditionally, to know, to give, to love.

As with education itself, teacher education under capitalism will exist to support the philosophical, economic and cultural dictates of capitalism. However, in countries that allow various forms of citizen debate and participation, there will be opportunities to refine the harshness of economic dominance and to amend educational arrangements for more social and democratic outcomes. In accord with Table 5.7 in Chapter 5, therefore, this chapter discusses a major aspect of teacher education that can realistically be strengthened across all programs and become one of its defining features. In some respects, the notion of *practice-theorising* for teacher education is not new, but within the context of Table 5.7 does take on vastly added significance. For example, Hagger and McIntyre (2006, p. 170) point out,

> Practical theorising needs initially to be a social activity, led by the mentor, who provides a model by asking appropriate questions about the observed lesson, using an appropriate range of criteria and drawing on a range of appropriate sources of evidence. By the end of the programme, it needs to be a mental activity in which the beginning teacher engages habitually, competently and fluently.

In this way, Hager and McIntyre connect the social and the mental such that there is a fluid and shifting relationship between them, moving backwards and forwards. As this process continues, participants being to think more about practice and practice more their thinking, as they adapt and distil their understandings of experience. The connected components of *practice-theorising* become as one, indistinguishable in mind and action. This is the essential aspect of formal education and of teacher education that is a serious weakness in traditional approaches to teaching

## 148 *Appraising the practice turn*

and learning around the world (Biesta, 2015c). In discussing the nature of practice in more detail next, we review its historical context and its connections with the philosophy of pragmatism.

Two competing philosophies of humanity and of knowledge have existed throughout the twentieth century and continue today. First, a dominant conservative and rationalistic view that considers knowledge and understanding arise from human reason alone. Second, a progressive and experiential view that deems all knowledge as involving social acts and inquiry including reflection on those acts. For over 30 years, neoliberalism in its own interests has exacerbated this difference such that the understanding and development of theory is seen to be accessible by some, whereas practice, or applied theory, can be utilised by many. Perhaps the majority of schools strengthen this divide by considering some subjects to be theory, best taught before lunch where concentration is at a maximum, while other subjects are practical, best conducted in the afternoon with activity and energy. Teacher education has struggled to reconcile the fracture between theory and practice in knowledge and learning, especially when defending its location in universities. Conservative critics of teacher education argue that programs should be more closely related to the reality of schools and that more time for pre-service teachers should be spent in school classrooms rather than remote university lecture theatres. This notion of turning towards practice (sometimes called practice-based or school-based) usually centres on didactic and behaviouristic methods of teaching, where knowledge is known 'at a distance' from learners. A second interpretation of 'practice turn,' however, situates teacher education within a broad historical and philosophical tradition that emphasises social action, personal and community reflection and strategies for cultural change that seek a better world. The term *practice-theorising* is used in this chapter to describe the central process of this latter progressive tradition whereby all participants submit their practice and comprehensions to not only their own critique, but to the ongoing critique of colleagues, the literature and the integrity of social and professional practice.

Given attention to the 'practice turn' for teaching generally, the contemporary notion of 'practice' as identified by the practice theorist Schatzki (2001, p. 2), emergent and contested as it is, involves 'embodied, materially mediated arrays of human activity centrally organized around shared practical understanding.' These arrays of social activity are clearly evident in schools and comprise the majority and moral essence of teachers' work. Alasdair MacIntyre (1985, p. 187) had a similar view, but provided additional detail, especially important for teachers:

> Any coherent and complex form of socially established co-operative human activity through which goods internal to that form of activity are realised in the course of trying to achieve those standards of excellence which are appropriate to and partially definitive of that form of activity, with the result that human powers to achieve excellence and human conceptions to the ends and goods involved, are systematically extended.

*Appraising the practice turn*   149

What exactly constitutes the 'internal goods' of practice so defined is not entirely clear from MacIntyre's writing, but as an example, they could include dialogue regarding social purpose, processes of inquiry in the design, pursuit and evaluation of the activity, the use of language for expression and explanation and the confronting of ethical questions as they arise. Looked at in this way, the properties or 'internal goods' of teaching practice (and practices in other professions) are encountered and understood only by participation in teaching practice as teachers and students work together on areas of their interest. That is, such internal properties cannot be imposed externally, but must be experienced through practices that include and demonstrate discussion, inquiry, evaluation and ethical issues combined for social purpose. When ecologies of this type are created, teachers and students are involved in 'learning as social practice' across all levels of schooling and across all subject content (Jons, 2014). The implications of this proposal for knowledge, teaching and learning is discussed next. While it may not have been specifically spoken of as 'social practice,' schooling during the welfare state period (1945–1975) had a more civic and democratic orientation than today, with children from working families staying at school longer to become well-informed citizens. During the Neoliberal period (1980-present), this tendency has been reversed by policymakers in many countries with emphasis being placed on the economic imperatives of education with their competitive, private and market-positioning outcomes. For these reasons, schooling today is often construed as transmitting accepted truths and facts that can be adopted by students and then be repeated, measured and tested for accuracy. The notion that learning is a social practice comprising the experience of internal goods or properties as the basis of personal learning and understanding struggles to survive.

It may be understandable that schooling can be seen as primarily delivering factual knowledge to children, but an inquiry-based or practice-based approach has contested this view for a long time. Over the past 100 years, Dewey was a strong supporter of modern science and of its presence in the curriculum of schools. However, he was more concerned with its capacity for engaging children (indeed citizens) with worthwhile knowledge and the distinction between defensible knowledge, opinion and dogma. Dewey saw the importance of involving children with scientific content through the process of scientific method, but with his theory of pragmatic inquiry learning, he argued that method is not mandated as a set of procedures or rules, but emerges for each experimenter through ongoing investigation. In this sense, he is noting a division between how a particular experiment might be conducted and the specific steps involved and how science itself as a field of human activity – or practice – is conceived. As Dewey (2008, p. 254) pointed out,

> For though the existing state of science is *one* of the interests and cares that determine the selection of things to be investigated, it is not the only one. Problems are not self-selecting and the *direction* taken by inquiry is determined by the human factors of dominant interest and concern that affect the choice of the matters to be specifically inquired into.

150 *Appraising the practice turn*

This is salutary advice for how school curriculum is planned and implemented. Merely passing on facts and information that have been accumulated by others in other places at other times will not necessarily enthuse learners of any age, as they will be removed from community context and will most likely find it difficult to make connections between the interwoven threads and nodes of valued community experience. Immersing participants in experience as social practice is a non-sequential prerequisite for abstracting knowledge and meaning from social practice, without which learning is expected to occur in a vacuum. Any consideration of a 'practice turn' in education therefore must have strong justification of its epistemological purpose and direction.

## Epistemology: the nature of knowledge and learning

Little attention has been provided to epistemology during the neoliberal era. This has made it difficult for detailed responses to market-driven curricula to come forward, including more progressive proposals for teacher education. A broad definition of epistemology involves the nature of knowledge, where it comes from and how it is understood by citizens. This must be clear to execute a strong commitment that in all economies and not only the robust, public schooling should provide all children regardless of background with access to and meaningful investigation of the major ideas and schema of significant knowledge. This necessarily entails respect for the customs, culture and comprehension of local communities as the framework for the survey and analysis of accepted understandings as new learnings are considered (Aronson and Laughter, 2016). In this regard, 'learning as a social practice' (Mead, 1962) constitutes a central principle of learning and takes as a major principle the philosophy of pragmatism developed in particular by Peirce, James and Dewey. According to Peirce (1992/1999),

> Consider what effects which might conceivably have practical bearings we might conceive the object of our conception to have. Then our conception of the effect is the whole of our conception of the object.

Pragmatism can be misinterpreted as concentrating on the outcome of an event only and, with different observers engaging the outcome differently, can be seen as leading to knowledge relativism. It is clear, however, from the statement by Peirce that observing and interpreting the effect enables consideration and understanding of the object. That is, meaning is obtained through reflecting on the effect, not merely noting the effect alone. As more and more participants undertake the event and effect and consider the relationship between objects and effects, then meaning and understanding are consolidated over time. Making a cake by changing the ingredients and noting what happens not only provides evidence of the impact different ingredients make on the cake but also develops a new apprehension of the object 'cake' itself. Truthfulness of 'cake' emerges over time. What pragmatism advocated therefore was an active process of experience, experimentation and reflection out of which substantial and coalesced knowledge

*Appraising the practice turn* 151

would become apparent. Exactly how humans come to understand knowledge remains a mysterious process, except that different people might suggest that after an experience or combination of experiences over time, they have a different 'feeling' or 'awareness' regarding a particular concept than what they had before. This is congruent with Dewey's notion that learning involves the 'construction and reconstruction of experience' that must be undertaken by each person rather than ideas or propositions simply being accepted by each person. In this respect, each person must reinvent the wheel for him or herself and construct his or her own awareness and meaning.

In addition to the work of Dewy and colleagues on pragmatism and inquiry, the theories of the French sociologist Pierre Bourdieu can also provide a guide to the nature of learning and how we might conceptualise in more detail how humans come to participate with different knowledge structures. His concepts of habitus, field and various forms of capital such as the cultural and symbolic are central to his thought and method on these points. It is worth quoting at length the notion of habitus developed by Bourdieu (1990, p. 53) to begin our analysis of how practice and practical reasoning can establish a relationship between objective and subjective knowing:

> The conditionings associated with a particular class of conditions of existence produce habitus, systems of durable, transposable dispositions, structured structures predisposed to function as structuring structures, that is, as principles which generate and organise practices and representations that can be objectively adapted to their outcomes without presupposing a conscious aiming at ends or expressed mastery of the operations necessary in order to attain them. Objectively 'regulated' and 'regular' without being in any way the product of obedience to rules, they can be collectively orchestrated without being the product of the organising action of a conductor.

This is Bourdieu's attempt at explaining human creativity and improvisation against the pressure of conservative and traditional social forces (Zipin and Nuttall, 2016). Bourdieu accomplishes this task through the epistemological concepts of practical sense and reflexivity. Practical sense or doxa in Bourdieuian terms involves our understanding of a particular field of action, its rules and procedures and how progress is made within acceptable boundaries. Reflexivity and its historical, material and structural location assumes a deeper understanding of the field and its knowledges so that initiatives can be taken as the circumstances alter to benefit a particular social actor and to support agency. These two notions enable learning to be constructed as experience is gained, learning that occurs within the framework of the habitus and in relation to it. Like Dewey, Bourdieu's approach is descriptive in character and can therefore be criticised in descriptive terms. Conceptualising learning, however, as arising from continuing social practice such that a reflexive relationship can be established between field and habitus, indicates that learning is a dynamic social process incorporating personal and community experience, a process that is hampered or severed when access to experience and

152  *Appraising the practice turn*

the generation of new tentative experience is denied. This model of epistemology, where to be human is to learn and where all humans are understood as constructing their own knowledge from the basis of their own experience, stands in stark contrast to the view that knowledge is known externally and is transmitted by experts.

Philosophical considerations of epistemology, or the nature of knowledge, must of necessity raise questions of ontology or the nature of human existence, the context within which knowledge and learning occurs. Teachers, for example, can see themselves as learners, as co-producers of knowledge with students and colleagues, or as isolated experts who already 'know' knowledge and can accurately pass on meaning to others. The epistemological side of this equation can be stated as 'I think (act), therefore I am (exist),' or ontologically, 'I am (exist), therefore I think (act).' How humans came to exist and have become the way they are is difficult to answer for some in the latter case, whereas in the former case, humans have become the way they are through continuous acting and experience. It may be appropriate to suggest then that after thousands of years of acting, thinking and existing that we can see a reflexive dialectic between ontology and epistemology such that both are respected and taken into account for educational purposes. In this way, teachers develop a broad understanding of themselves as teachers and learners and their complicated social role and do not confine themselves to a mechanical or technical role of teaching in the classroom. If learning is characteristic of being human, then the epistemological-ontological dialectic creates humans as constantly learning from birth to death, of being in transformation as they seek more profound meaning from their thinking, acting and existence. There is an obvious choice to be made for teachers when planning curriculum and assessment.

## Practice as progressive or conservative teaching

Considering outcomes of the immersion of teachers and pre-service teachers in a broad understanding of professional practice leads to the notion of *practice-theorising*. As noted earlier, such an interpretation of practice situates teacher education within a broad historical and philosophical tradition emphasising social action, personal and community reflection and strategies for cultural change that seek a better world. The central feature of this progressive process involves all participants submitting their practice and comprehensions to not only their own critique, but to the ongoing critique of colleagues, the literature and the integrity of social and professional practice. It was also suggested earlier that the 'internal goods' of practice as suggested by MacIntyre could include attributes or properties such as dialogue regarding social purpose, processes of inquiry in the design, pursuit and evaluation of the activity, the use of language for expression and explanation and the confronting of ethical questions as they arise throughout the practice. While this description gives a thorough and complex definition of practice, it also goes beyond a view of teachers and teaching that is confined to the transmission of subject content as the sole means by which the 'quality' of teaching and learning is determined. Thoughtful and reflexive human engagement with the social and physical worlds cannot be directed externally through regulation and method, but it relies on internal purpose and interest as meaning and significance are investigated. Biesta (2013) takes up this question when he comments on what he calls 'virtuous professionals' and how teachers might become 'educationally wise.' These matters will be discussed more fully later in the chapter. What follows now are three school scenarios of how progressive teaching and learning settings can support the generation of *practice-theorising* for teachers and students alike:

## Scenario 1: mathematics

Working in learning circles of about four members each, Year 8 students negotiated a series of projects regarding the mathematics of flowers. One group decided to monitor the surface area of rose petals as the blooms expand over time and to see if there are any connections with the changing colour of the flowers and weather conditions. They have enlisted the support of the school's caretaker who has tended a rose garden at the front of the school for many years as his pride and joy. Over a period of weeks, each student carefully unravelled a number of blooms to isolate individual petals, placing each on a sheet of squared paper to estimate area. As a group, they discuss their accumulated data and graph area against colour estimated through a colour chart they have devised. Recognising their results as a first approximation, they report to the class that the total area of petals seems to reach a maximum that is roughly proportionate to the intensity of colour, which is then maintained depending on the amount of sunlight and water available. 'Aren't roses beautiful, I've never taken much notice of how the petals fit together before.' Classmates suggest that an excursion to the local botanical gardens could provide further information regarding the various properties of flowers and whether or not the use of fertiliser makes any difference. One student said that she had heard her mother talking about a 'blue' rose and that she thought interfering with nature was quite wrong.

## Scenario 2: science

Year 9 students were busily engaged in groups of two in conducting a series of small experiments regarding the states of matter. They were able to proceed at their own pace through many experiments that had been outlined on iPad files, discussing with the teacher any problems, results and other research that caught their interest. One group was gently heating a small amount of an orange power in an ignition tube. Suddenly, the orange powder transformed itself into a grey sludge in the bulb of the tube, prompting excited comments such as 'Did you see that?' 'Can we do that again?' and 'What happened?' Coming over, the teacher suggested that the experiment be conducted again to see if the same result could be obtained. Holding up the second product of grey sludge, the teacher asked whether any clue could be gained from the name of the powder, mercuric oxide? 'Mercuric – sounds like mercury,' puzzled one student with a frown 'and oxide sounds like oxygen.' As other suggestions were made, the teacher pondered that perhaps the powder was a compound made up of mercury and oxygen together and that as it was heated with

154  *Appraising the practice turn*

the Bunsen flame, the bond holding them together was broken. 'This might drive the oxygen off and leave mercury in the bottom, isn't that amazing?' 'I thought mercury was that stuff in thermometers,' exclaimed a student who had wandered over from another group, 'perhaps we could make one if we could heat enough powder!' 'But anyhow, what's a bond?'

## Scenario 3: literature

Small groups of Year 10 students were scattered around the classroom discussing the current book they were reading. They were very familiar with a wide range of computer-based devices including their indispensable smart phones and surveillance cameras they saw in many of the streets and shopping centres of town. Based on numerous videos they had watched, the message from George Orwell about 'Big Brother' was realistic and a worry, although some could see both sides of the issue. 'It might be possible that someone has a bomb and even to catch a robber, we have to be prepared.' 'Besides, most people follow the law, so there's no harm.' Sitting down and catching the end of this conversation, the teacher wondered how an author like Orwell could predict the future and raise difficult issues that would continue to confront citizens after so many years. 'He must have had a wild scary imagination, Miss, just like J. P. Rowling, where they step outside their own lives, science fiction is like that too.' Another student who had been very quiet, said hesitatingly that more people should have taken serious notice of Orwell's predictions as they seemed to be becoming true and were changing how we thought about each other. 'Well, I think it's just a story, just like Harry Potter that we know isn't true and what's more important is how it's written and how situations and feelings are described, it's all in the language. We know that C. S. Lewis was just telling a story about Narnia, don't we!' Their exploration lapsed into silence for a moment as they returned to the next paragraph they were reading as a group, each with their own thoughts, each being changed by meaning and exploits on the page.

For teachers and pre-service teachers involved in classrooms depicted earlier, there is rich potential for *practice-theorising* of teaching and learning for all participants. It should be noted that a major difference with reflective practice is the continuing process of *practice-theorising* applying rational knowledge so created to new situations, the step of investigating rational knowledge in social practice. In the scenarios, described topics and projects of mutual interest are being negotiated and investigated, observations are discussed along the way without judgements being imposed, those with more experience are able to comment and suggest when outcomes need some explanation and all activities can be located in historical and ethical frameworks. Knowledge is integrated to allow for key ideas to be linked across domains when needed. For school students, issues that emerge from practice are open to theorising by the groups concerned, whether this involves the structure of plant species, the nature of the chemical bond, or the purpose of literature. For teachers and pre-service teachers, contemplation involves the manner by which school students connect their prevailing cultural knowledge with new experience, how personal and community interest can be extended to embrace systematic

*Appraising the practice turn* 155

explanation and how 'knowledge gives a sense of delight and of intellectual travel beyond the information given' (Bruner, 1979, p. 109) is grasped by all students. Bruner went on to suggest that arising from this perspective, depth and continuity rather than coverage are crucial for teaching and that an educated person 'should have a sense of what knowledge is like in some field of inquiry, to know it in its connectedness and with a feeling for how the knowledge is gained.' It is significant that progressive approaches to teaching and learning as noted earlier recognise that an over-emphasis on the formalities of teaching can distract from and diminish learning. Rather, flexible and open learning environments are created that encourage students to genuinely experiment with their social and physical worlds in the active and continuing construction and reconstruction of their experience. The conservative view that encourages the acceptance of exotic experience imposed by others, can only alienate and frustrate.

## Emerging arrangements of teacher education: core practices, clinical, praxis

To relate the philosophy – or ideology- of practice more closely to current programs in teacher education (Miles, Lemon, Mitchell and Reid, 2016) and to attempt to ascertain whether a 'practice turn' of some type has been adopted, three emerging approaches in teacher education that are either gaining in application or audience have been identified for discussion: core practices, critical praxis and clinical approaches. Each will need to be analysed on the basis of current evidence or intent regarding an explicit definition of practice and whether or not this constitutes a shift in understanding of practice from previous programs. At this early stage of their development, it may be the evidence available for each arrangement is limited, but the direction being investigated and implemented may be distinctly discernible. In the brief summaries that follow, emphasis is restricted to philosophical detail rather than information regarding school placements, role of mentors, numbers of pre-service teachers involved, necessary resources etc.

### Core practices

Initiated mainly in the United States of America, the core practices approach distinguishes itself from traditional views of teacher education in a number of key ways. Firstly, challenging the common view of teaching as something that can be mostly learned through experience, core practices instead conceptualises teaching as unnatural, intricate, interactional and improvisational work. Secondly, recent efforts have focused on a 'deliberate orientation toward "ambitious" teaching in which subject matter figures prominently' (Fornazi, 2014, p. 360), distinguishing current core practices work from prior attempts at practice-based teacher education to orient teacher education around practice (Fornazi, 2014). Grossman (2009) argues that to do this, teacher educators need to add pedagogies of enactment to their existing repertoire of pedagogies of investigation and reflection (Grossman, 2009). By utilising representations, decompositions and approximations of practice in professional

## 156  *Appraising the practice turn*

education, enactment pedagogies, such as video analysis and rehearsal, acknowledge the endemic difficulties of teaching defined in these ways, while trying to help novices learn to manage them (Fornazi, 2014). Currently, teacher education programs appear to be caught in the status quo of an 'add-on' type of response when addressing calls for change in teacher education or when complying with policy directives, allowing the rigid separation among and between methods and foundation courses, and between university courses and field placements, to remain unchanged. Re-organisation of programs around a set of core practices, strikes at the heart of this 'add-on' response, challenging teacher educators instead to redesign programs 'in ways that allow pre-service teachers to learn about the multiple aspects of teaching in an integrated fashion' (Grossman, 2009).

### Clinical approaches

The notion of 'clinical' approaches in education and teacher education is difficult to pursue because of the lack of research data and evidence to date. However, according to the University of Melbourne (MGSE, 2016) clinical teachers proceed by inter alia monitoring and evaluating their impact on learning and adapting the lesson to meet the needs of each student, using evidence about what each student knows and understands at the start of the teaching period to inform their teaching interventions, constructing appropriate teaching and learning environments for every student and continuously evaluating the impact of their teaching, to inform next steps (McLean, 2013). It has been difficult to obtain detail regarding the notion of clinical approaches to teaching, but this description seems to be unaware of what teachers actually do in classrooms and the manner by which they go about their work. It is unfortunate that the notion of 'clinical' denotes a medical connection, with the inference that education can be improved by importing a process from another profession; it is not clear why medicine is preferred. Questions regarding clinical approaches and what counts as evidence, how are professional decisions made and what happens when the expected results are not obtained, remain to be answered. Not only is discussion of evidence-based medicine more complicated in practice than what is assumed, but that attempting to impose the ideology of evidence-based medicine on education subverts the philosophy of education and learning as a social practice. It subverts the role of the teacher as researcher in making professional judgements in the interests of local communities, families and students (Biesta, 2015a; Fordham, 2016; Hulse and Hulme, 2012). Professionals in all fields do not merely apply outcomes from randomised control trials, but are responsible for considering the wide range of evidence at their disposal and the social, cultural and political contexts within which learning and social participation occurs.

### Praxis learning

In moving beyond *practice* as professional activity to achieve particular educational consequences that are governed by a set of theorised parameters to ensure consensus of participants, to *praxis* as cycles of ethically framed action or

*Appraising the practice turn* 157

rationality regarding what is good and appropriate, based on a system of values and judgement rather than rules or laws to improve teaching and learning, a major philosophical leap is being made (Biesta, 2015b). Schooling is being imbued with a moral purpose about what teaching and learning are for in the mutual interest of participants. Teaching and learning practice can be guided by a *praxis inquiry protocol* (Arnold, Edwards, Hooley and Williams, 2012a) that involves participants describing, explaining, theorising and changing practice. Depending on the social, economic and educational conditions that prevail, however, it is also possible to consider the notion of *critical praxis*, defined as cycles of ethically framed action or rationality regarding what is good and appropriate, based on a system of values rather than rules or laws and requires judgements in practice to be made. Critical praxis brings together the ideas of ideology critique, self-reflexive consciousness and emancipatory action for improved teaching and learning and the public good. Establishing the conditions for both praxis inquiry and critical praxis within regular professional practice will be a complicated, long-term task. For teacher education constrained as it is by university, registration and employment requirements, it may be that a comprehensive set of conditions may only be possible in a small number of locations and will need to be constantly refreshed. Alternatively, a number of the suggested conditions may be possible and that some progress can be made towards becoming more critical for some participants.

It is clear that each of the three arrangements noted earlier has attempted to give greater weight to classroom practice than previous programs for teacher education. This is indicated by comments such as 'utilising representations, decompositions and approximations of practice in professional education' (core practices), 'monitoring and evaluating impact on learning and adapting the lesson to meet the needs of each student' (clinical) and 'a system of values and judgement rather than rules or laws to improve teaching and learning' (praxis). The extent to which this direction has been implemented is not obvious, or whether the nature of practice envisaged is significantly different to what went before. If the intended result is to further establish teacher dominance in classrooms, then a conservative teacher education is becoming more conservative. None of the three arrangements, however, has provided specific detail on particular approaches to classroom pedagogies, although it is consistent with the overall approach to consider core practices as supporting a learner-centred approach, clinical teaching as supporting a knowledge-centred approach and praxis learning as a society-centred approach. Zeichner (2012, p. 377) suggests that practice-based teacher education has a long history and has renewed attention, but there remains considerable variation across the United States (for example) as to what should be taught. This general proposition also applies to the three initiatives discussed earlier until such time as more research data become available.

## Researching practice and teacher education

There is a significant ideological difference between envisaging schooling, teaching and learning as merely a 'practical' activity whereby knowledge that is known and privileged is passed from expert to novice, compared with learning about the

## 158 *Appraising the practice turn*

nature of knowledge itself and the identification of worthwhile knowledge for use and meaning. In strategic terms, a 'practice turn' can be appropriated to support either imperative, with the former conservative practice emphasizing more classroom-based know-how and the latter progressive practice supporting more practice-theorising know-that. Each approach needs to locate personal learning in agenda of established knowledge for either autocratic acceptance or democratic investigation. In their extensive survey of research on teacher preparation, Cochran-Smith and Villegas (2015, pp. 8–12) suggest a framework of 'research as historically situated social practice.' They argue that this is required to take into account the political, economic and social forces that impact education and to recognise the interests and epistemologies of researchers that guide the research they undertake. Additionally, they refer to Bourdieu in recommending a research perspective of 'social practice' rather than 'paradigm,' as a means of allowing these features to be admitted and incorporated. Teacher education research at present is, however, somewhat inadequate in providing a database for robust discussion of educational practice and for policy determinations (Darling-Hammond, 2016). However, small-scale research projects of teaching practice and utilising both qualitative and quantitative methods provide useful insights at the local level, but need more rigorous interrogation for broader application. Longitudinal and large-scale projects of teaching practice appear to be in the minority, especially those that are multifaceted as described by Cochran-Smith and Villegas earlier.

A powerful argument for having a clear understanding of the purposes of education is provided by Biesta (2013, p. 134), when he raises the question of being 'educationally wise' and making 'wise judgements.' In referring to Aristotle, Biesta writes, 'Practical wisdom is not to be understood as a set of skills or dispositions or a set of competences, but rather denotes a certain quality or excellence of the person.' As discussed earlier, he draws on the notion of *praxis* to contend that teachers need to live well and construct educational settings that have the best interests of students at heart and where knowledge and learning can be pursued without fear or favour. Again noting Aristotle, Biesta calls being encouraged to make wise educational judgements as a values or 'virtues-based approach to teacher education' (p. 135). For teachers and students, a virtuous life will involve living and learning for the public good and of attempting to act appropriately and as knowledgeably as possible in everything that is done. In this sense, acts of virtue may involve courage in undertaking uncertain and risky projects, generosity when working and learning with others, humility when sharing observations and options and persistence when projects are difficult and confusing. Defining teacher 'quality' as teacher 'character' in this way radically redefines schooling and teaching and provides much greater articulation of 'practice turn.' A narrow understanding of skills and competences has always been rejected by progressive educators in favour of student-centred approaches to knowledge and learning. It has been difficult, however, to establish the conditions for a 'practice turn' to *practice-theorising* capable of realizing in practice questions of equity and virtue. More often than not, progressive intent is nominated without the mechanisms for enactment.

*Appraising the practice turn* 159

Accordingly, researching teacher education and pre-service teacher education needs to occur within an explicit understanding of educational purpose that is then pursued through wise and prudent action and judgement by all participants. It needs to take into account the social setting in which knowledge is constructed and incorporate both small-scale and large-scale projects with continuity and rigour. In recognizing itself as social practice, all educational research needs to grapple with the historical and situated understanding of practice and how practice and theory/theorising come together in human experience. These questions were of central concern to Dewey (2012, p. 252) who, in summarizing his perspective of modern philosophy, commented,

> Certain assumptions regarding the nature of knowledge sense have persisted throughout pretty much the whole course of philosophical discussion. Certain other assumptions, used as premises in defining knowledge, account for that division into opposed schools that marks modern epistemological theory. The most important assumption in the first class is, in all probability, that which treats knowledge as purely *theoretical* in the sense in which that word is completely antithetical to *practical.* In the second class are the considerations that have produced the conflict of the empiristic and the rationalistic, the a posteriori and a priori schools in modern philosophy – a division historically associated with its attendant separation of perception-conception, induction-deduction, particulars-universals, probability-certainty.

These philosophical divisions continue to bedevil schooling and constitute the key problems that educational research has not resolved epistemologically or methodologically. They are at the heart of the frustration and alienation of large numbers of families and school students. If a conservative or progressive 'practice turn' in teacher education is under way, then teacher education research needs to move well beyond the skill and competency, measurement and accountability distraction to teaching and delve deeply into the contradictions and purposes of living and learning, the practices of equity and virtue and the structures of knowledge and consciousness. These are issues that, through democratic social practice, transform the character of teachers and students alike and not only the artefacts, texts and metrics under examination. Teacher education research can contribute to human satisfaction, compassion and destiny, or not.

## Acknowledgement

This chapter draws on the research and scholarship of Dr Kirsten Sadler, College of Arts and Education, Victoria University Melbourne, in relation to core practices, clinical approaches and praxis education.

# 9 Critical schooling for all

Privileged circumstance narrows view
contributing little to human contentment
of alleviating anguish and regret
yet fissures expand to generous ideas
informing practice with artistic acumen
provoked to inhabit a better world
every change an act of history evolved.

It is not possible to prescribe a detailed model of education or of teacher education that can be implemented everywhere, in different countries and under different situations, but it is possible to identify specific characteristics that can be considered everywhere. This book has argued that despite different cultures, histories and economic demands, a broadly discursive and democratic approach to education and teacher education provides an appropriate framework for all children regardless of background to explore, construct and critique meaning and knowledge in their own interests. (For an extensive discussion of current approaches to teacher education in Australia, see Brandenburg, McDonough, Burke and White (2016) and Bahr and Mellor (2016)). Such an approach is supportive of all children whether male or female, older or younger, living in urban or country areas, having access to an extensive or limited range of educational resources and the support of teachers with qualifications that the country can provide. Social context including poverty and family income generally, health and housing and the state of political openness existing, all impact on education and learning of all members of the community, how we engage the world and come to personal understandings of it, is essentially epistemological in character and occurs despite pressures to constrain and control (Comber, 2016). It has been argued throughout previous chapters that American Pragmatism as a 'living philosophy,' a philosophy about living and a philosophy that is itself living and changing, offers the best strategy of thinking about and investigating these issues (Garrison, 2012). Whether or not American Pragmatism involves a continuing working out of the different views of its founders, or a continuing working out of a range of different features in the context of changing social conditions, is up to each participant to decide. Maintaining a principled stance towards pragmatism in the era of dominant and mature neoliberalism has

_Critical schooling for all_   161

proven itself to be an incredibly difficult undertaking whether in education or in any other human field of endeavour. Contrasting a cohesive and integrated view of education as a philosophy of practice with six other philosophies has produced a set of values, principles and practices that are consistent with pragmatism and which are now available for implementation around the world. The central characteristic of such a program is action – the authorisation of all participants to act together in coming to understand and to resolve. This is the notion of being critical.

## Formation of critical life

Three main themes run throughout the chapters of this book in establishing the framework for and practice implications of a critical stance towards society, education, teaching and learning. First, a comprehensive, integrated and cohesive approach to the social context of knowledge and of knowledge itself means that an all-sided and open-minded view of the issues under consideration is taken, rather than a narrow and limited view. It is accepted that complex issues and problems require all evidence and understandings to be assembled if the most appropriate options are to be available for decision making and execution. Raising issues regarding six philosophies of practice that can then offer support and criticism of education illustrates an all-sided view of thoroughness and rigour in strengthening education as a field of practice in its own right. Second, the emphasis on epistemology, or the nature of knowledge and what it means to learn and know, ensures that how humans act in pursuing knowledge and their humanity, or, more particularly, what is good or evil, is the main imperative of education and teaching. Third, being critical is necessarily a philosophical endeavour where acting, reflecting and making sense of the world raises questions of human consciousness or continuing general awareness of our histories and cultures such that our decisions are located within contextual frameworks that both guide and change as experience accumulates. These three themes of open-mindedness, social action and philosophical appreciations are the opposite of neoliberal imperatives and, when taken together, establish the conditions for democratic lifeworlds. The overall narrative of the book has drawn heavily on the work of philosophical pragmatism and major theorists such as Dewey and Biesta as they suggest understanding the world by engaging with it, where humans construct their own knowledge in association and discourse with their social and physical environments. Being critical is not a feature of education systems worldwide, although it must be said that fully developed primary systems with an emphasis on play, experimentation, care and well-being and sociality provides a very sound basis. In theorising educational practice and criticality, the concept of praxis has been proposed for realistic implementation by educators and systems around the world.

## Intersubjective praxis

Where social action takes us is mired, absorbed in history and culture. It takes us to the question of truth, of perception, fact and value. Amongst the early pragmatists there were different opinions of truth ranging from all action leading at

## 162 *Critical schooling for all*

some point to a unified understanding of what is, to approximate correspondence between an external object and internal representation, to an agreement amongst participants regarding what they are considering and acting upon. This raises the question of relativism, of whether or not each person has a 'true' understanding of a rock, river, bridge or circle, or whether each of which cannot accurately be determined. As Dewey put it, the 'quest for certainty' has been a constant search by humans forever, but it is not a problem if truth exists through each expressing their understanding as accurately as they can. As mentioned earlier, Dewey's response to what might be called an 'end point' of human understanding was his concept of 'warranted assertability' (Dewey, 1941, p. 172):

> The position which I take, namely, that all knowledge, or warranted assertion, depends upon inquiry and that inquiry is, truistically, connected with what is questionable (and questioned) involves a sceptical element, or what Peirce called 'fallibilism.' But it also provides for probability and for determination of degrees of probability in rejecting all intrinsically dogmatic statements, where 'dogmatic' applies to any statement asserted to possess inherent self-evident truth. That the only alternative to ascribing to some propositions self-sufficient, self-possessed and self-evident truth is a theory which finds the test and mark of truth in consequences of some sort is, I hope, an acceptable view.

Locating teacher education within pragmatism, as praxis (Bernstein, 1971/1999) connects closely with the notion of 'warranted assertability.' That is, through democratic and collaborative inquiry, humans come to a justification of their beliefs at a particular time, based on the experience they have of particular situations. Whether or not there is an ultimate truth or good is, of course, a belief in itself that cannot be justified necessarily by current human experience. In this sense then, it is possible to link the notions of praxis and subjective knowledge produced from the mutual experience of groups of people, to consider what can be called 'intersubjective praxis,' or the process towards understanding embarked upon by an assembly or gathering of people as they act on the world to change their thinking and practice for the public good (Bottero, 2010). By this manner, they become more human, more subjective, more aware of their existence as humans in relation to each other and to the universe generally. Throughout this journey, each person will construct their own warrants of truth and asset them as they see fit, in co-operation with friends, colleagues and opponents as best that is possible at the time. Such warrants will establish habits of thought and practice that can be tentative or determining depending on the totality and intensity of experience that accrues. At this stage of human history, philosophy and science, it is not possible to explain why certain experience generates thoughts, practices and habits of, for example, guilt and shame, joy and sadness, fear and courage, frustration and optimism. These emotions and feelings emerge somehow as past and current experience come into alignment and produce the new. The connection or spectrum between reason and emotion can only be described speculatively rather than be detailed as a causative process, from act to outcome. Following on from our previous discussion of

*Critical schooling for all*   163

consciousness as the 'hard problem' of philosophy, it may be that thinking about 'intersubjective praxis' as the point of singularity for thought and therefore of reason and emotion, is similar to thinking about the origins of the universe and the point of singularity of the big bang and what continues to have followed today. What we can think about with a little more precision, is how to establish settings of becoming for humans of all ages, to investigate what they and others think, and whether or not what they think can be warranted in some way. For the time being. Human ethics is a case in point.

## Acting for what is right

In Chapter 4, a discussion of ethical conduct and the nature of virtue was begun to locate education within a broader historical and philosophical context. Teacher education, for example, then becomes not a mere institutional formality, but a way of formatting living for all involved. As was noted, Aristotle suggested that human happiness comes about not so much as a permanent state of mind, but through living well over a lifetime, through attempting to conduct oneself as well as possible and to be reflective and contemplative of personal actions. Happiness could be fleeting, but whether or not a virtuous life such as this had been attempted and therefore whether happiness had been achieved, could only be judged as life came towards its end. Aristotle defined a number of virtues to guide consideration of the meaning and purpose of human life, virtues such as honesty, justice, courage and modesty. There was a middle path or 'golden mean' to be taken for each rather than going to extremes. With the virtue of courage, for example, we could either be reckless or cowardly, with modesty, one could either be arrogant or detached. In his discussion of intellectual virtues and virtue epistemology, Baehr (2011) has raised questions regarding the place of virtue in learning and whether or not certain intellectual and character virtues are necessary for learning and knowledge production. It is difficult to separate such considerations from the sum total of socio-cultural experience and it is certainly difficult to conceive of knowledge being created in a virtuous vacuum. What is the relationship between memory, speech and hearing, for example, when a young child encounters a chair and table for the first time and relates this experience to that of 'bed' as part of daily culture? How is a true and justified belief of 'chair and table' constructed from very limited contact and performance? Virtue, then, envisaged as significant and excellent practice that guides experience and habit over a lifetime is central to our humanity and how we become. It therefore is a central aspect of education and learning that should be made explicit for all involved.

The question now becomes whether or not it is possible or desirable to contemplate an education system that involves *praxis* learning emerging from a matrix of practices and social acts that are associated with appropriate educational virtues. The notion of educational virtue is being raised from an epistemological perspective. That is, can a number of the properties of practice be identified such that they will involve acting in a certain way in terms of knowledge participation and production? If so, will these properties, acts and virtues assist learning that is

164  *Critical schooling for all*

personal, creative and independent? In this sense, virtues are not seen as values or as psychological traits to be imposed for personality development or character education. The list of virtues to be considered will need to be extensively debated amongst practitioner philosophers and the manner by which they can be included in the range of educational practice. It may be appropriate for the list of virtues to be few in number so that broad agreement can be reached (at least in the first instance) and the matrix of practice to not be over complicated for initial analysis. Table 9.1 shows a draft set of virtues and their possible application:

*Table 9.1* Educational virtues of practice and application (for discussion)

| Educational Virtues of Practice | Curriculum Application | Connection with Aristotelian Virtues |
| --- | --- | --- |
| Dialogue | Expressions of ethical experience with colleagues | Wise deliberation |
| Inquiry | Cycles of negotiated projects involving design, explanation, evaluation, new design | Open-mindedness |
| Respect | Explore knowledge, production of knowledge, views of colleagues | Justice |
| Judgement | Personal acts based on viewpoint, advice of others, reference to authorities | Courage |
| Responsibility | Rigorous consideration of projects | Truthfulness |
| Reflection | Monitoring of projects and appraisal of outcomes | Friendliness |

It can be seen from Table 9.1 that each draft educational virtue is described as an action, in doing words, to be undertaken by each learner, both individually and collectively, as epistemological lives are constructed in schools and classrooms. The distinction between epistemology and psychology is clear. As mentioned earlier, MacIntyre (1985) has argued that moral conduct results from engagement with the 'internal goods' of social practice, although the exact nature of such goods is unclear. Similarly, as noted by Ferkany and Creed (2014, p. 571), virtuous action is taken in relation to a 'stock of knowledge' that has been developed as a result of practice decision making, in the same way 'as a musician's deployment of her musical knowledge in a performance.' Teachers and students involved in educational practices of this type will also respond from their 'stock of knowledge' as they see fit to the conditions they experience. It is accurate to argue that not all cultures may support schooling so arranged, but this is also true of the argument earlier, that many students do not appreciate the dominant conservative approach of many schools and subject areas at present. However, a broadly democratic approach that encourages maximum student participation with their learning will enable many more children to become immersed in the practices of knowledge

*Critical schooling for all* 165

production rather than narrow systemic imposition. Each culture, political system and education profession will make their own decisions accordingly.

Questions of educational equity are usually approached from a sociological rather than epistemological viewpoint. These often involve the economic background of families, funding of schools, private and public systems of schooling and implications regarding test results. Attention is given to admission to various types of schools via select entry procedures and the costs associated with elite schools (Teese, 2013). While these issues are important, a focus on general access to schooling has not made major inroads into learning success that the majority of children should experience at school regardless of background. A shift to *praxis* learning constitutes a shift to an emphasis on epistemology, the nature of knowledge and learning and the conditions by which knowledge can best be produced by learners both in and out of school. Raising the issue of educational virtue links the practice of learning with the broad historical consideration of human satisfaction and fulfilment that neoliberalism casually discards. Equity does not mean equality, so different learners involved in a democratic *praxis* curriculum will achieve different understandings and outcomes, not in a relative sense as all personal knowledge is of equal significance, but in the sense that all learners are constructing their own journeys towards interacting with the world in self-fulfilling ways. Whether or not all children of a certain age should come into contact with a certain set of ideas at the same time – the area of rectangle, the music of Bach, a red blood cell, the poems of Robbie Burns – is one of the great political conundrums of formal schooling, but not of democratic learning. All children do not need to be on an assembly line of this type for them to be totally engrossed in the social and physical worlds and to be establishing the groundwork for a productive and civic life. Educational equity means coming to appreciate in due course and regardless of economic standing, the beauty of a butterfly, the mystery of the clouds, the coldness of the stream and empathy with the distressed mother on page 57 of the novel. Identifying the properties of practice as educational *and* human virtues that all children and teachers have the chance to live and experience over time embraces an epistemological equity that rejects the shallowness and callousness of neoliberal condescension.

## Pragmatism and signature pedagogies

In the grand tradition of university work, different academics will approach their units of study and interactions with students in different ways. This is particularly so with application of the praxis model, given that it depends on the availability of situations that will encourage each participant to pursue their interests in relation to the interests of colleagues and of systemic requirements (Arnold, Edwards, Hooley and Williams, 2012b; Gudjonsdottir et al. 2007). This occurs within the context that all pre-service teachers have enrolled in a series of units that have a published timeline and outcomes. The praxis model is therefore intended to establish a balanced and integrated approach across units such that all pre-service teachers and lecturers alike are involved in a continuing process of educational projects that involve participatory social action and collaborative discourse for explanation and meaning. It is to be expected that all units will involve a combination of negotiated and researchful projects, engagement with major professional ideas and practices through online and face-to-face activities, academic readings and discussion and group and individual presentations. Organisation of groups into learning circles such that investigations are as autonomous as possible is to be preferred. There are a number of factors or practices that impact the practices of praxis teacher education in a dialectical relationship with the lifeworld of participants, involving communities, families, teachers and school students. In this regard, we are now able to define praxis teacher education in the following way:

> A praxis model of teacher education within a materialist philosophy of the social and physical lifeworlds, investigates major aspects of society, education and teacher education as arrays of social practices and seeks to enact social and ethical practices arising for the public good.

Teacher education therefore exists within a 'three world' context of lifeworld, or the world of social experience, the world of inquiry or relationship and interaction with the objects of experience and the conscious world of human subjective experience (Figure 9.1).

Within this broad understanding, the particular units and studies of a specific course of teacher education attempt to adopt a fluid and interactive relationship with each other, such that the practices and ideas of each unit are informing and are informed by each other. Each of the five components of the praxis model of teacher education discussed next exists in a dynamic and dialectical relationship with each other and with the signature pedagogies. There is thus movement and interchange between components and signature pedagogies such that learning of participants can occur at any point at any time. In this sense, the model exists

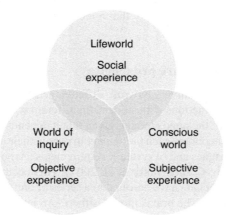

*Figure 9.1* Three world's context of teacher education

as a three-dimensional arrangement of motion and transformation, in a similar way to how atomic structure is envisaged as materials/particles with various properties circulating a set of other materials/particles and properties in a cloud of entangled energy and matter. While a praxis model of teacher education is integrated and fluid at all times, the different processes that are involved can be represented in Figure 9.2:

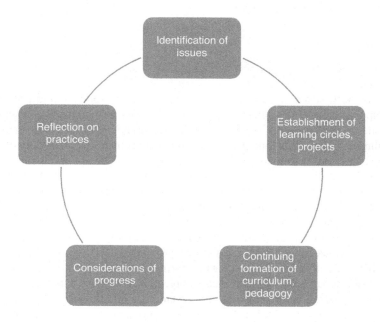

*Figure 9.2* Integrated process of praxis teacher education

Each of the specific components of Figure 9.2 is described as follows:

## *Curriculum*

With this conception of motion and change, a practice perspective could define curriculum as transforming discourses, practices and ideas that result from creative interaction between generative themes and rich tasks. Key features of curriculum under praxis conditions would most likely include the generation of major ideas from the interests of students through portfolio dialogue, action arising regarding what is done with these ideas and subsequent action through rich tasks and engaging in problematising which leads to points of departure for ongoing learning.

## *Pedagogy*

From the point of view of practice, pedagogy can be defined as repertoires of formal, informal and transitional practices to engage and investigate ideas, problems

## 168 *Critical schooling for all*

and practices. Under these conditions, participants bring together their experience of recognised and authorised pedagogical methodologies with their more informal lifeworld understandings of dialogical practices. This results in the formation of new, intersubjective pedagogical practices that become available for application as deemed appropriate. Participants are not dominated by predetermined approaches to teaching and learning, but rely on their community experience to judge the most appropriate methodology to pursue.

### Teaching

As a specific subset of practice pedagogy, consideration has been given to the main features of a praxis teaching and learning environment. *Listening* was identified as the first feature, taken to mean an intense or concentrated process of participants attempting to identify key words and ideas that are used in discussion as thoughts and issues are reported and described and any underlying themes or meanings emerge. When one person or group comes to an understanding of what is being said, they can then respond with ideas of their own. Participants are not seeking to have their current views accepted by this process, but to understand the views of others by which held viewpoints can be refined and recast. *Language* use is therefore central to meaning making as discussion proceeds and new ideas and concepts are constructed by each participant. It is usual for comments to be made and questions asked to clarify what is meant and to move understanding forward. Various strategies are used as discussion and *dialogue* proceeds, such as the *scaffolding* of ideas and concepts as participants seek meaning, the bringing to bear of a broad base of experience and tacit knowledge to particular concepts and the incorporation of community understandings into the network of language and practices being considered. Throughout this process of listening, language and dialogue, participants will encounter different *critical perspectives* or world views that may be their own or those of others. They will be in the position of taking risks in expressing hidden or uncertain views and ideas that may not be accepted, they will struggle to understand the different viewpoints of others so that they are in a position to explore further and to redraft their own thinking in comparison. Generally and hopefully if the conditions permit, they express through their words and deeds an intention of working in concert, side by side, with others to understand and fashion a better world by so doing.

### Assessment

In theorising that teaching can be understood as 'intersubjective practice,' it follows that learning environments should enable all participants to consider issues of their interest that of necessity will draw upon background personal and community culture and will involve fertile language situations of conversation, description, initiative and creativity. There is thus a combination of experience, experimentation and interest as current ideas and practices are transformed into the new. A proposed practice analysis as the basis of assessment within intersubjective praxis

*Critical schooling for all* 169

teaching and learning environments will need to include conceptual understandings of practice situated, practice engaged and practice emergent. Accordingly, assessment is taken to mean practice analysis of learning environments and the identification and monitoring of new practices so created. A contemporary discussion and critique of current assessment practices can be found at Lingard, Thompson and Sellar (2016).

## *Research*

In a similar manner, the practice of research can be conceptualised as engagement with reflective discursive practices that establish dialogue between participants to transform current practices into intersubjective praxis knowledge. As with all practice components, practice research can reproduce current accepted methodologies or set about creating innovative approaches to meet non-traditional situations. Researching with Indigenous communities for Indigenous interests is a case in point. It may be that research should enable a process of 'bricolage,' whereby communities and researchers adopt and adapt local methodologies, those methodologies and approaches that are 'at hand,' at least in the first instance. Research should not be seen as a series of predetermined processes for mechanical application, but an imaginative, creative process of community problem solving within the context of recognised procedures (Blackmore, 2014; Menter, 2014; Stenhouse, 1981).

Where a person constructs their understanding of teaching and learning through action, by observing, experiencing and discussing the context of learning and teaching practice, they enter into a relationship between their own current understanding and the possibility of emerging and new understandings informed by more formal and more informal social and educational practices. This process involves engagement in discursively reflective activities that promote pre-service teachers to ask questions and examine their current understanding of a situation (Loughlan, 2014). When these discussions occur in an open and trusted environment, which Habermas refers to, as the public sphere, new understandings can emerge leading to frames of practice expanding. The process is dynamic with processes and practices within the praxis model changing and being modified to suit the context of the learning environment. The five practices represented in the diagram in Figure 9.2 come together to inform praxis teacher education. There is a dialectic relationship between the components, rather than being seen as separate activities and involving constant restlessness, motion, change and transformation.

A praxis model of teacher education needs to be able to identify key structural elements around which programs are arranged and which describe the key approaches to teaching and learning so undertaken. The eight signature pedagogies shown in Table 9.2 map the landscape of praxis teacher education for lecturers and pre-service teachers alike. The signature pedagogies provide a language by which all participants can describe their learning journey and the social and educational acts embarked upon. Each signature pedagogy may act differently to other signature pedagogies in a program of study. Some may 'act at a distance' across all programs and units in the same way, or in different ways. Some may

*Table 9.2* Signature pedagogies of praxis teacher education

| Signature Pedagogies | Characteristics of Signature Pedagogies | | |
|---|---|---|---|
| Professional Practice (Schatzki, Kemmis, Green) | Recognises personal learning from immersion in practice | Supports communities of practice to support inquiry for improved learning environments and student learning | Continuing critique of practice for change of conditions to formulate ideas of new practice |
| Repertoires of Practice (Kalantzis, Cope) | Identifies and articulates features of pedagogical, curriculum, assessment practices | Links key features of pedagogy, curriculum, assessment for change and improvement | Critiques repertories of educational practice as social activity that supports satisfaction and progress |
| Teacher as Researcher (Stenhouse) | Systematically investigates own practice for improvement | Participates as member of school-based research team/s | Relates local, national and global research, policy and practice |
| Case Conferencing (Shulman) | Generates case and commentary writing for understanding of practice | Participates in case conferencing and concept analysis for production of teachers' knowledge | Encourages articulation and analysis of teachers' knowledge in relation to theories of curriculum and teaching |
| Community Partnership (Gonzalez, Moll & Amanti; Sizer) | Connects with local communities | Integrates community culture and knowledge into curriculum | Investigates community to understand local aspiration, history, knowledge, language |
| Praxis Learning (Freire) | Investigates/ provides description, explanation, theorising and change of practice in response to reflection on practice | Demonstrates a curriculum developed from praxis and in response to reflection | Constructs learning environments of ethically informed action for the public good |
| Participatory Action research (Kemmis, Brennan) | Identifies and advocates key issues of policy and participates in collecting data for analysis | Contributes to project discourses with internal and external team members | Theorises and critiques research findings in the public domain |
| Portfolio Dialogue (Freire, Dewey, Brookfield) | Compiles and discusses artefacts of personal learning over time | Participates with artefact and knowledge discourses that show understandings of meanings of practice | Demonstrates a coherent philosophy consistent with personalised practice and community change for public good |

Copyright © 2014 by Neil Hooley

act much more locally and specifically in different programs and units and with different participants. A more nuanced view of the signature pedagogies and their application will enable a better understanding of their influence and what changes or adjustments need to be made. Rather than considering the signature pedagogies as a map of teacher education only, the map can be recast as a three-dimensional 'panorama of the lifeworld.' That is, teacher education is brought into the mainstream of social life intimately connected with all other social, educational and political practices and is not placed outside, in isolation. The practices of the lifeworld thereby become practices of education, meaning that the culture and history of communities are strongly connected and respected, again, not isolated. This has particular implications for the five components of teacher education noted earlier.

Given that the map of signature pedagogies noted earlier is based on the understanding of praxis as social action for the public good, the practice of signature pedagogies is essentially ethical in character. That is, there is a very strong correlation between understanding human ethical conduct as acting in an appropriate manner for the general good of others and community and the concept of praxis as the means of enacting the human disposition of living well. It may be, however, that the map needs to be expanded to ensure that it is essentially democratic and can take account of issues such as power and influence, discrimination, bias and the like. A brief example of the enactment of each signature pedagogy from the pre-service teacher point of view is also shown next:

1   Professional practice
    Small teams of pre-service teachers and mentor teachers redraft a unit of work for school students to encourage open-ended investigations and different explanations.
2   Repertoires of practice
    Documentation and implementation of different approaches to teaching to ascertain which features appear to engage school students more personally with a particular topic.
3   Teacher as researcher
    Pre-service teachers participate with mentor teacher professional learning group in the gathering and analysis of data regarding student written expression
4   Case conferencing
    Learning circles of pre-service teachers write, discuss and annotate cases regarding their classroom experience and generate themes across all cases that result in the concept mapping of teachers' knowledge.
5   Community partnership
    Members of local community invited to describe their local experience with pre-service teachers and school students so that a more complete understanding of the history and culture of community lifeworld can be understood and respected.

## 172 *Critical schooling for all*

6 Praxis learning
   Pre-service teachers emphasise learning for school students based on personal action and reflection so that curriculum can incorporate intersubjective understandings of as many students as possible.
7 Participatory action research
   Pre-service teachers theorise their own collective school experience and invite comment from more experienced colleagues to critique and discuss ways of strengthening public education.
8 Portfolio dialogue
   Ongoing compilation and discussion of artefacts of culture and experience so that themes of meaning and learning are identified and can be problematised for further investigation.

## Significance of the model

In positioning education and teacher education in the lifeworld of ordinary experience, the praxis model of teacher education described earlier theorises a view of humanity that is democratic and noble and respects the culture and knowledges of all citizens. It conceives the lifeworld as being the assemblage of experience, meanings and values that have arisen from community practice and which guide ongoing social acts of purpose and explanation. The lifeworld provides memories, evidence and sustenance for love, integrity and honesty that are necessary resources for meeting all the challenges of the unjust and indecent. It respects the dignity and validity of how citizens go about making sense of their social and physical worlds and how decisions are made for the public good. Seen in this way, the geography of teacher education expressed as eight signature pedagogies, in fact provides a broad description or 'panorama' of the lifeworld of ordinary experience and by so doing, connects the lifeworld of ordinary experience with the schoolworld of students and teachers; integrated fully, they become as one. From a practice perspective, not only do the praxis model components also become integrated, but they establish a dialectical relationship with the lifeworld and schoolworld so that they become accessible at all times to participants. It needs to be recognised that a deeper understanding of lifeworld features is a beginning point for community and school experience and learning and that other experience from different lifeworlds needs to be considered to inform and critique current perspectives. That is, communities or groups that may enter into discussion of particular issues for strategic ends, to win or dominate, need to accept that other viewpoints are of equal importance and require communicative processes, to understand and incorporate. Beginning with the lifeworld familiar and ordinary, participants engage with other ideas and perspectives, adopting different thoughts, proposals, practices and plans as they pursue knowing. Recognising that education and teacher education are positioned in the lifeworld experience with dialectical relationships being created between all aspects of praxis social action conceptualises personal and community learning as an emancipatory rather than an enslaving human capability.

## Linked reason and emotion

Whether or not formal learning or schooling should involve the emotions remains contested around the world. This is distinct from both teaching about the emotions as in a psychology class and informal living where the emotions are concerned every day. Which emotions are being considered for education and learning? There are different compilations but, as a starting point and according to Aristotle, the emotions involve feelings such as anger, friendship, fear, shame, kindness, pity, indignation, envy and love. It is difficult to see how these as a group can or should be built into a curriculum. For some, we can consider their opposite such as anger/ calmness, but this is a case of picking and choosing to suit, why not cruelty as compared with kindness? Again, the distinction must be made with what students feel as a consequence of learning, not what a teacher has arranged beforehand. It should be hoped that students in science classes feel confident in conducting experiments and using scientific equipment when they experience the wonder of chemicals reacting to form new compounds. I would hope that students in my mathematics class are enthralled by the realisation that a circle has the dialectical properties of no beginning or end. Similarly, students will sometimes shed a tear through sadness or compassion when they encounter human stories in literature, poetry and song. Whether they do of course, is up to them, not me. These responses are democratic and occur spontaneously through personal experience, community, shared and individual, as we explore the physical and social worlds. Indeed, it could be argued that to try and artificially create emotional situations for children through formal schooling, is immoral.

American pragmatism (Menand, 1997) may offer us a philosophical way into these questions. If social life is the great teacher and we come to know though bringing our current understandings and cultures into close alignment with indeterminate situations, then the generation of new situations will constitute our learning and our responses. Under these democratic situations, all participants can give their best imaginations, their best hopes, their best actions and their best advice to others so that deeper understandings occur. This is what Dewey called 'becoming whole' in two senses, a continuing process of 'becoming' as we experience and of moving beyond the current into a more expansive or 'whole' life. When we become and know, we have a different relationship to the world than before and see it differently, understand it differently. In the formal education or curriculum sense therefore, emotions are not a given at the start, somehow created by teachers or the state, to insist that students appreciate certain predetermined events such as plays and art, but emotions may arise as a result of experience that cannot be predetermined. I cannot preordain that students are fascinated by school mathematics, but I can situate students in personal and shared experience that may reveal the beauty of snowflakes and polyhedra. Experience itself, according to the pragmatists, is not solid and graspable as such, truth just waiting to be inhaled, but can be accepted, taken in and made our own, in our own way. Whether or not all students in my class have the same understanding of my definition of a circle cannot be ascertained, but they have their own understanding for sharing and meaning.

174 *Critical schooling for all*

So where does that leave us on emotion in formal schooling? Dewey comments that readiness to learn involves accepting what life and experience offers as opportunities to transform indeterminate situations into more determinate possibilities. This is an ongoing process, of becoming. He suggests that readiness to learn in the general life sense involves open-mindedness, wholeheartedness, responsibility and directness. Open-mindedness requires us to readily consider the new, the challenging and the somewhat uneasy or unfamiliar. Our efforts at engaging experiences enthusiastically, fully and entirely in an all-sided manner, is called wholeheartedness. Being a responsible learner means accepting the consequences of what we do and of our investigations. Finally, Dewey thought that directness means trusting human action as the way forward rather than being resigned to what is and of not being distracted from the course of action. This seems to me to be good advice in dealing with human emotions in school, dominated by an oft-imposed and depersonalised curriculum. They seem to provide a way of approaching life head-on, of constructing plans with others of problem solving and then, of responding to what happens in the way you deem fit. This is not set beforehand, but emerges from experience, from practice, in the fullness of life itself, not from the state, curriculum developers or textbook writers. Children need to experience their own experience, to make sense of what they think for themselves, to make their own tentative judgements and to navigate their worlds from a practice perspective (Kwak, 2015). Of course, lonely Sunday afternoons are a part of that, as too sadness at the most recent mistake, frustration at just not getting it, pleasantness at walking by the river with a friend, worrying that someone close is safe. But these are democratic emotional responses that emerge from our experience; they are not to be artificially imposed.

## Radical action, knowledge, education, democracy

What then can we say about education and teacher education that sets about establishing a process of becoming for all participants regardless of background, often running counter to dominant cultural economical and political pressures, a radical view of a flourishing humanity rather than one of oppression and constraint? It is clear that most education systems around the world are not this, highly conservative rather than radical, where knowledge is seen to be known, exists in small slices for acceptance and adoption and where teachers are not prepared to be creative, to take risks and to be wrong. In this sense, public education dos not act in the interests of the vast majority of ordinary people, but seeks to contain thinking within narrow boundaries that enclose imagination, curiosity and investigation. As a starting point for the recovery of subjectification, all teachers whatever their circumstances can make a personal and professional commitment to implementing the following summary principles:

- theorising subjectification as the ongoing construction of humanness by all humans based on the dialectical materialism of existence for all communities;

Critical schooling for all 175

- recognising the cultures and systems of lifeworlds as the context within which the process of subjectification and objectification occurs;
- authorising a negotiated rather than imposed curriculum based on the interests of all students working collaboratively;
- enabling all students in all subjects to become immersed in the social act of investigation involving language, inquiry and reflexivity;
- endorsing a range of signature pedagogies that constitute practice, partnership and praxis approaches to knowledge and understanding;
- constructing continuing narratives of epistemology for all students that describe the process and outcomes of intersubjective praxis;
- recognising and integrating the human spectrum of reason and emotion such that all capabilities are respected and incorporated; and
- establishing continuing acts and processes of monitoring subjectification as personal narratives of knowledge, creativity, understanding and insight.

These guidelines for subjectification within education and teacher education do not form a prescribed pathway, but outline a journey of personal action and creation. They of course embrace and build upon many forms of knowledge that have been accepted until now and those forms of knowledge that are uncertain and emerging today. They do, however, see knowledge as the context for human becoming, rather than the static or final outcome. They do not express a desire to understand fixed truth, or God's view, sometimes argued as mathematics and physics, but accept we are all attempting to know ourselves and the universe as best we can. This is the philosophical view of American Pragmatism, again not a fixed dogma to be applied, but a framework for investigation as the world and all the humans on it proceed, then as now, together. Mass systems of schooling around the world struggling under the dictates of neoliberalism and its demand to reify and dehumanise social life including education, can respond with more of the same or construct their own moral purpose in the interests of all ordinary families and children. We need to delve into the great works that have been left to us, the great ideas and practices of philosophy, science, literature, arts, mathematics, humanities and technologies, but these need to inform our own thinking and critique, not dominate them. Rather than the obscenities of neoliberalism, this will be our legacy.

It is fitting that some final thoughts must go to Dewey. His concluding chapter in *Experience and Nature* takes up questions of existence, value and criticism where he discusses again the continuity between the natural and social worlds and where human values originate. These questions of course refer to the very basis of humanity and whether or not how we are today can be explained through experience and culture. Dewey's concept of experience was identical to that used by the American jurist, Oliver Wendell Holmes (1841–1935), often associated with the early pragmatists, who famously stated in his book *The Common Law* (2012) that 'the life of the law has not been logic; it has been experience.' In this regard, Dewey (1958, pp. 428–429) wrote,

176 *Critical schooling for all*

All knowing and effort to know starts from some belief, some received and asserted meaning which is a deposit of prior experience, personal and communal. In every instance, from passing query to elaborate scientific undertaking, the art of knowing criticises a belief which has passed current as genuine coin with a view to its revision. It terminates when freer, richer and more secure objects of belief are instituted as goods of immediate acceptance. The operation is one of doing and making in the literal sense. Starting from one good, treated as apparent and questionable and ending in another which is tested and substantiated, the final act of knowing is acceptance and intellectual appreciation of what is significantly conclusive.

This statement is an explicit summary of the pragmatists' view of what it means to be human and why it is unnecessary to posit the existence of external influence beyond combinations of matter and energy. Earlier in the chapter noted earlier, Dewey had quoted Holmes as suggesting that all that is necessary is to realise that the universe has produced us and all that we believe and love. It is from this understanding, that we set about formal systems of education, where fact and value, reason and desire, profane and sacred, past and present, sadness and delight, expected and unpredicted collide. Whether or not intersubjective social action will take us closer to some type of 'ultimate purpose' remains to be seen, but it can open to us the 'immediate subjectification purpose' of the human family and the historical and physical context in which we live, learn and love, the context of becoming. Public systems of education that embrace the vast majority of the world's peoples, cultures and backgrounds need to be characterised by these radical democratic values and perspectives.

## Epistemology

Knowing the infinite seems improbable
except for those anointed uncertain and fragile
yet the interactions between matter and energy
forever shaping time, space and humanity
create at once scenarios of brutality and love
dialectics of connection, pattern and neuron
in constant formation and antagonism
incongruous that scattered specks coalesce
enabling the very idea of imagination
and curious capacity to be aware of universals
beauty and morality dependent on physical structure
resonating between yellow giants and double helices.

Miracle a misnomer, there is nothing else
confined by this matrix of transience, new patterns
struggle to explain the absorb and mysterious
whether centred or decentred, superficial or deep

*Critical schooling for all* 177

as cascading waves bring illumination and confusion
there emerges realisation, matter and energy spinning
vibrating particles and strings raised in imagination
knowledge exists between the logical and biological
increasing in complexity, passing new thresholds
but contradictions persist casting doubt on origins
our influence predetermined and entombed
our place, our fate a random process.

A tortuous expedition of enlightenment to excise
superstition and prejudice for personal authority
relying on our own sensibilities and reason
mechanical, predictable macro visions challenged
by seemingly chaotic weird micro arrangements
and elusive theories that confound practice
truth a property of matter in contest with conversation
exploration and confluence integrates perception
bringing observation and explanation into alignment
liberating boundaries of established thought;
meanwhile children languish in cells of alienation
as the delicate bourgeois ponder echelon and sip tea.

# Part III reflections

As is always the case, each reader, learner and traveller, will need to evaluate their personal journey in relation to the aspirations and values of the community with which they live and work. The previous four chapters have attempted to outline some principles and strategies by which a critical and cohesive approach to education can be implemented to benefit the vast majority of participants. Some comment has been provided regarding a social class view of education from which key policy and practice decisions can be made. This suggests of course that social class including economic factors dominate social life, but that specific lifeworlds within general socio-economic conditions can struggle for a more independent existence. One chapter raises specific questions of Indigeneity as a significant issue internationally regarding the striving of Indigenous peoples for justice and democracy. True democracy will not have been achieved in human history until this issue has been resolved. A further chapter argues that teacher education has also come under enormous strain as neoliberal imperatives move further and further away from the 'sweetness and light' of all that is meaningful and virtuous and which should be expected from public systems of education by ordinary families and children around the world. The destination we have arrived at proposes education as a philosophy of practice in its own right and outlines a series of principles and practices for adoption that are critical in intent, practice-based in implementation and democratic in association. This concept of education takes a giant leap beyond education being primarily concerned with transmitting what is already known involving slices of predetermined information, to a concept that supports a flourishing humanity for each community, family and child as they engage their social and personal lives. It is a concept that dignifies the character, intellect and knowledge of each participant as sensuous and cultural species-beings dedicated to living well in the interests of a compassionate, peaceful and knowledgeable humanity.

# References

Aristotle. (2014). *Aristotle's Ethics: Writings From the Complete Works*, Revised Edition, Edited and with an Introduction by Barnes, J. and Kenny, A., Princeton: Princeton University Press.

Arnold, J., Edwards, T., Hooley, N. and Williams, J. (2012a). Conceptualising teacher education and research as 'critical praxis,' *Critical Studies in Education*, 53(3), 281–295.

Arnold, J., Edwards, T., Hooley, N. and Williams, J. (2012b). Theorising on-site teacher education: Philosophical Project Knowledge (PPK), *Asia-Pacific Journal of Teacher Education*, 40(1), 67–78.

Arnold, M. (1932/1984). *Culture and Anarchy*, Edited and with an Introduction by Wilson, J. D., Cambridge: Cambridge University Press.

Aronson, B. and Laughter, J. (2016). The theory and practice of culturally relevant education: A synthesis of research across content areas, *Review of Educational Research*, 86(1), 163–206.

Attenborough, D. (2002). *Life on Air: Memoirs of a Broadcaster*, London: BBC Books.

Audi, R. (2011). Epistemology: A Contemporary Introduction to the Theory of Knowledge, 3rd Edition, New York and London: Routledge.

Baehr, J. (2011). The Inquiring Mind: On Intellectual Virtues & Virtue Epistemology, Milton Keynes: Oxford University Press.

Bahr, N. and Mellor, S. (2016). *Building Quality in Teaching and Teacher Education*, Australian Education Review, Camberwell: ACER Press.

Bellmann, J. (2014). The changing field of educational studies and the task of theorising education, in Biesta, G., Allen, J. and Edwards, R. (Eds) *Making a Difference in Theory: The Theory Question in Education and the Education Question in Theory*, London and New York: Routledge, 65–82.

Bernstein, B. (2010). Vertical and horizontal discourse: An essay, *British Journal of Sociology of Education*, 20(2), 157–173.

Bernstein, R. J. (1971/1999). *Praxis & Action: Contemporary Philosophies of Human Activity*, Philadelphia: University of Pennsylvania Press.

Biesta, G. J. J. (1998). Mead: Intersubjectivity and education: The early writings, *Studies in Philosophy and Education*, 17, 73–99.

Biesta, G. J. J. (2013). *The Beautiful Risk of Education*, Boulder and London: Paradigm.

Biesta, G. J. J. (2015a). What is education for? On good education, teacher judgement and educational professionalism, *European Journal of Education*, 50(1), 75–87.

Biesta, G. J. J. (2015b). On the two cultures of educational research and how we might move ahead: Reconsidering the ontology, axiology and praxeology of education, *European Educational Research Journal*, 14(1), 11–22.

## 180  References

Biesta, G. J. J. (2015c). Freeing teaching from learning: Opening up existential possibilities in educational relationships, *Studies in Philosophy and Education*, 34(3), 229–243.

Biesta, G. J. J. (2015d). Teaching, teacher education, and the humanities: Reconsidering education as a *Geisteswissenschaft*, *Educational Theory*, 65(6), 665–679.

Biesta, G. J. J., Allen, J. and Edwards, R. (Eds) (2014). *Making a Difference in Theory: The Theory Question in Education and the Education Question in Theory*, London and New York: Routledge, 65–82.

Birmingham, C. (2004). Phronesis: A model for pedagogical reflection, *Journal of Teacher Education*, 55(4), 313–324.

Blackmore, J. (2014). Cultural and gender politics in Australian education, the rise of edu-capitalism and the 'fragile project' of critical educational research, *Australian Educational Researcher*, 41(5), 499–520.

Blumer, H. (1969). *Symbolic Interactionism: Perspective and Method*, Berkeley: University of California Press.

Bottero, W. (2010). Intersubjectivity and Bourdieusian approaches to 'identify,' *Cultural Sociology*, 4(1), 3–22.

Bourdieu, P. (1990). *The Logic of Practice*, California: Stanford University Press.

Bourdieu, P. (2004). *Science of Science and Reflexivity*, Chicago: University of Chicago Press.

Bourdieu, P. and Passeron, J.-C. (1977). *Reproduction in Education, Society and Culture*, London: Sage Publications.

Bradatan, C. (2015). *Dying for Ideas: The Dangerous Lives of the Philosophers*, New York, London, New Delhi and Sydney: Bloomsbury Press.

Brandenburg, R., McDonough, S., Burke, J. and White, S. (2016). *Teacher Education: Innovation, Intervention and Impact*, Singapore: Springer.

Brooks, M. (2013). Invest in minds not maths, *New Scientist*, 220(2948–2949, December), 38–39.

Bruner, J. (1979). *On Knowing: Essays for the Left Hand*, Cambridge and London: Harvard University Press.

Burridge, P., Hooley, N. and Neal, G. (2016). Creating *frames of practice* for teacher education, *Asia-Pacific Journal of Teacher Education*, 44(2), 156–171.

Butler, J. (1986). Sex and Gender in Simone de Beauvoir's Second Sex, *Yale French Studies* No. 72, Simone de Beauvoir: Witness to a Century and New Haven: Yale University Press, 35–49.

Butler, J. (2016). *Notes on and Quotations From and About Judith Butler*, accessed at http://studymore.org.uk/xybut.htm, July.

Cassidy, D. (1995). *Einstein and Our World*, Atlantic Highlands, NJ: Humanities Press.

Chalmers, D. (2003). Consciousness and its place in nature, in Stich, S. and Warfield, T. (Eds) *Blackwell Guide to Philosophy of Mind*, MA: Blackwell, accessed at http://consc.net/papers/nature.pdf, 2, July 2016.

Chernus, I. (2016). *Religion as a Cultural System: The Theory of Clifford Gertz*, accessed at www.colorado.edu/ReligiousStudies/chernus/4800/GeertzSummary.htm, July.

Clandinin, D. J. and Connelly, F. M. (2000). *Narrative Inquiry: Experience and Story in Qualitative Research*, San Francisco: John Wiley and Son.

Cochran-Smith, M. and Villegas, A. M. (2015). Framing teacher preparation research: An overview of the field, part 1, *Journal of Teacher Education*, 66(1), 7–20.

Collyer, M. (2015). Practices of conformity and resistance in the marketization of the academy: Bourdieu, professionalism and academic capitalism, *Critical Studies in Education*, 56(3), 315–331.

## References 181

Comber, B. (2016). Poverty, place and pedagogy in education: Research stories from frontline workers, *Australian Educational Researcher*, 43(4), 393–417.

Connell, R. (2007). Southern Theory: The Global Dynamics of Knowledge in Social Science, Crows Nest: Allen & Unwin.

Cox, B. and Cohen, A. (2016). *Forces of Nature*, London: Harper Collins Publishers.

Dakich, E., Watt, T. and Hooley, N. (2016). Reconciling mixed methods approaches with a community narrative model for educational research involving Aboriginal and Torres Strait Islander families, *Review of Education, Pedagogy and Cultural Studies*, 38(4), 360–380, doi:10.1080/10714413.2016.1203683

Darder, A. (2013). *Freire and Education*, New York and London: Routledge.

Darling-Hammond, L. (2016). Research on teaching and teacher education and its influences on policy and practice, *Educational Researcher*, 45(2), 83–91.

da Silva, F. C. (2007). *G. H. Mead: A Critical Introduction*, Cambridge: Polity Press.

de Beauvoir, S. (1973). *The Second Sex*, New York: Vintage Books, 301.

Deen, P. (2012). *Unmodern Philosophy and Modern Philosophy: John Dewey*, Carbondale and Edwardsville: Southern Illinois University Press.

Deflem, M. (2016). Tonnies, Ferdinand (1855–1936), in Craig, E. (Ed) *Routledge Encyclopedia of Philosophy Online*, London: Routledge, accessed at http://deflem.blogspot.com/2001/08/tonnies-ferdinand-1855-1936-2001.html, July.

Delpit, L. (2006). Lessons from teachers, *Journal of Teacher Education*, 57(3), 220–231.

Dennett, D. 2003. Explaining the 'magic' of consciousness, *Journal of Cultural and Evolutionary Psychology*, 1, 7–19

Denzin, N. K. and Lincoln, Y. S. (2000). *SAGE Handbook of Qualitative Research*, 2nd Edition, Thousand Oaks, CA: Sage Publications.

Denzin, N. K. and Lincoln, Y. S. (2008). Preface, in Denzin, N. K., Lincoln, Y. S. and Smith, L. T. (Eds) *Handbook of Critical Indigenous Methodologies*, Los Angeles: Sage Publications, ix–xv.

Dewey, J. (1906/2008). John Dewey, the Later Works 1925–1953, Volume 9: 1933–1934, Essays, Reviews, Miscellany and a Common Faith, Edited by Boysdon, J. A., Carbondale: Southern Illinois University Press, 9.

Dewey, J. (1916). *Democracy and Education*, London: Collier Macmillan Publishers.

Dewey, J. (1927/1952). *The Public and Its Problems*, Athens: Swallow Press and Ohio University Press.

Dewey, J. (1939). First published in *John Dewey and the Promise of America*, Progressive Education Booklet No. 14, Columbus, OH: American Education Press, 1939, from an address read by Horace M. Kallen at the dinner in honour of John Dewey in New York City on 20 October 1939; reprinted in The Later Works, Vol. 14.

Dewey, J. (1939/1969). *The Theory of Valuation*, Chicago: The University of Chicago Press.

Dewey, J. (1941). Propositions, warranted assertability and truth, *The Journal of Philosophy*, XXXVII, 169–186.

Dewey, J. (1958). *Experience and Nature*, New York: Dover Publications Inc.

Dewey, J. (2008). *John Dewey: The Later Works 1925–1953, Volume 16: 1949–1952*, Edited by Boydston, J. A., Carbondale: Southern Illinois University Press.

Dewey, J. (2012). *Unmodern Philosophy and Modern Philosophy*, Edited and with an Introduction by Deen, P., Carbondale and Edwardsville: Southern Illinois University Press.

Durst, A. (2010). Women Educators in the Progressive Era: The Women Behind Dewey's Laboratory School, New York: Palgrave Macmillan.

## 182  References

Edwards-Groves, C. and Kemmis, S. (2016). Pedagogy, education and praxis: Understanding new forms of intersubjectivity through action research and practice theory, *Educational Action Research*, 24(1), 77–96.

Ellis, V. (2011). Reenergising professional creativity from a CHAT perspective: Seeing knowledge and history in practice, *Mind, Culture and Activity*, 18(2), 181–193.

Engels, F. (1954). *Dialectics of Nature*, Moscow: Foreign Languages Publishing House.

Engestrom, T. (2007). Putting Vygotsky to work: The change laboratory as an application of double stimulation, in Daniels, H., Cole, M. & Wertsch, J. V. (Eds.), *The Cambridge Companion to Vygotsky*. Cambridge: Cambridge University Press, 363–383.

Eriksen, E. O. and Weigard, J. (2003). *Understanding Habermas: Communicative Action and Deliberative Democracy*, London and New York: Continuum.

Exley, S. and Ball, S. J. (2014). Neo-liberalism and English education, in Turner, D. and Yolcu, H. (Eds) *Neo-Liberal Educational Reforms: A Critical Analysis*, London: Routledge.

Feenberg, A. (2014). The Philosophy of Praxis: Marx, Lukacs and the Frankfurt School, London and New York: Verso.

Feinberg, W. (2012). The idea of a public education, *Review of Research in Education*, 36, 1–22.

Ferkany, M. and Creed, B. (2014). Intellectualist Aristotelian character education: An outline and assessment, *Educational Theory*, 64(6), 567–588.

Flyvbjerg, B. (2001). Making Social Science Matter: Why Social Inquiry Fails and How It Can Succeed Again, Cambridge, UK: Cambridge University Press.

Fordham, M. (2016). Realising and extending Stenhouse's vision of teacher research: The case of English history teachers, *British Educational Research Journal*, 42(1), 135–150.

Fornazi, F. M. (2014). Understanding core practices and practice-based teacher education: Learning from the past, *Journal of Teacher Education*, 65(4), 357–368.

Fraser, N. (1992). Rethinking the public sphere: A contribution to the critique of actually existing democracy, in Calhoun, C. J. (Ed) *Habermas and the Public Sphere*, Cambridge: MIT Press, 109–142.

Freire, P. (1972). *Cultural Action for Freedom*, Harmondsworth, UK: Penguin Books.

Freire, P. (1970/2000). *Pedagogy of the Oppressed*, 30th Anniversary Edition, New York, London, New Delhi and Sydney: Bloomsbury Press.

Gardner, H. (1983). *Frames of Mind: The Theory of Multiple Intelligences*, New York: Basic Books.

Garrison, J. (2012). 2012 Dewey lecture: Making meaning together beyond theory and practice, *Education & Culture*, 29(2), 5–23.

Geertz, C. (1993). The Interpretation of Cultures: Selected Essays, New York: Basic Books.

Giddens, A. (1979). Central Problems in Social Theory: Action, Structure, and Contradiction in Social Analysis, Berkeley and Los Angeles: University of California Press.

Giddens, A. (1984). *The Constitution of Society*, Cambridge: Polity Press.

Giddens, A. (1998). *The Third Way: The Renewal of Social Democracy*, Cambridge: Polity Press.

Gonzalez, N., Moll, L. and Amanti, C. (Eds) (2009). *Funds of Knowledge: Theorising Practices in Households, Communities and Classrooms*, New York and London: Routledge.

Grande, S. (2004). *Red Pedagogy: Native American Social and Political Thought*, Lanham, Boulder, New York, Toronto and Oxford: Rowman & Littlefield Publishers Inc.

Greer, G. (2008). *The Female Eunuch*, New York: Harper Collins Publishers.

## References   183

Grossman, P. (2009). Redefining teaching, re-imagining teacher education, *Teachers and Teaching: Theory and Practice*, 15(2), 273–289.

Gudjonsdottir, H., Cacciattolo, M., Dakich, E., Davies, A., Kelly, C. and Dalmau, M. (2007). Transformative pathways: Inclusive pedagogies in teacher education, *Journal of Research on Technology in Education*, 40(2), 165–182.

Habermas, J. (1981/1987). The Theory of Communicative Action: Lifeworld and System, a Critique of Functionalist Reason, Volume 2, Boston, MA: Beacon Press.

Habermas, J. (1984). *The Theory of Communicative Action*, Volumes 1 and 2, London: Heinemann.

Habermas, J. (1992). The Structural Transformation of the Public Sphere: An Inquiry Into a Category of Bourgeois Society, Translated by Burger, T. and Lawrence, F., Cambridge, MA: The MIT Press.

Hagger, H. and McIntyre, D. (2006). Learning Teaching From Teachers: Realising the Potential of School-based Teacher Education, Maidenhead and New York: Open University Press.

Hancock, I. (2002). *We Are the Romani People*, Hatfield, UK: University of Hertfordshire Press.

Hare, R. M. (1989). *Essays in Ethical Theory*, Oxford, UK and New York: Clarendon Press and Oxford University Press.

Harvey, D. (2010). *The Enigma of Capital and the Crises of Capitalism*, Oxford, UK: University of Oxford Press.

Hirst, P. H. (1974). *Knowledge and the Curriculum: A Collection of Philosophical Papers*, London and Boston: Routledge and Kegan Paul.

Hirst, P. H., Barrow, R. and White, P. (1993). *Beyond Liberal Education: Essays in Honour of Paul H. Hirst*, London and New York: Routledge.

Hooley, N. (2009). *Narrative Life: Democratic Curriculum and Indigenous Learning*, Dordrecht, Heidelberg, London and New York: Springer.

Hooley, N. (2015). Learning at the Practice Interface: Reconstructing Dialogue for Progressive Educational Change, London and New York: Routledge.

Hooley, N. and Levinson, M. (2014). Investigating networks of culture and knowledge: A critical discourse between UK Roma Gypsies, indigenous Australians and education, *Australian Educational Researcher*, 41(2), 139–153.

Hulse, B. and Hulme, R. (2012). Engaging with research through practitioner enquiry: The perceptions of beginning teachers on a postgraduate initial teacher education program, *Educational Action Research*, 20(2), 313–329.

Hursh, D. and Martina, C. A. (2016). The end of public schools? Or a new beginning? *The Educational Forum*, 80(2), 189–207.

Jackson, P. W. (1998). *John Dewey and the Lessons of Art*, New Haven and London: Yale University Press.

James, W. (1899/2015). Talks to Teachers on Psychology and to Students on Some of Life's Ideals, Mineola, NY: Dover Publications Inc.

Joas, H. (1985/1997). G. H. Mead: A Contemporary Re-Examination of His Thought, Cambridge, MA: MIT Press.

Joas, H. (1993). *Pragmatism and Social Theory*, Chicago and London: The University of Chicago Press.

Joas, H. (1996). *The Creativity of Action*, Chicago: University of Chicago Press.

Jons, L. (2014). Learning as calling and responding, *Studies in Philosophy and Education*, 33(5), 481–493.

Kemmis, S. (2001). Educational research and evaluation: Opening communicative space, *Australian Educational Researcher*, 24(1), 1–30.

## 184  References

Kemmis, S. and McTaggart, R. (2005). Participatory action research: Communicative action and the public sphere, in Denzin, N. K. and Lincoln, Y. S. (Eds) *The SAGE Handbook of Qualitative Research*, 3rd Edition, London: Sage Publication, 559–603.

Kincheloe, J. L. (2004). Refining rigour and complexity in research, in Kincheloe, J. L. and Berry, K. S. (Eds) *Rigour and Complexity in Educational Research: Conceptualising the Bricolage*, New York: Open University Press, 23–49.

Kincheloe, J. L. (2009). *Critical Pedagogy Primer*, 2nd Edition, Peter Lang: New York.

Kincheloe, J. L. (2011). Describing the bricolage: Conceptualising new rigour in qualitative research, in Hayes, K., Steinberg, S. R. and Tobin, K. (Eds) *Key Works in Critical Pedagogy: Joe L. Kincheloe*, Rotterdam: Sense Publishers, 177–190.

Kincheloe, J. L. and Steinberg, S. R. (1998). Addressing the crisis of whiteness: Reconfiguring white identity in a pedagogy of whiteness, in Kincheloe, J. L., Steinberg, S. R., Rodriguez, N. M. and Chennault, R. E. (Eds) *White Reign: Deploying Whiteness in America*, New York: St Martins Griffin, 3–30.

Kovach, M. (2009). *Indigenous Methodologies: Characteristics, Conversations and Contexts*, Toronto, Buffalo and London: University of Toronto Press.

Kuhn, T. S. (1962/2012). *The Structure of Scientific Revolutions*, 50th Anniversary Edition, Chicago: Chicago University Press.

Kwak, D.-J. (2015). The implications of Arendt's concept of judgement for humanistic teaching in a postmetaphysical age, *Educational Theory*, 65(6), 681–697.

Leiviska, A. (2015). The relevance of Hans-Georg Gadamer's concept of tradition to the philosophy of education, *Educational Theory*, 65(5), 581–600.

Levinas, E. (1969/1991). *Totality and Infinity*, Dordrecht: Kluwer Academic Publishers.

Levinson, M. P. (2007). Literacy in English Gypsy communities: Cultural capital manifested as negative assets, *American Educational Research Journal*, 44(1), 5–39.

Levinson, M. P. (2009). Cultural difference or subversion among Gypsy Traveller youngsters in schools in England: A question of perspective, in Danaher, P. A., Kenny, M. and Leder, J. R. (Eds) *Traveller, Nomadic and Migrant Education*, New York and London: Routledge, 59–73.

Levinson, M. P. and Hooley, N. (2014). Supporting the learning of nomadic communities across transnational contexts: Exploring parallels in the education of UK Roma Gypsies and indigenous Australians, *Research Papers in Education*, 29(4), 373–389.

Levi-Strauss, C. (1966). *The Savage Mind*, Chicago: Chicago University Press.

Lévi-Strauss, C. (1978). *Myth and Meaning*, New York: Schocken Books.

Lingard, B. and Sellar, S. (2014). The OECD and the expansion of PISA: New global modes of governance in education, *British Educational Research Journal*, 40(6), 917–936.

Lingard, B., Thompson, G. and Sellar, S. (Eds) (2016). *National Testing in Schools: An Australian Assessment*, London and New York: Routledge.

Livingston, J. (2001). Pragmatism, Feminism and Democracy: Rethinking the Politics of American History, New York and London: Routledge.

Loughran, J. (2014). Professionally developing as a teacher educator, *Journal of Teacher Education*, 65(4), 271–283.

Lukes, S. (1985). Emile Durkheim: His Life and Work, a Historical and Critical Study, Stanford: Stanford University Press.

MacIntyre, A. (1985). *After Virtue: A Study in Moral Theory*, 2nd Edition, London: Duckworth.

Makkreel, R. A. and Rodi, F. (Eds) (1989). *Wilhelm Dilthey: Selected Works Volume 1, Introduction to the Human Sciences*, Princeton, NJ: Princeton University Press.

## References    185

Ma Rhea, Z. (2012). Partnership for improving outcomes in Indigenous education: Relationship or business? *Journal of Education Policy*, 27(1), 45–66.

Marks, G. N. (2010). What aspects of schooling are important? School effects on tertiary entrance performance, *School Effectiveness and School Improvement*, 21(3), 267–287.

Marx, K. and Engels, F. (2015). *The Communist Manifesto*, Los Angeles: Millennium Publications.

McLean Davis, L. (2013). Masterly preparation: embedding clinical practice in a graduate preservice teacher education programme: The clinical praxis exam in the Master of Teaching, *Journal of Education for Teaching: International Research and Pedagogy*, 39 (1), 93–106

Mead, G. H. (1962). Mind, Self, and Society: From the Standpoint of a Social Behaviourist, Chicago: University of Chicago Press.

Menand, L. (Ed) (1997). *Pragmatism: A Reader*, New York: Vintage Books.

Menter, I. (2014). BERA presidential address 2013: Educational research – What's to be done? *British Educational Research Journal*, 40(2), 213–226.

MGSE. (2016). Melbourne Graduate School of Education, University of Melbourne, Australia, accessed at http://education.unimelb.edu.au/, July.

Miles, R., Lemon, N., Mitchell, D. M. and Reid, J-A. (2016). The recursive practice of research and teaching: Reframing teacher education, *Asia-Pacific Journal of Teacher Education*, 44(4), 401–414.

Mishler, E. G. (1990). Validation in inquiry-guided research: The role of exemplars in narrative study, *Harvard Educational Review*, 60(4), 415–440.

Moll, L. C. (2014). *L. S. Vygotsky and Education*, London and New York: Routledge.

Moll, L. C., Amanti, C., Neff, D. and Gonzalez, N. (2009). Funds of knowledge for teaching: Using a qualitative approach to connect homes and classrooms, in Gonzalez, N., Moll, L. and Amanti, C. (Eds) *Funds of Knowledge: Theorising Practices in Households, Communities and Classrooms*, New York and London: Routledge, 71–87.

Naidoo, R. and Williams, J. (2015). The neoliberal regime in English higher education: Charters, consumers and the erosion of the public good, *Critical Studies in Education*, 56(2), 208–223.

Nakata, M. (2002). Indigenous knowledge and the cultural interface: Underlying issues at the intersection of knowledge and information systems, *IFLA Journal*, 28(5/6), 281–291.

Norman, J. (2013). *Edmund Burke: The First Conservative*, New York: Basic Books.

Osberg, D. and Biesta, G. (Eds) (2010). *Complexity Theory and the Politics of Education*, Rotterdam, Boston and Taipei: Sense Publishers.

Osberg, D., Biesta, G. and Cilliers, P. (2008). From representation to emergence: Complexity's challenge to the epistemology of schooling, *Educational Philosophy and Theory*, 40(1), 213–227.

Parsons, T. (1937/1968). *The Structure of Social Action*, New York: Free Press.

Peirce, C. S. (1992/1999). *The Essential Peirce*, two volumes edited by the Peirce edition project, Bloomington: Indiana University Press (1992/1999), 1, 132, cited in Pragmatism, *Stanford Encyclopaedia of Philosophy*, accessed at http://plato.stanford.edu/ entries/pragmatism/, July 2016.

Penrose, R. (2009). Shadows of the Mind: A Search for the Missing Science of Consciousness, London: Vintage.

Pihlstrom, S. (2015). *The Bloomsbury Companion to Pragmatism*, London, New Delhi, New York and Sydney: Bloomsbury.

Pring, R. (2005). Philosophy of Education: Aims, Theory, Common Sense and Research, London and New York: Continuum.

## 186  References

Puddlephatt, A. (2009). The search for meaning: Revisiting Herbert Blumer's interpretation of G.H. Mead, *The American Sociologist*, 40(1), 89–105.

Quine, W. V. O. (1976). *The Ways of Paradox and Other Essays, Revised and Enlarged Edition*, Cambridge, MA: Harvard University Press.

Ravitch, D. (2014). Reign of Error: The Hoax of the Privatisation Movement and the Danger to America's Public Schools, New York: Vintage Books.

Reay, D. (1998). Rethinking social class: Qualitative perspectives on class and gender, *Sociology*, 32(2), 259–275.

Roberts, P. (2015). 'It was the best of times, it was the worst of times. . .': Philosophy of education in the contemporary world, *Studies of Philosophy and Education*, 34(6), 623–634.

Rodriguez, G. M. (2013). Power and agency in education: Exploring the pedagogical dimensions of funds of knowledge, in Faltis, C. and Abedia, J. (Eds), *Review of Research in Education*, 37, 87–120.

Rorty, R. (1979). *Philosophy and the Mirror of Nature*, Princeton and Oxford: Princeton University Press.

Rorty, R. (1982/2011). *Consequences of Pragmatism*, Minneapolis: University of Minneapolis Press.

Russell, D. C. (2013). Virtue ethics, happiness and the good life, in Russell, D. C. (Ed) *The Cambridge Companion to Virtue Ethics*, New York: Cambridge University Press.

Savage, M., Divine, F. and Cunningham, N. (2013). A new model of social class: Findings from the BBC's Great British Class Survey experiment, *Sociology*, 47(2), 219–250.

Schatzki, T. R. (2001). Introduction: Practice theory, in Schatzki, T. R., Cetina, K. K. and Savigny, E. V. (Eds) *The Practice Turn in Contemporary Theory*, London and New York: Routledge, 1–14.

Seddon, T. (2015). Re-making education in contexts of uncertainty: Governing, learning and contextual understanding, *Australian Educational Researcher*, 42(5), 527–548.

Seigfried, C. H. (1993). Shared communities of interest: Feminism and pragmatism, *Hypatia*, 8(2), 1–14.

Shulman, L. S. (1987). Knowledge and teaching: Foundations of the new reform, *Harvard Educational Review*, 57(1), 1–21.

Shulman, L. S. (2005). Signature pedagogies in the professions, *Daedalus*, 134(3), 52–59.

Sonnert, G. (2005). *Einstein and Culture*, New York: Humanity Books.

Stapp, H. (2009). *Mind, Matter and Quantum Mechanics*, Verlag, Berlin and Heidelberg: Springer.

Stenhouse, L. (1981). What counts as research?, *British Journal of Educational Studies*, 29(2), 103–114.

Strhan, A. (2016). Levinas, Durkheim and the everyday ethics of education, *Educational Philosophy and Theory*, 48(4), 331–345.

Teese, R. (2000/2013). *Academic Success and Social Power: Examinations and Inequality*, Melbourne: Australian Scholarly Publishing.

UK. (1967). The Plowden Report. Children and Their Primary Schools: A Report of the Central Advisory Council for Education (England), London: Her Majesty's Stationery Office.

US. (2016). No Child Left Behind: Elementary and Secondary Education Act (ESEA), Department of Education, accessed at www2.ed.gov/nclb/landing.jhtml, July.

van der Veer, R. and Valsiner, J. (1994). *The Vygotsky Reader*, London: Blackwell, 338–354.

## References    187

Vuyk, R. (1981). *Overview and Critique of Piaget's Genetic Epistemology 1965–1980*, Volume 1, London, New York, Toronto, Sydney and San Francisco: Academic Press.

Vygotsky, L. S. (1987). *The Collected Works of L. S. Vygotsky*, Volume 1, Edited by Reiber, R. and Carton, A. S., New York and London: Plenum Press.

Williams, R. (1989). Culture is ordinary (1958), in Gable, R. (Ed) *Resources of Hope: Culture, Democracy, Socialism*, London: Verso, 3–14.

Wollstonecraft, M. (1792/2016). *A Vindication of the Rights of Woman*, Chapter XII *On National Education*, available in *The Informal Education Archives*, accessed at www. infed.org/archives/e-texts/wollstonecraft_on_national_education.htm, July.

Wright, P. R. and Pascoe, R. (2015). Eudaimonia and creativity: The art of human flourishing, *Cambridge Journal of Education*, 45(3), 295–306.

Young, M. F. D. (2008). Bringing Knowledge Back In: From Social Constructivism to Social Realism in the Sociology of Education, Abington: Routledge.

Zeichner, K. (2012). The turn once again toward practice-based teacher education, *Journal of Teacher Education*, 63(5), 376–382.

Zipin, L. and Nuttall, J. (2016). Embodying pre-tense conditions for research among teacher educators in the Australian university sector: A Bourdieusian analysis ethico-emotive suffering, *Asia-Pacific Journal of Teacher Education*, 44(4), 348–363.

# Index

abstract knowledge 7
acts, properties of 20
Addams, Jane 124–5
aesthetic experience 104–5
aesthetic form, five conditions of 104
akrasia 44
Allen, J. 69
Amanti, C. 138–40
American Pragmatism 8–9, 20, 160–1, 175; collective consciousness 22–3; and Continental philosophy 21
analysis 54
anticipation 104
application of educational virtues 163–4
applied fields of study 69
Aristotle 13, 29, 45, 87, 158, 163, 173; politics 46
Arnold, Matthew 32, 76–7
Aronson, B. 150
assessment 51, 62; criticism of 109–10; No Child Left Behind Act 48; practice analysis 48–9; results as marker of economic progress 107; in teacher education praxis model 168–9
assimilation, Native American view of 135
associative learning 77, 129–30
Attenborough, David 129
axiology 17

Baehr, J. 163
Ball, S. J. 48
becoming whole 173
belief, and knowledge 103
Bernstein, B. 14
Biesta, G. J. J. 22–3, 50, 69, 158
Blair, Tony 93
Blumer, H. 126
Bohr, Niels 36
Bourdieu, P. 29, 99–100, 104, 127, 151–2

bourgeois world view 119–20
Bradatan, C. 61
bricolage approach to research 131–2, 140–3
*Bringing Knowledge Back In* (Young, 2008) 8, 9
Burke, Edmund 87
Butler, Judith 125–6

capitalism 12, 92–3; bourgeois world view 119–20; cultural capital 128; neoliberalism 83; objectification of human workforce 22; and religion 72; social democracy 89–90
cardinal virtues, justice 45–6
case conferencing 170–2
case studies: learning with the senses 124–6; social class in education 120–2; uniforms of convention 127–30
Cassidy, D. 107
categories 106–7
Change Laboratory 21
Chernus, I. 72
church states 74
Clandinin, D. J. 53
class categories 122
class consciousness 122
clinical approaches to teacher education 156
Cochran-Smith, M. 158
cognivist teaching 17–18
collective consciousness 10, 22–3
commodity fetishism 88
*Common Law, The* (Holmes, Oliver Wendell, 2012) 175–6
communication 51, 62
communicative action 11, 88; gesture 105–6; lifeworld 31–2; shared experience 30

*Index* 189

community 39; Habermas' view of 40; moral nature of 40; protocol for practitioner and community research 140–1

comparing: bourgeois and proletarian characteristics 119–20, 129; conservative and neoliberal views of education 12–13

complexity theory 34–6; computer modelling 34; dissipative structures 35; human consciousness 35

computer modelling, in complexity theory 34

Comte, Auguste 72–3

concrete knowledge 7

Connell, R. 128–9

Connelly, F. M. 53

conscientisation 33

consciousness 9, 36–8, 52, 106; class consciousness 122; collective consciousness 10; in complexity theory 35; conscientisation 33; exemplars 54; and experience 37; in Marxism 105; social class, connection with the human mind 122

conservation 104

conservatism 25; in the classroom 25–7; correlation with education 109; and education, tensions between 78–80; and neoliberalism 87; political-democratic features of 108; social justice impact 25; tension with education 109

conservative sociology 4

constructivism 17

Continental philosophy 21

continuity 104

control over curriculum 47–9; No Child Left Behind Act 48; practice analysis 48–9

Copenhagen Institute for Theoretical Physics 36

core practices approach to teacher education 155–6

correlations between education and philosophy 109

courage 163

Cox, Brian 129

creative action 51, 62; in Marxism 103

creative democracy 43; justice 45–6

critical complex epistemology 18

critical consciousness 33

critical pedagogy 142

critical praxis 157

criticism of testing 109–10

cultural hybridity 138

cultural interface 132–4

cultural mediation 21

cultural reproduction 127

Cultural-Historical Activity Theory (CHAT) 21

culture 51, 62, 71; aspects of 32; conscientisation 33; European theory, dominance of 128–9; and experience 9; FoK 138–40; Geisteswissenschaften 50; Gonzalez' view of 138; Indigenous groups, marginalisation of 132–4; and meaning 32; and religion 76–8; religion 72, 73; schools, cultural stance of 127; Williams' view of 134

cumulation 104

Curie, Marie 96

curriculum 51, 62; control over 47–9; designing 65–6; discursive approach 131; education as knowledge discipline, scenario 63–7; FoK 138–40; model for Discursive Cultural Knowledge Formation 144–5; national curriculum 65; No Child Left Behind Act 48; Plowden Report 47; principles of discursive learning 136–7; scope and sequence 99; standards and assessment 48; in teacher education praxis model 167

da Silva, F. C. 71

da Vinci, Leonardo 104

de Beauvoir, Simone 125

decline of social class 121–2

Delpit, L. 138–40

democracy 38–41, 51, 62; community 39; creative democracy 43; and ethical conduct 45; justice 45–6; parameters 38–9; public spheres 40–1; representative democracy 93; secularism 73; shared experience 39; social democracy 89–90

*Democracy and Education* (Dewey, 1916) 8–9; see *also* Dewey, John

democratic learning 15

Denzin, N. K. 140

Descartes, René 19

designing curriculum 65–6; scope and sequence 99

Dewey, John xvii, 10–11, 30, 39, 43, 71, 76, 86, 94, 121–6, 149, 159, 173; American Pragmatism 9; creative

## 190    Index

democracy 43; ends and means 86–7; Great Community 27–8; pragmatism 20
dialectical materialism 9, 105, 119, 130; consciousness 38
dialogue 164; portfolio dialogue 170–2
directness 174
disciplinary knowledge, education as 61–3, 68
discursive approach to schooling 131, 134–7, 160
Discursive Cultural Knowledge Formation 132, 144–5
dissipative structures 35
doxa 151
Durkheim, Emile 10, 72

economic systems, formal education xiv
education: American Pragmatism 8; comparing conservative and neoliberal views of 12–13; conservative view of 12; control over curriculum 47–9; cultural stance of schools 127; equity 165; formal education 50; Geisteswissenschaften 50; goals of 59; human learning 7; as knowledge discipline 60–3, 68; learning by doing 4–5; neoliberalism 12; normative categories 52; ontology 52; philosophy 14; as philosophy of practice 50–1, 107; public education xiii; questions underpinning 1; reflexive sociology of education 15; relationship to fields of human activity xiv; relationship to philosophies xiii–xiv; scope and sequence 99; social class 120; social class in 120–2; socio-economic issues xiv, 5–7; standards and assessment 48; three domains of 52; and virtue 163; Vygotsky's view of 9; see also philosophies of practice
educational research 112
educational virtues 163–4
Edwards, R. 69
Einstein, Albert 96, 99, 106–7
elements of experience: philosophy 3–4; sociology 3–4
emotion, linking reason with 173–4
emotional experience 121
empirical view of epistemology 16
empty vessel view of learning 35
ends and means 86–7
Engels, Friedrich 101
episteme 13–14

epistemology 7, 149–50; in the classroom 25–7; cognivist knowledge 17–18; conservatism 12–13; conservative 25; critical complex epistemology 18; empirical view of 16; experience 9; genetic epistemology 17; human learning 7; knowledge 8; naturalised 19; neoliberalism 12–13, 25; practice interface 15; praxis 14; progressive 25; progressivism 13; rationalist view of 16; social conditions, impact on 28; social justice impact 25
equilibrium 35
equity 51, 62; educational equity 165; marginalised groups 132
ethical conduct 43–6, 51, 62; akrasia 29; as cardinal virtue 45; democratic conduct 45; educational equity 165; educational virtues 163–4; happiness 163; practical reasoning 44–5; virtues 46
eudaimonia 45, 87
European theory, dominance of 128–9
examples of discursive schooling 136–7
exemplars 53–4; sense making 54
Exley, S. 48
experience 8–9; aesthetic experience 104–5; empirical view of epistemology 16; evolution of self 81; fusion of horizons 112; narrative inquiry 53; perezhivanie 121; profane knowledge 10; shared experience 30, 39; subjectivity 37; three domains of human existence and education 52
Experience and Nature (Dewey, 1958) 30, 175–6

faith, and knowledge 103
fascism 10
feeling of knowing 71–2
Female Eunich (Greer, 1970) 125
feminism 123–4; gender and sex 126; learning with the senses case study 124–6
field 151
fields of knowledge 61–3; applied fields of study 69; see also disciplinary knowledge; knowledge
five conditions of aesthetic form 104
'flywheel of habit' metaphor 89
formal education xiv, 50, 57; as field of human activity xiv
formal schooling xii; emotion in 174
frames of practice 67–8

## Index 191

Franklin, Rosalind 96
freedom of the mind 94–5
Freire, Paulo 10, 18; conscientisation 33; control over curriculum 49
funds of knowledge (FoK) 135, 138–40; model for Discursive Cultural Knowledge Formation 144–5
fusion of horizons 112

Galileo 96
Gardner, H. 70
Geertz, C. 72
*Geisteswissenschaften* 50
*Gemeinschaft – Gesellschaft* contrast 128
gender, and sex 126
generalised other 24–5, 126
generation of human selfhood 82–3
genetic epistemology 17
gesture 105–6
Giddens, A. 29, 67, 93, 111–12
goals: of education 59; of research 50; of scenarios in Part II 113
Gonzalez, N. 138
Grande, Sandy 135
Great Community 27–8, 38–41; public spheres 40–1; see *also* democracy
Greek philosophy 29; akrasia 44; eudaimonia 45, 87; phronesis 14, 29; Plato 94; politics 46; praxis 14, 29
Greer, Germaine 125, 129
guide to life 72
guidelines for subjectification 174–5
Gypsy Roma Traveller (GRT) children 146; cultural interface 132–4; marginalisation of 132

Habermas, Jurgen 10, 29, 31, 81–3; communicative action 11; lifeworld 31–2, 52; view of community 40
habits 117–18
habitus 151
Hager, H. 147
happiness 87, 163
Heisenberg, Werner 36
Hirst, Paul 61
historical materialism 105
historical pragmatism 130
Hooley, Dr Neil 145
horizontal knowledge structures 14
Hull House 124–5
human brain see consciousness
human existence, three domains of 52
human learning 7

human selfhood, generation of 82–3
Hursh, D. 48

identity politics 123; feminism 123–4
ideologies: conservatism 12; moderate forms of 88; neoliberalism 11–15; religion as 74
implementing FoK 139–40
inclusion, Native American view of 135
Indigenous Australian (IA) children: cultural interface 132–4; marginalisation of 132
Indigenous groups: bricolage approach to research 140–3; discursive approach to schooling 134–7; FoK 138–40; model for Discursive Cultural Knowledge Formation 144–5; Native Americans 135
inquiry 52, 164; exemplars 54; narrative inquiry 53; praxis inquiry protocol 156–7
insight 54
integrated educationists 60
intellectual virtues 87
interaction 62
interaction between education and philosophy: conservatism 78–80; Marxism 101–4; neoliberalism 83–6; religion 74–6; science 95–8; social democracy 90–2
internal goods of practice 148–9
interpreting research 53
intersection of political-democratic tensions 89
intersubjective praxis 161–3
intersubjectivity 22, 24, 62, 105; collective consciousness 22–3

Jackson, P. W. 104
James, W. 89, 129–30
Joas, H. 20, 25, 82
judgement 164
justice 45–6; intent 46

Kant, Immanuel 16, 99–100
key features of religion 73
Kincheloe, J. L. 18, 142
knowledge: applied fields of study 69; cognivist 17–18; communicative action 11; concrete 7; education as knowledge discipline 61–3, 68; epistemology 7; exemplars 53–4; feeling of knowing 71–2; fields of 61–3; FoK 135; genetic

## 192 *Index*

epistemology 17; horizontal knowledge structures 14; human learning 7; linking with praxis 14; naturalised epistemology 19; powerful knowledge 15; profane 10; reliance on faith 103; requirements for teaching 66; sacred 10; scientific 7; social knowledge 105; socio-transcendental conditions of 100; transformational 51; vertical knowledge structures 14
Kovach, Margaret 140
Kuhn, T. S. 96–9; exemplars 53–4; paradigm shift 19

labour parties 94
language 30; communicative action 11; in learning 10; and myth 74
Laughter, J. 150
Law of Three Stages 73
learning 7, 51, 62, 112, 129–30; assessment 48; associative 77; bricolage approach 140–3; CHAT 21; comparing conservative and neoliberal views of 12–13; democratic learning 15; discursive approach 134–7; education as knowledge discipline, scenario 63–7; empty vessel view of 35; intersubjectivity 22; language 10; Mead's view on 22; Piaget's view on 17; practice analysis 48–9; as social act 16; social acts 42; as social practice 148–50; theory of action 16, 19; and virtue 163
learning by doing 4–5
Leiviska, A. 111–12
Levinson, Martin 145
Lévi-Strauss, Claude 73
Lewis, C. S. 154
lifeworld 31, 32, 52; culture 32; development of 106; evolution of self 81; exemplars 54
Lincoln, Y. S. 140
linguistic turn 11, 30–2
linking reason with emotion 173–4

MacIntyre, Alasdair 148–9
marginalised knowledge 132; cultural interface 132–4; model for Discursive Cultural Knowledge Formation 144–5
Martina, C. A. 48
Marx, Karl 10, 29, 72, 100–1
Marxism 9, 32; commodity fetishism 88; correlation with education 109; dialectical materialism 9, 105, 130;

materialism 105; political-democratic features of 108; proletarian world view 119–20; tension with education 101, 109
mass testing 109–11
materialism 105
mathematics case study, social class in education 120–2
McIntyre, D. 147
Mead, George Herbert 22, 71, 99, 105, 123–4, 126, 150; generalised other 24–5
meaning: of being human 71; and culture 32; and myth 74
measurement, effect on wave function 36
meta-insight 54
mind-body dualism 21
model for Discursive Cultural Knowledge Formation 144–5
moderate forms of ideologies 88
Moll, L. C. 71, 138–40
*Mona Lisa* (da Vinci) 104
moral nature of community 40
morality 51, 62
multiple intelligences 70
myth 73

Nakata, Martin 132–3
narrative dialogue 54
narrative inquiry 53–4
national curriculum 65
Native Americans, issues of inclusion 135
naturalised epistemology 19
neoliberalism 11–15, 25, 31, 83; in the classroom 25–7; and conservatism 87; control over curriculum 47–8; correlation with education 109; ends and means 86–7; intersubjectivity 22; objectification of human workforce 22; political-democratic features of 108; social justice impact 25; tension with education 83–6, 109
Newton, Isaac 96
No Child Left Behind Act 48
normative categories 52

objectification of human workforce 22
observation, effect on wave function 36
offshoring 122
ontology 52, 152
open-mindedness in formation of critical life 161
Orwell, George 154
Osberg, D., Biesta, G. and Cilliers, P. (2008). *From representation to*

*emergence: Complexity's challenge
to the epistemology of schooling*,
Educational Philosophy and Theory 34

paradigm shift 19
paradigms 96, 98–9, 101
parameters, of democracy 38–9
parrhesia 14
Parsons, T. 19
participatory action research 170–2
Passeron, J. C. 127
pedagogy: signature pedagogies 165–72;
   in teacher education praxis model 167–8
*perezhivanie* 121
philosophies of practice 51, 62;
   conservatism 25, 78–80; correlations
   with education 109; exemplars
   53–4; formation of critical life 161;
   intersection of political-democratic
   tensions 89; Marxism 101; neoliberalism
   83; normative categories 52; political-
   democratic features of 107–8; questions
   for education as 110–11, 118; religion
   72–4; science 95; social democracy
   89–92
philosophy: consciousness 36–8;
   epistemology 7; Greek philosophy 29;
   progressive 4; questions underpinning
   3; and sociology 4; as a way of life 14;
   world views 4
*Philosophy and the Mirror of Nature*
   (Rorty, 1979/2009) 3–4
phronesis 14, 29
Piaget, Jean 17–18
Plato 94
Plowden Report 47
political-democratic features of
   philosophies of practice 107–8
politics 46; class politics 123; feminism
   123–4; identity politics 123; intersection
   of political-democratic tensions 89;
   labour parties 94; national curriculum
   65; third way values 93–4
Popper, Karl 96
portfolio dialogue 170–2
post-structuralism 22
powerful knowledge 15
practical reasoning 44–5
practical sense 151
practical wisdom 29, 158
practice 51–2; frames of practice 67–8;
   internal goods of 148–9; and theory 120;
   turning towards 148

practice analysis 48–9
practice turn 148–50, 158
practice-theorising 147; clinical
   approaches 156; critical praxis 157;
   historical context 148; praxis inquiry
   protocol 156–7; as progressive teaching
   152–5
pragmatism 20, 51, 62, 71, 77–8, 82,
   117, 160–1; creative democracy 43;
   feminism 123–4; historical pragmatism
   130; signature pedagogies 165–72;
   socio-transcendental conditions of
   knowledge 100
praxis 14, 29, 51, 62; critical praxis 157;
   intersubjective praxis 48, 161–3; teacher
   education 166–72
praxis inquiry protocol 156–7
predestination 72
primary frames of practice 67–8
principles of discursive learning 136–7
processes in teacher education praxis
   model: assessment 168–9; curriculum
   167; pedagogy 167–8; teaching 168
profane knowledge 10
professional practice 170–2
progressive epistemology 13
progressive philosophy 4
progressivism 25; in the classroom 25–7;
   practice-theorising 152–5; social justice
   impact 25
proletarian world view 119–20
properties of acts 20
protocol for practitioner and community
   research 140–1
*Public and Its Problems, The* (Dewey,
   1927/1952) 39
public education xiii
public spheres 40–1
purposes of education 59

quantum mechanics 36–8; and
   consciousness 37; measurement, effect
   on wave function 36
*Quest for Certainty, The* (Dewey,
   1906/2008) 77
questions for education as philosophy of
   practice 110–11, 118
questions underpinning formal education 1
Quine, W. V. O. 19

rational action 20
rationalist view of epistemology 16
Ravitch, D. 48

194  *Index*

reason 10; linking with emotion 173–4; practical reasoning 44–5
Reay, D. 121–2
reflection 164
reflexive sociology of education 15
reflexivity 151
reification 22
relativism 162–3
religion 63, 72–4; and capitalism 72; church states 74; correlation with education 109; and culture 73, 76–8; and education, tensions between 74; as guide to life 72; as ideology 74; key features of 73; political-democratic features of 108; tension with education 109
repertoires of practice 170–2
representative democracy 93
research 51, 62; bricolage approach to 142–3; Change Laboratory 21; critical pedagogy 142; educational research 112; goals of 50; interpreting 53; narrative inquiry 54; participatory action research 170–2; in practice 157–9; protocol for practitioner and community research 140–1; reliance on theoretical input 69; in teacher education praxis model 169–72
respect 164
responsibility 164, 174
Rodriguez, G.M. 139
role of the sociologist 15
Roma 146
Rorty, Richard 4; see *also Philosophy and the Mirror of Nature* (Rorty, 1979/2009)
Rowling, J. P. 154
Russell, D. C. 87

sacred knowledge 10
Sadler, Dr Kirsten 159
Sartre, Jean-Paul 125
scenarios: conservatism, tension with education 78–80; education as knowledge discipline 63–7; goals of 113; Marxism, tension with education 101–4; neoliberalism, tension with education 83–6; for practice-theorising 152–5; religion, tension with education 74–6; science, tension with education 95–8; social democracy, tension with education 90–2
Schatzki, T. R. 148
schooling: bricolage approach 131, 140–3; cultural stance of schools 127;

discursive approach 131, 136–7, 160–1; education as knowledge discipline, scenario 63–7; formal xii; meta-epistemological perspective 18; model for Discursive Cultural Knowledge Formation 144–5; public education xiii; subjectification as main purpose of 22; theory of action xii
science 95; correlation with education 109; exemplars 53–4; paradigms 99–101; political-democratic features of 108; quantum mechanics 36–8; tension with education 95–8, 109
scientific knowledge 7
scope and sequence in education 99
secondary frames of practice 67–8
secularism 73
selfhood, generation of 82–3
sense making 54
sensory perception: learning with the senses case study 124–6; naturalised epistemology 19
sex and gender 126
shared experience 30, 39
Shulman, Lee 66
signature pedagogies 66–7, 165–72
social acts 24, 42; as basis for education as philosophy of practice 49–51; creative democracy 43; gesture 106; properties of 20; as requirement for critical life 161; as requirement for learning 42
social class in education 120; class categories 122; connection with the human mind 122; decline of 121–2; mathematics case study 120–2; offshoring 122
social conditions, impact on epistemology 28
social democracy 89–90; correlation with education 109; freedom of the mind 94–5; political-democratic features of 108; tension with education 90–2, 109; third way values 93–4
social facts 10
social justice: epistemologies, impact on 25; justice as cardinal virtue 45–6; practice interface 15
social knowledge 105
social reproduction 127
society: church states 74; communicative rationality for 31; pluralist 73; secularism 73

socio-economic issues: in education xiv, 5–7; position and culture 127–30
sociology 3; Durkheim, Emile 10; as horizontal knowledge structure 14; Law of Three Stages 73; and philosophy 4; practice interface 15; reflexive sociology of education 15; role of the sociologist 15
socio-transcendental conditions of knowledge 100
standards and assessment 48; No Child Left Behind Act 48
strategic action 11
structuration 29
*Structure of Social Action, The* (Parsons, 1937/1968), theory of action 19
subjectification 22, 174–5
symbolic interactionism 126

teacher education: core practices 155–6; curriculum 167; guidelines for subjectification 174–5; pedagogy 167–8; practice-theorising 150–5; research 169–72; researching 157–9; signature pedagogies 170–2; teaching 168; three world's context 166–7; virtues-based approach 158; warranted assertability 162–3
teacher education praxis model, significance of 172
teaching 51, 62; bricolage approach 140–3; cognivist 17–18; comparing conservative and neoliberal views of 12–13; discursive approach 131, 136–7; education as knowledge discipline, scenario 63–7; integrated educationists 60; knowledge requirements 66; national curriculum 65; signature pedagogies 66–7
techne 13
Teese, R. 48
tensions between education and philosophy 109; conservatism 78–80; Marxism 101–4; neoliberalism 83–6; religion 74–6; science 95–8; social democracy 90–2
tertiary frames of practice 68
testing: criticism of 109–10; international test results 107; No Child Left Behind Act 48; results as marker of economic progress 107
themata 106–7

themes in FoK 139
theory: Discursive Cultural Knowledge Formation 132; European dominance of 128–9; and practice 120; practice-theorising 147; *see also* practice-theorising
theory of action xii, 16, 19; CHAT 21; communication 30; practical wisdom 29; properties of acts 20; rational action 20
*Theory of Communicative Action: Lifeworld and System, a Critique of Functionalist Reason, The,* Volume 2 (Habermas, 1981) 31
third way values 93–4, 111–12
three domains of human existence and education 52; context for teacher education 166–7; exemplars 54
transformational knowledge 51, 62
Travellers 146

unifying spirit 107

validity claims 11
values, third way 93–4, 111–12
vertical knowledge structures 14
Villegas, A. M. 158
virtues: courage 163; educational virtues 163–4; intellectual virtues 87; justice 45–6
virtues-based teacher education 158
Vygotsky, Lev 9, 10, 121; CHAT 21; cultural mediation 21

warranted assertability 162–3
wave function, effect of measurement on 36
wave-particle duality 36
Weber, Max 10, 31, 72
welfare systems 91
well-being 45
weltanschauung 106
weltbild 106
Westminster system of government 46, 91
wholeheartedness 174
Williams, Raymond 32, 71, 134
Wollstonecraft, Mary 123
world views 4

Young, Michael F. D. 9

Zeicher, K. 157
zone of proximal development 10, 71